# Visual Communication in Digital Design

YoungJin.com Y.

# Visual Communication in Digital Design



ISBN: 978-89-314-3434-7
Printed and bound in the Republic of Korea.

**How to contact us:**

E-mail: support@youngjin.com

Address: YoungJin.com
3F Mapo Tower Bldg, 418-1 Mapo-dong, Mapo-Gu, Seoul 121-734, Korea

**Credits**

Production Manager: Suzie Lee
Developmental Editor: Rachel Lake, Publication Services, Inc.
Project Manager: Lorie Donovan, Publication Services, Inc.
Editorial Services: Publication Services, Inc.
Book Designer: Litmus
Cover Designer: Litmus
Production Control: Jay Won, Misook Kim

# Preface

There are many principles, elements, and considerations requisite in creating a piece of visual work, but the application of these elements varies widely. Acquiring design principles and integrating them into the design process is difficult and requires much practice. To fill the gap between knowledge and practice, this art should ideally be approached with both active study and consistent practice.

Visual works are difficult to explain, and must be carefully analyzed to understand their underlying concepts. Experience is essential in visual design to enable you to appeal to the audience's aesthetic values, which are often subconscious. Design principles are merely general instructions, suggesting several ways to find an answer.

Visual Communication in Digital Design is intended as a guide and a resource for those who are interested in both graphic design and digital design. This book has two main elements: design theory and design practice. Each of the 12 chapters presents a separate topic, such as lines, shapes, color, and typography, while several Design Studio sections offer relevant, hands-on activities to guide you through the principles.

This book is intended to be studied sequentially, to progress from general applications to more specific projects such as poster design and web interface design. Spend as much time as you need to on the Design Studio activities, and review topics as occasion demands.

Ji Yong Park

August 2007

Rockhampton, Queensland, Australia

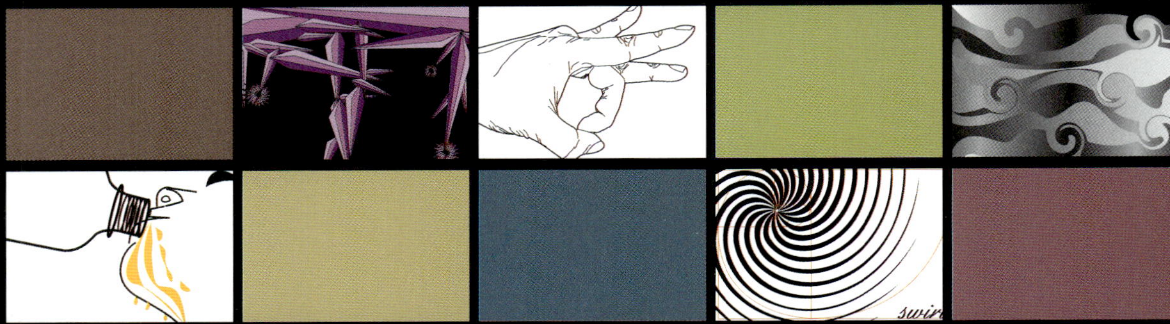

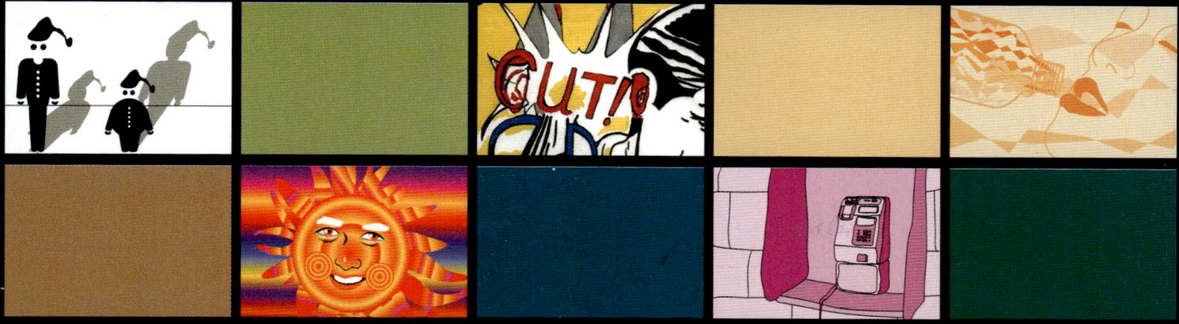
CUT!

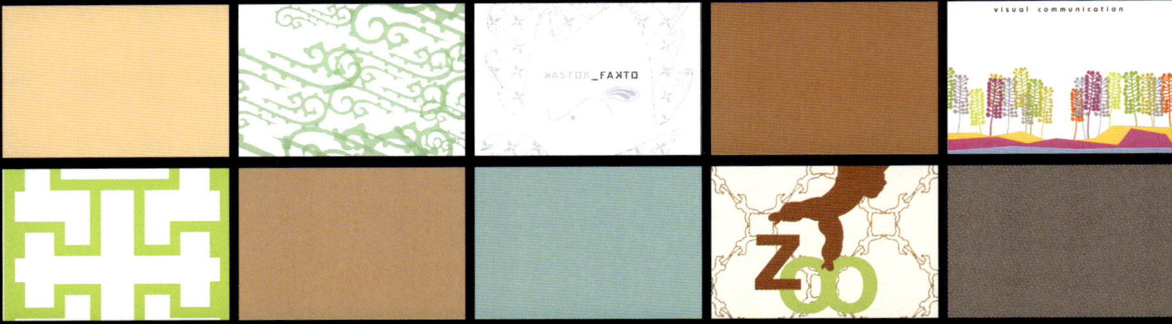
visual communication

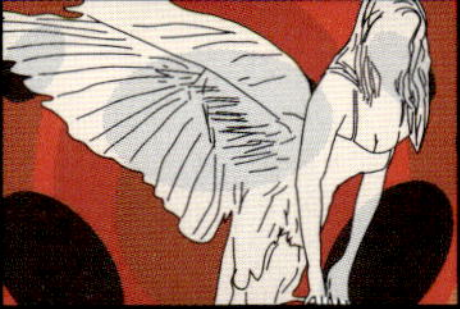
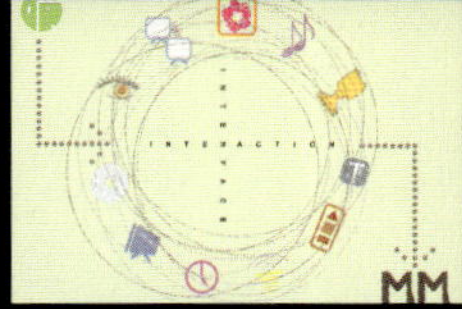
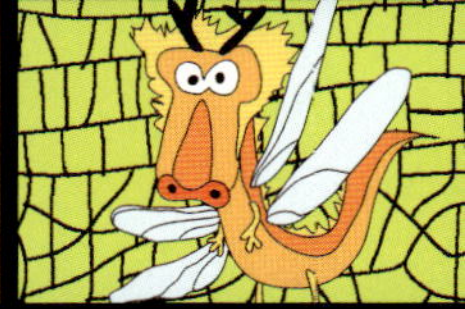
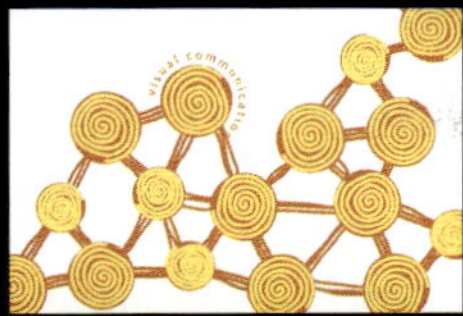
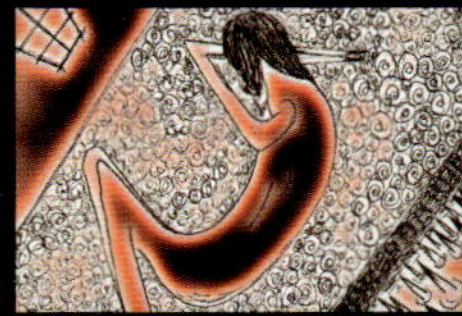

## About the Author

Dr. Ji Yong Park (Doctor of Design) is a lecturer of Digital Innovation at Central Queensland University, Rockhampton, Queensland, Australia. He has over six years of teaching experience in higher education and mainly taught visual communication and digital design. His research interests are in the development of training methodology for designers and design students via online in terms of interactive learning experience design and web site evaluation methodology in terms of user experience.

## Acknowledgments

Special thanks to Bradley John Acutt for his hard work and dedication to this book. Thanks to Joy Reynolds for helping me by giving constructive criticism. Many thanks to Sandi Weedon and Jason Fairchild for reading this book from the readers' point of view and giving me great feedback.

My sincere thanks to Suzie Lee (Soo-Jung Lee), Overseas Business Division Manager at YoungJin.com, for giving me this great opportunity, her support, and contribution to this work.

My biggest thanks must go to my wife, Eun-Sook Lee—an editor, a partner, a consultant, and a friend—who always encourages me to be the best that I can be and supports me.

## Special Thanks

Special thanks to my students who gave me their permission to publish their works. The following are the students' full names:

Bradley John Acutt
Chelsea Sutherland
Douglas (Chak Cheung) Tsang
Elise Sondergeld
Joy Reynolds
Justin Andrew Hawley
Karina Maree Voss
Kaylene Court
Krista Avila
Michael Ignatius Horoba
Natalie Gaye Clarke
Sandra Mary Weedon

Chapter

# [ 01 ]

# Graphic Design and Elements

Graphic design is the art of visual communication that is manipulating various visual elements, such as text and images, to present information in an aesthetically pleasing manner according to user needs.

# Graphic Design

Graphic design seeks to find the most appropriate balance between aesthetic and functionality, between tradition and creativity, in accordance with the user's needs and preferences.

Graphic design is a type of visual communication that is a process of arranging and manipulating design elements, such as text, color, and image, in order to deliver an effective visual message. A graphic designer always cares about how the target user perceives and understands the visual design outcome, because it communicates with people on a visual level only. Understanding who the target user is and what they want is the most important procedure in any design process and suggests to the designer how to effectively communicate the design's function and message. Therefore, it is fair to say that the process of graphic design is all about the target user in terms of visual communication.

**Note** | That book distinguishes between the terms "the user" and "the audience" for visual design. The term "user" is more pertinent to digital design and visual communication in that consumers in a digital environment are more participational and better receive the communicational aspect rather than from print. On the other hand, the "audience" is a viewer or an appreciator who is observing a visual work.

As shown in Figure 1-1, the purpose of graphic design is to find the perfect balance of the four key concepts: aesthetics, functionality, creativity, and tradition.

Aesthetics define the style and communication methods of design products to users in terms of the user's visual and emotional experience. The designer must visualize the relationship between the user's experience and the functionality of the design without reducing effectiveness. Functionality incorporates the necessary features of a design product in a visual design form and organizes them to be clear to the target user. Aesthetics and functionality often conflict within environments involving racial characteristics, contemporary ideas, culture, and technology.

Tradition suggests adhering to established principles and methods of design. Creativity, on the other hand, involves invention through breaking down existing values and traditions. Creativity and tradition also conflict with each other in design and, in conflict, new values are produced from old. Therefore, graphic design is always influenced by the relational conflict between aesthetics and functionality and between creativity and tradition.

Graphic design seeks to find the most appropriate balance between these four features using design elements. In other words, graphic design pursues an effective visual communication of a design product through the tuning of these four features to meet user needs and desires.

Graphic design is tailored to the user's needs, which are located between the four features. This determines the relationship and the priorities of the four features (see Figure 1-2). Ultimately, the designer's role in digital environments is to define the user experience in terms of visual communication and to solve visual communication issues in a functional, creative, and aesthetically pleasing manner.

1 2

1 Figure 1-1. Four aspects of graphic design
2 Figure 1-2. User needs in graphic design

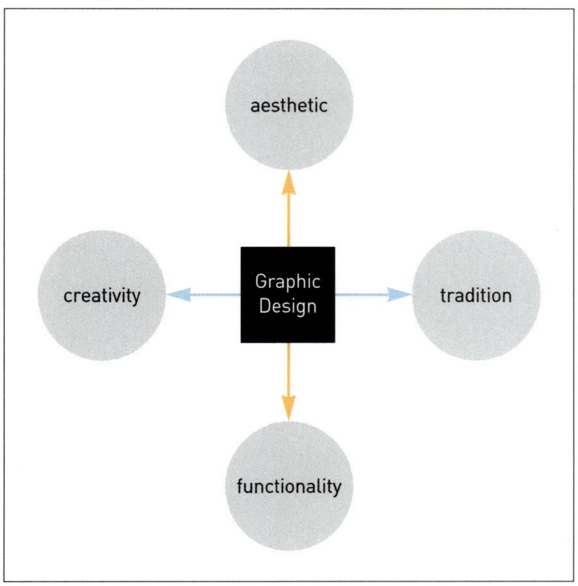


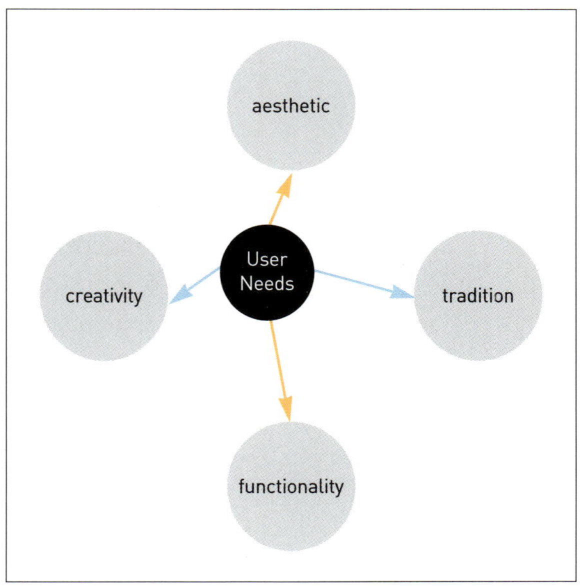

# Elements of Design

The design elements are the constituents of a visual composition and the designer defines their relationships to create an effective layout and design.

The elements of design are the basic parts constituting a composition in a visual design. A point, a line, and a shape are formative objects that can be manipulated, arranged, and formed to create a particular visual composition.

For example, a point creates a line that creates a form. These are formative elements in a visual design that create a definite visual structure. There are also formless elements such as texture, space, size, and color.

These do not have a definite shape, but can be used to form a visual structure by being associated with and arranged around the formative elements.

The following seven basic elements, both formative and formless, can produce many different layouts depending on how they are used. It is important to note that using these seven design elements appropriately in a visual design requires much practice.

In this section we will look at each element briefly.

## Point

—

A point is the smallest and unbreakable unit that can be used to compose a form. A single point represents position in terms of space. A set of points can be used to represent a line or a shape. Points can have various characteristics by using the concepts of scale, distance, and direction.

Figure 1-3 shows that the point produces a sense of stability because it is positioned in the middle of the document.

Figure 1-4 shows that the point sticking to the top in this plane produces a sense of instability and movement. Gravity appears to be pulling it down. On the other hand, Figure 1-5 shows the point looking lonely and isolated because it is positioned in the right bottom corner.

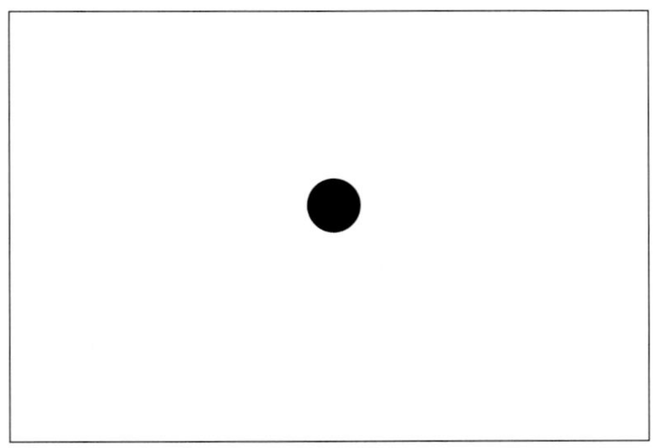

1 Figure 1-3. A single point in stable position
2 Figure 1-4. A single point in an unstable position
3 Figure 1-5. A single point in isolated position

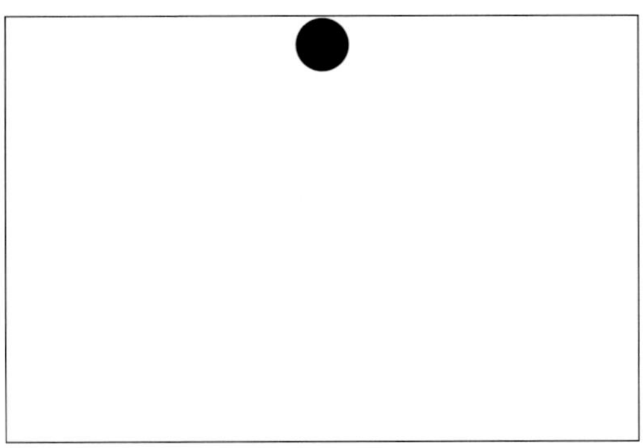

So far, the examples have shown that a single point is able to produce an emotional mood by its position in the space. A plain document is transformed into defined space due to the positioning of the point. This shows how a point (the formative element) and space (the formless element) work together to create a visual design.

A set of points can create a powerful relationship between negative and positive space. The positive space is the area of space that a shape forms in the plane (positive space = yang), whereas the negative space is the space that the shape does not fill in the plane (negative space = yin).

Repetitive position and scale of objects produce a pattern that defines space in terms of visual design. Figure 1-6 is an example of pattern design with points.

A group of points can be a creative tool with connection or repetition. Points that are close together become a shape or a direction. Multiple points can create a line or a form. As shown in Figure 1-7, a group of points suggest a direction, that the points are moving away from the left to the right.

1 2

1 Figure 1-6. A pattern of points
2 Figure 1-7. Points indicating a direction

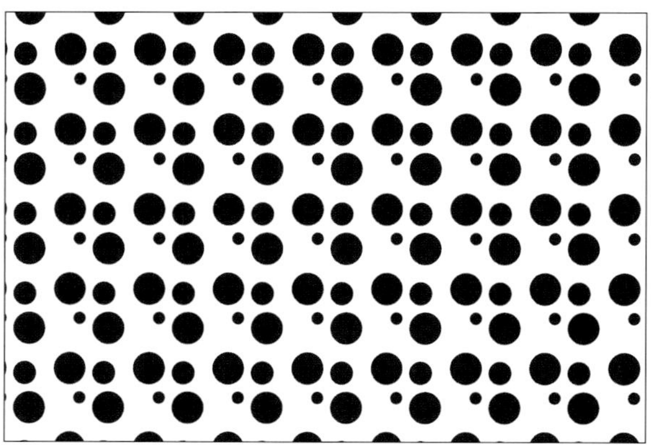

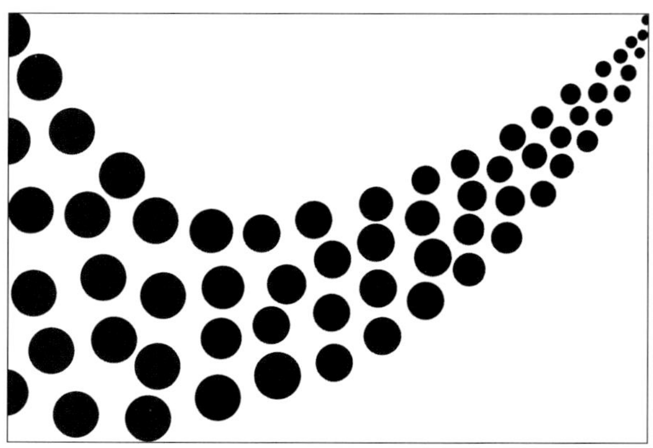

The point serves as the focus of attention to highlight important information. Drawing a circle on a date in the calendar means that it is an important day to remember (see Figure 1-8).

A point (or a dot) can highlight a key part of an object. Several points in combination may represent a more complicated object. Points can recreate an object in a simplified form by emphasizing its key features. As shown in Figure 1-9, the apple image is reproduced in a simplified form of dots, demonstrating the effective use of points to create a visual design.

| August | | | | | | |
|---|---|---|---|---|---|---|
| | 1 | 2 | 3 | 4 | 5 | 6 |
| 7 | 8 | 9 | 10 | 11 | 12 | 13 |
| 14 | 15 | 16 | 17 | 18 | 19 | 20 |
| 21 | 22 | 23 | 24 | 25 | 26 | 27 |
| 28 | 29 | 30 | 31 | | | |

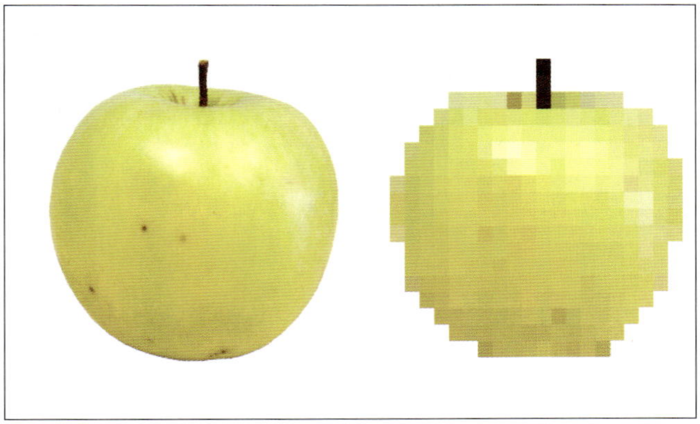

1
2

1 Figure 1-8. A red circle focuses the viewer's attention
2 Figure 1-9. Apple comprised of dots

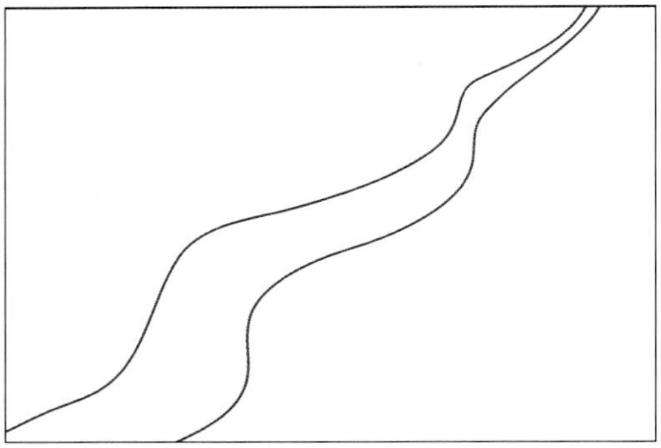

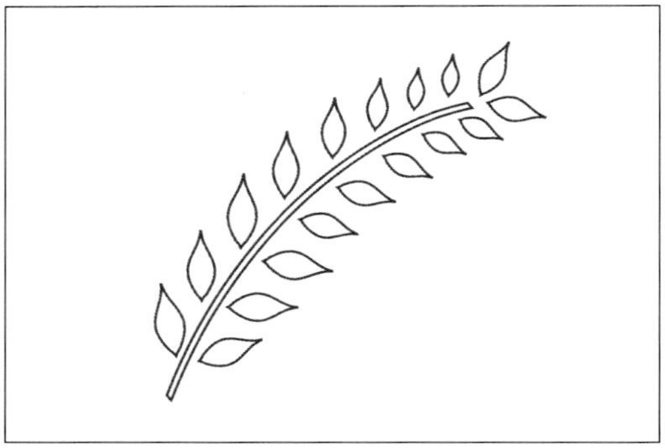

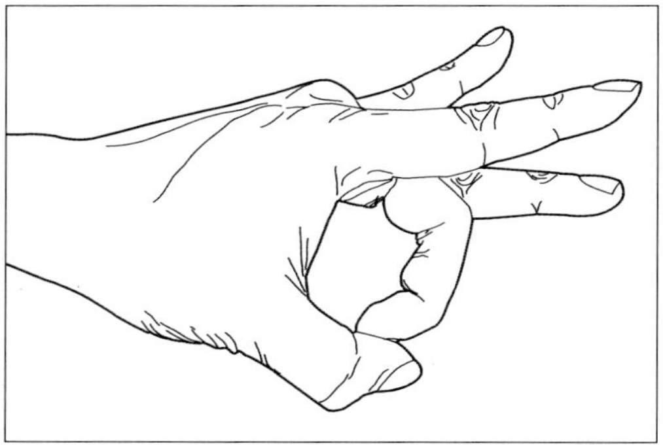

## Line

—

A line represents direction and length. Lines also create outlines of forms and can have expression and emotion. Lines are an important element in creating a perspective view.

A line can be defined as a path that leads the viewer in a certain direction. In Figure 1-10, one line is parallel to another so that, together, they visually create a winding path. This also produces a perspective direction that can be used to guide the audience's attention to a certain point in a layout.

Outlining often simplifies an object. The contour drawing in Figure 1-11 represents a general shape of leaves without any detailed information. A contour drawing in visual design eliminates unnecessary information from an object and delivers the information in a simpler format to the audience.

Lines can not only define an object simply, but also communicate quickly. The contour of an object enables audiences to identify it easily and quickly. Figure 1-12 shows a contour drawing of a posed hand.

1
2
3

1 **Figure 1-10.** Lines direct the viewer's gaze
2 **Figure 1-11.** Lines as contour drawings
3 **Figure 1-12.** Contour lines communicate efficiently

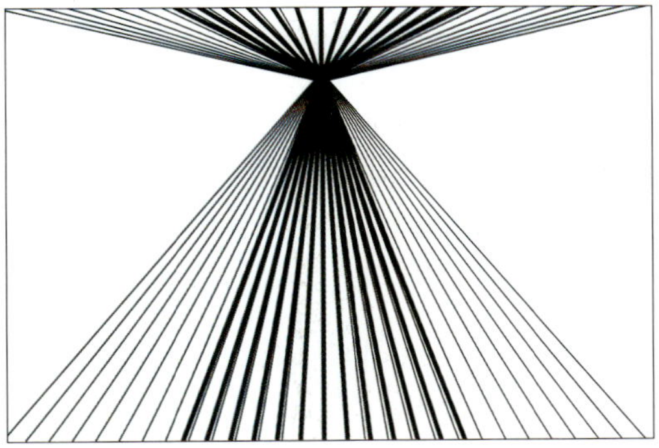

Lines often play an important role in visual structures that create a composition. As Figure 1-13 shows, the lines construct an impressive visual structure. This example produces a dynamic mood because the viewpoint is moving from the ground to the sky. It is as if you are standing on the ground and looking up at skyscrapers.

One purpose of design objects in a layout illustrated by line drawings is to present a basic visual structure. This allows the designer to determine whether the layout is appropriate (or effective). Other design elements such as color and texture often interrupt the designer's visual assessment. Figure 1-14 is an example of a line drawing layout outlining the design objects that portray a calendar page.

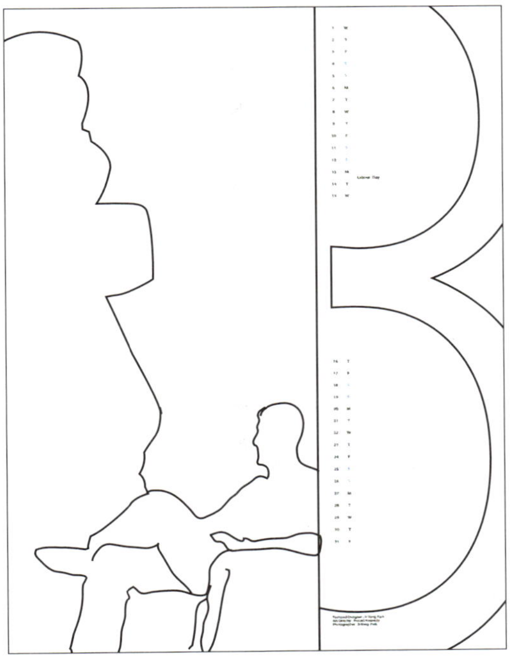

A line is a continuation of points. A line can express various ideas by manipulating width, length, types (curved, straight), and directions (horizontal, vertical, diagonal). These characteristics of lines are often used in information designs such as the subway map shown in Figure 1-15.

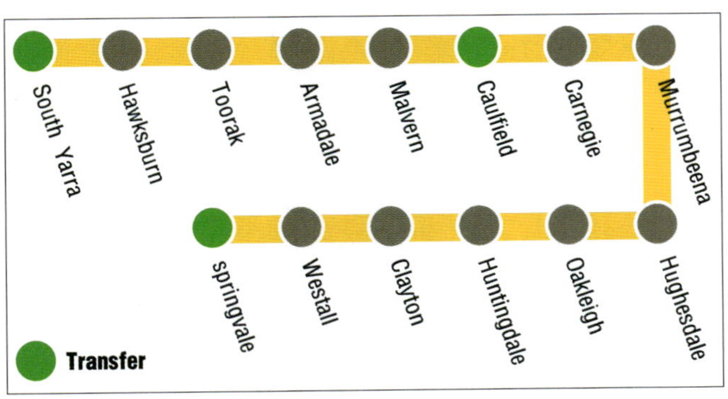


1 Figure 1-13. Lines create a sense of composition
2 Figure 1-14. Lines used in design layout
3 Figure 1-15. Lines connect pieces of information

## Shape

A shape is a defined area of a form. It is a fundamental unit that creates a space. There are three primitive shapes: circle, rectangle, and triangle. Shapes create two-dimensional and three-dimensional forms.

In the design, shapes create a positive area and the background becomes a negative area. The relationship between the positive and the negative areas produces a sense of space. The white lines in Figure 1-16 appear to partition into subdivisions (spaces); on the other hand, the black rectangle shapes create the white boundaries between themselves.

Shapes can enhance a sense of space with three-dimensional form. Figure 1-17 shows that the black shapes (or the white lines) organized like cobwebs create a three-dimensional atmosphere. Figure 1-17 is more dynamic than Figure 1-16 due to its three-dimensional space.

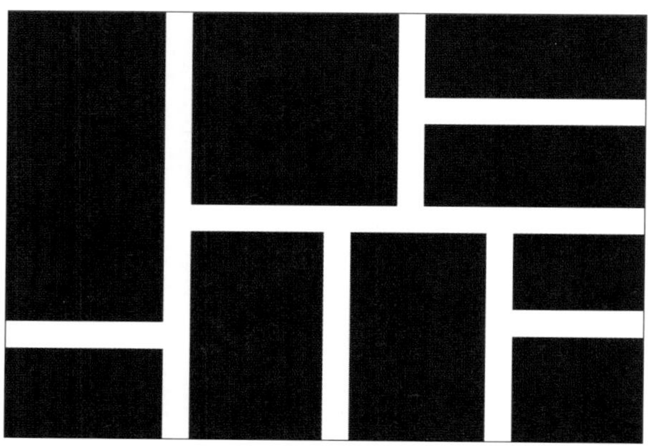

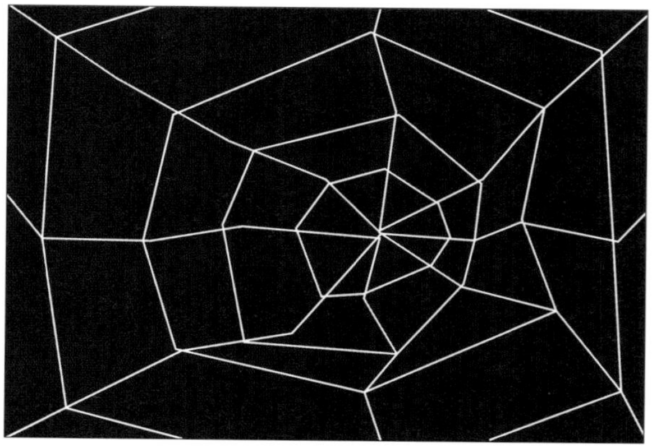

1
2

1 Figure 1-16. Shapes occupy and define space
2 Figure 1-17. A three-dimensional shape

Typically, shapes can be grouped into two categories: organic and geometric. Organic shapes are shapes with an irregular contour, such as leaves and trees that appear in nature. Organic shapes are typically complex and are inspired by the natural environment. They are visually rich and lively (see Figure 1-18).

Geometric shapes describe shapes with regular contours such as rectangles and circles. These are usually mechanical shapes that are man-made. Geometric shapes are drawn from a mechanical-type environment. They are typically regular, simple, structured, and stable (see Figure 1-19).

A shape, alone or in combination with other shapes, creates a visual composition that conveys information. Shapes in layout design are used to create and organize various forms in terms of visual communication.

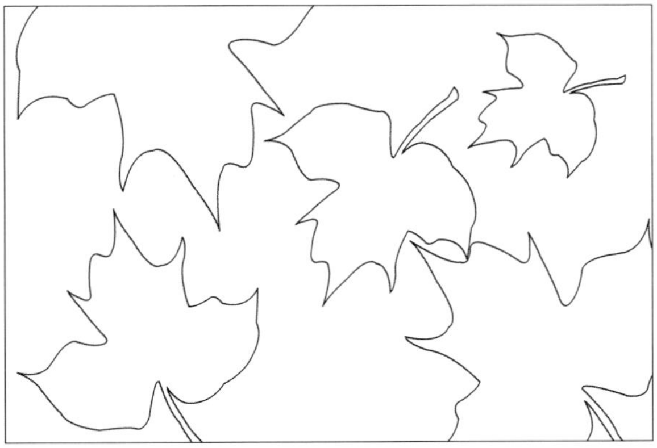

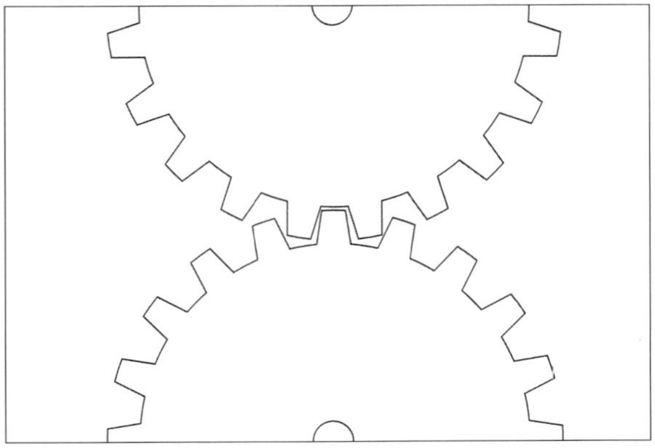

**1** **Figure 1-18.** An organic shape
**2** **Figure 1-19.** Geometric shape

## Texture

The texture of something is the way that it feels when you touch it. Visual texture is associated with the touch experience of an object; for example, how smooth or rough it is. That is, visual texture creates an illusion of a tactile experience. The texture of objects in terms of visual design adds richness and depth to a layout and can generate various emotions and moods.

In Figure 1-20, an irregular unevenness of texture creates a mysterious and enigmatic mood. The audience may never have physically experienced this surface characteristic, but their visual understanding is developed by their previous association with similar tactile experiences. Figure 1-21 is a photo of an ordinary brick wall that conveys a feeling of roughness. This texture may not require any explanation because the audience is very familiar with the surface.

Designers often create textured effects on the basis of tactile experiences in order to enrich visual communication. As Figure 1-22 shows, the pattern design emulates a tactile experience, which implies that the pattern is raised slightly from the surface.

1
2 3

1 Figure 1-20. Uneven texture
2 Figure 1-21. Rough texture
3 Figure 1-22. Embossed pattern texture

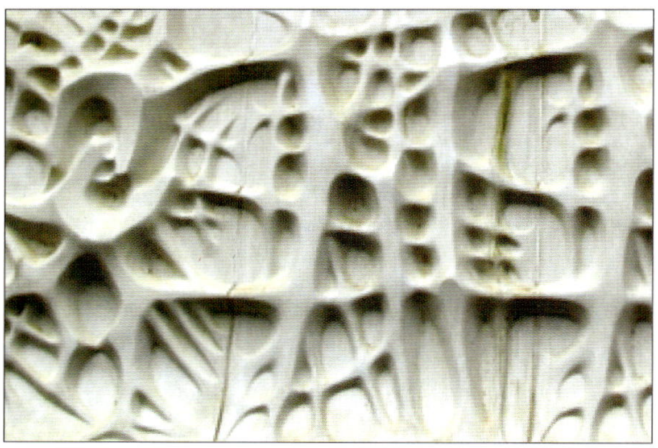

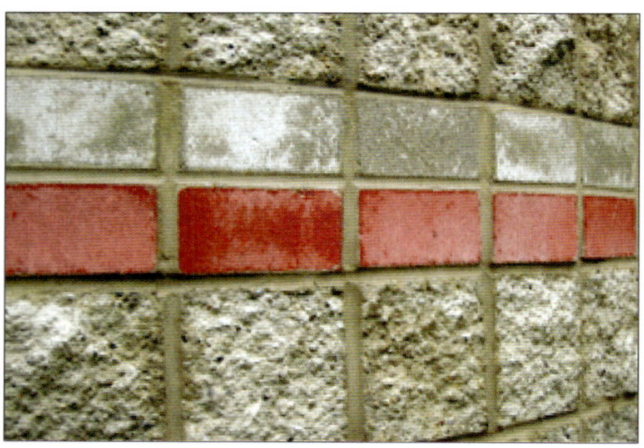

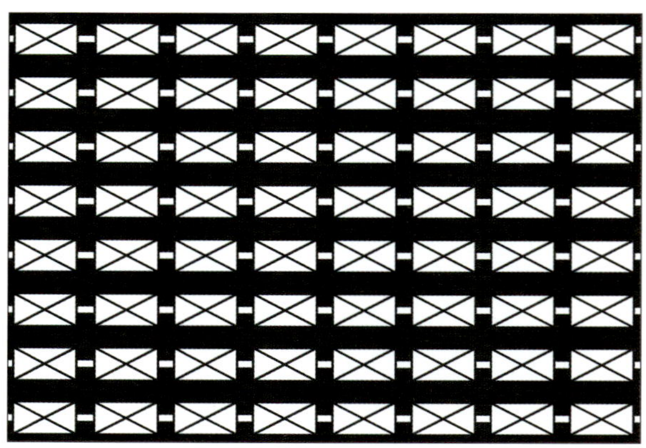

## Space

—

All design objects exist within space. In other words, shapes in a plane automatically create space. Space in visual design refers to an area that is available or empty within a layout. Space is also the area that can facilitate movement and direction. Space can be separated or unified by manipulating the design objects.

Space has a positive and a negative area; positive space is where shapes exist, and negative space is the empty space around shapes. The designer must have a good sense of visual balance. In an image, the result will vary depending on which space is dominant: either negative or positive space. As Figure 1-23 shows, the image on the right, in which negative space is dominant, is stronger and more impressive than the image on the left.

Organizing spaces in visual design is equivalent to arranging design elements or parts of a design element. As shown in Figure 1-24, empty area(s) connect the split parts of the word to convey its meaning: space.

The distance between objects determines their readability and composites a visual structure. As Figure 1-25 portrays, the example on the left is much more readable than the one on the right. However, their aesthetic assessments differ. The first image looks ordered, simple, and stable, whereas the second looks full, structured, and impressive.

1
2 3

1 Figure 1-23. Distinguishing figure and ground by positive and negative area
2 Figure 1-24. Creating ties between elements
3 Figure 1-25. Visual rest and readability

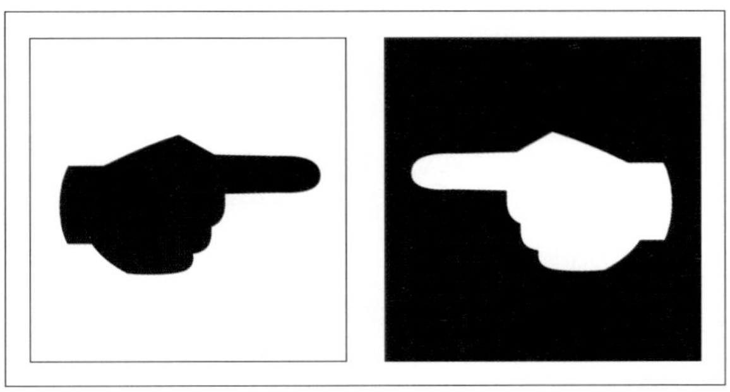

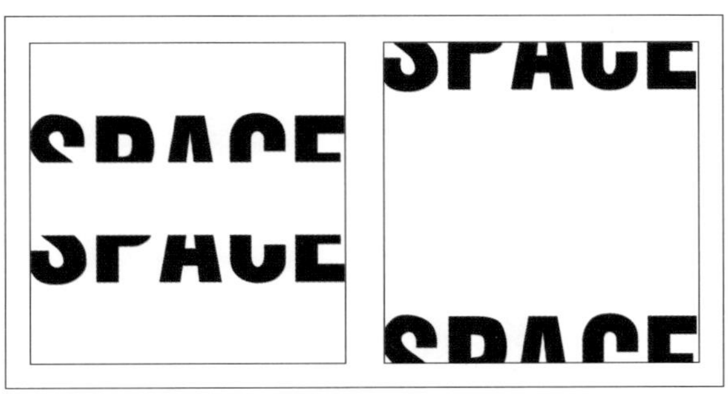

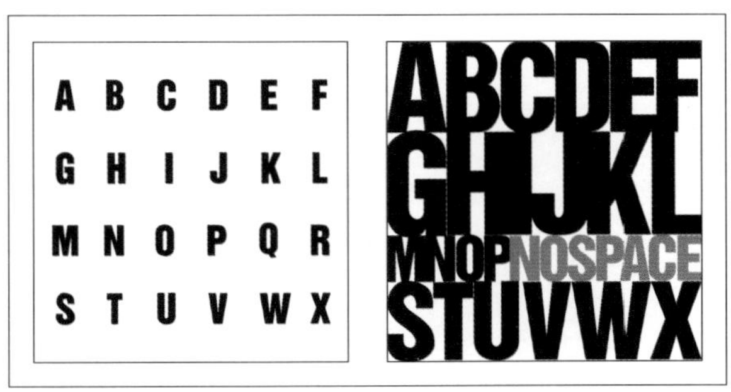

## Size

—

Size is how big or small something is. In visual design, an object's size is relative to other objects in the layout. Size determines the relationship between objects and space, and, in terms of visual design, refers to functionally and aesthetically organizing the design objects in a layout.

Figure 1-26 demonstrates that different sizes of the same design object can produce a totally different result. It also shows how size in visual design can be used to attract the audience's attention.

Size refers not only to the difference between objects, but also the balance between objects in terms of visual weight. In Figure 1-27, the different visual weights of layout design create different moods. Both designs are well-organized structures, but the design on the left looks firmer and more solid because the upper parts (banner and navigation) and the lower parts (columns) are systematically balanced in terms of visual weight.

As Figure 1-28 shows, the number 8 is maximized in the first design and minimized in the second design. Both emphasize number 8, but their visual impact differs in terms of the scale design. Size in visual design refers to scale, which is used to create a more attractive and effective solution and convey the message by adjusting the sizes of the design elements, including the background.

1 Figure 1-26. Relative size
2 Figure 1-27. Organizing elements in a consistent layout
3 Figure 1-28. Relative proportion

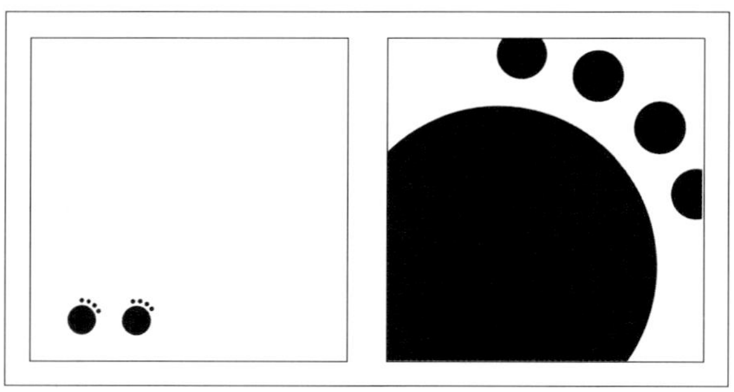

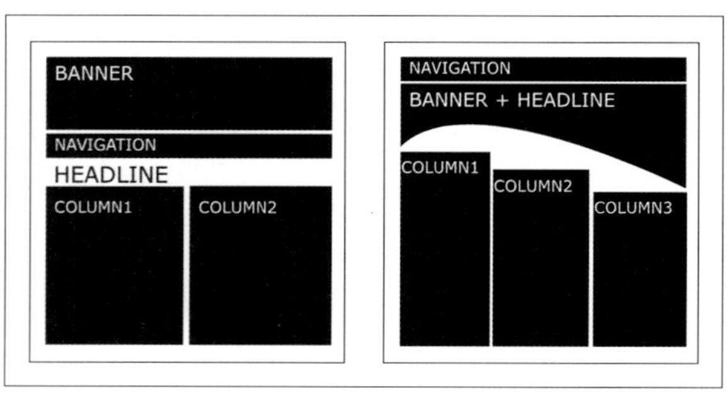


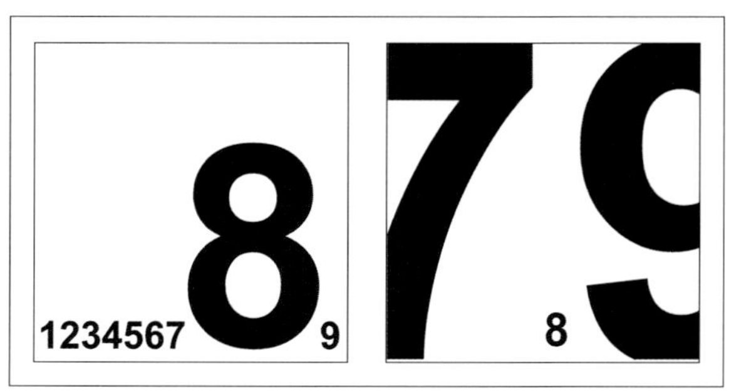

## Color

Color distinguishes objects, conveys moods in layouts, and attracts the eye to a particular point or object. Color also creates images and produces shapes. Selecting colors is often determined by psychological experience. For example, red often represents passion and power, yellow can represent warning or optimism. Figure 1-29 demonstrates how the design can have a different effect depending on its color. The right-hand bamboo image in sky blue is more palatable with our normal experience of bamboo: solid, cold, and sleek.

Color can separate one object from others to readily attract the audience's attention (see Figure 1-30). When used in layout, color allows the designer to give objects distinctive visual identities. Additionally, different colors create different moods and effects.

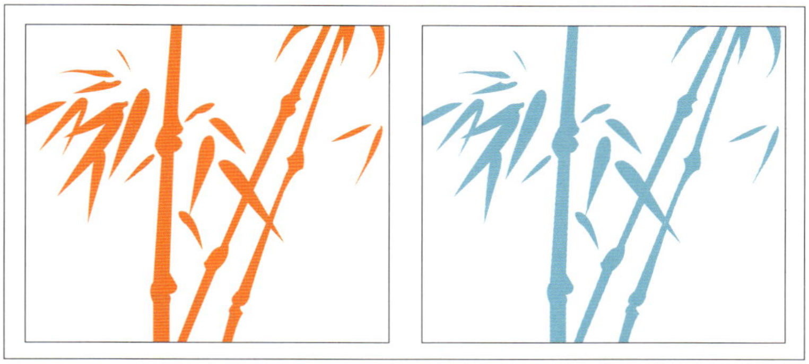

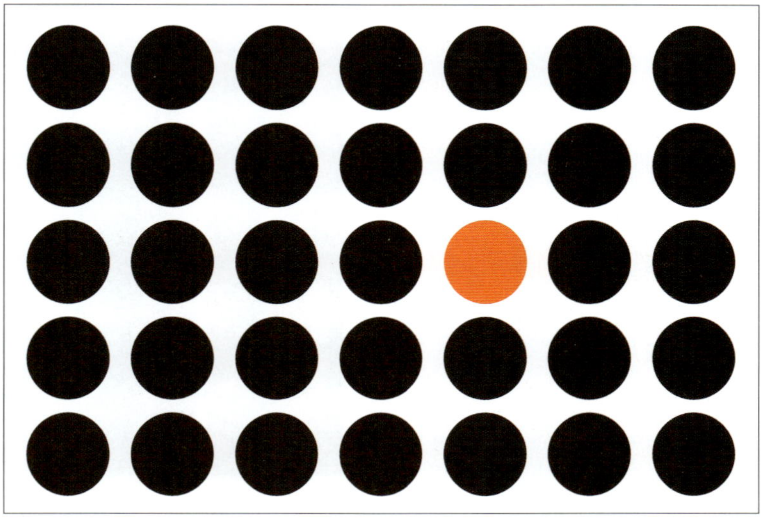

1
2

1 Figure 1-29. Color to create different moods
2 Figure 1-30. Color to focus attention

Color can also be used to create shapes. Figure 1-31 illustrates a liquid running down the throat. A shape with a color enriches its visual identity. The liquid in Figure 1-31 could represent water, but the audience associates the liquid with an orange drink.

Just as color creates a shape, it also creates a visual structure when combined with other shapes. Figure 1-32 presents an abstract composition with violet tones that emit a mood of cyberpunk style.

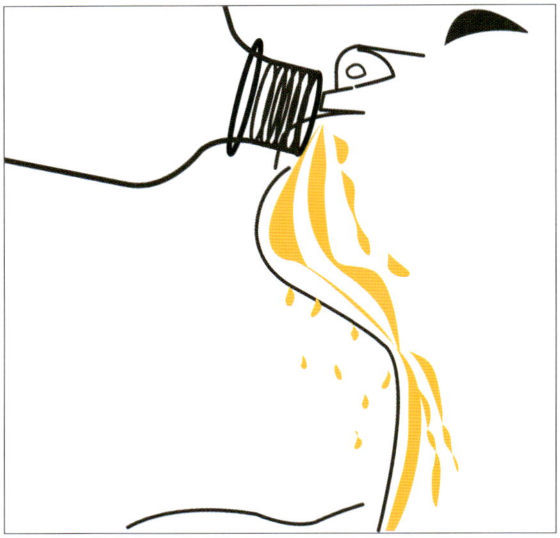

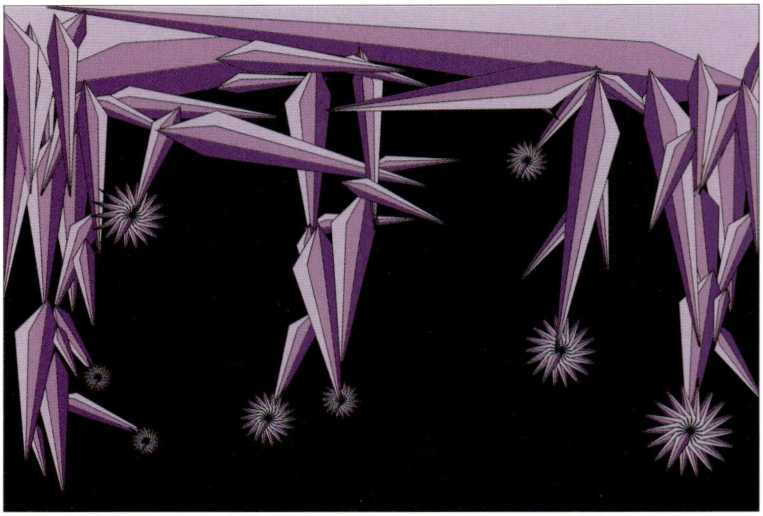

1 Figure 1-31. Color as shape
2 Figure 1-32. Color as structure

Chapter

# [ 02 ]

# Design Principles - Part 1

Layout design is the term used to describe the visual structure of the composition. Layout design is essential to arranging and manipulating the design elements in terms of creating its look and feel, also referred to as the theme. Practicing layout design is helpful for improving your visual assessment skills. There are many factors that contribute to a well-structured layout. The ten most fundamental principles to achieving good layout design will be introduced in this chapter and Chapter 3.

# Stability and Balance

A stable and balanced layout does not mean a dull and boring layout. It is as if gentle waves are crashing on the beach.

## Stable and Balanced

Stability often refers to balance and vice versa. Both refer to visual calmness and quietness. In a stable layout, there is no sense of movement because all elements are firmly fixed in position. The concept of balance is often adopted in creating a stable layout. When you balance one element with other elements, each element has the same dimension and importance in terms of visual weight. Therefore, a balanced layout of elements often produces a stable design. When you break the balance between elements, the sense of stability disappears.

In terms of visual design, stability represents symmetrical and balanced structures that do not appear likely to move or fall. Stable and balanced structures appear sound and their mood does not change suddenly or drastically. It is like looking at a calm and boundless expanse of the sea (see Figure 2-1).

In Figure 2-2, the sun (circle) and the horizon (straight line) are arranged with stability and balance within a rectangular frame that produces a stable, motionless layout. Figure 2-1 is more peaceful than Figure 2-2, but more monotonous. In this way, balancing the visual weights of elements in a layout can create different moods.

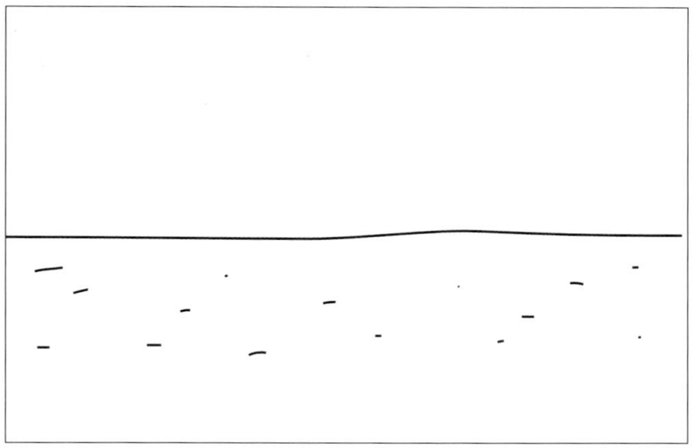

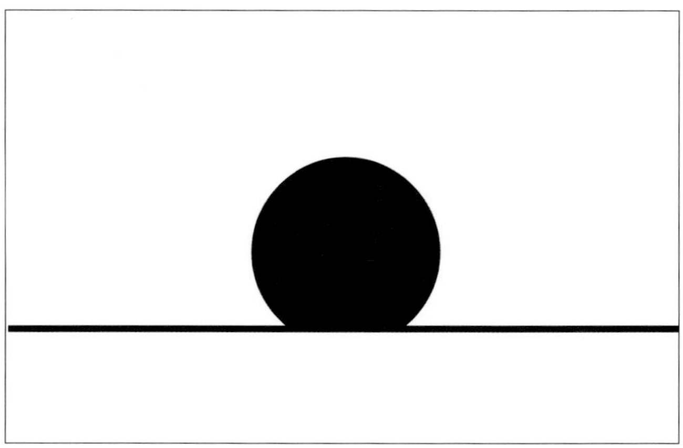

1
2

1 **Figure 2-1.** Stable horizon
2 **Figure 2-2.** Stable and balanced sunset/sunrise

## Symmetrical Stability

—

Most web sites, especially information-focused sites, are designed with a stable structure to display a large amount of information effectively and efficiently. A stable and balanced layout provides a sense of stability so that the user can access the information comfortably. Text information especially will have higher readability within this type of layout.

To balance one design element with other design elements, its visual importance must be weighed relative to the others. A sense of balance and symmetry emerges when each element's strength and importance is promoted in dimension, visuality, and structure.

Symmetrical balance in a visual design means that both sides from the center of the design vertically and horizontally are almost identical or perfectly centered compositions like a mirror image. Figure 2-3 and Figure 2-4 are symmetrical layouts that have visual weight in balance. Figure 2-3 divides the page symmetrically using stacked halves, and Figure 2-4 does so with quadrants.

1 2

1 Figure 2-3. Symmetrically stable using stacked halves

2 Figure 2-4. Symmetrically stable using quadrants

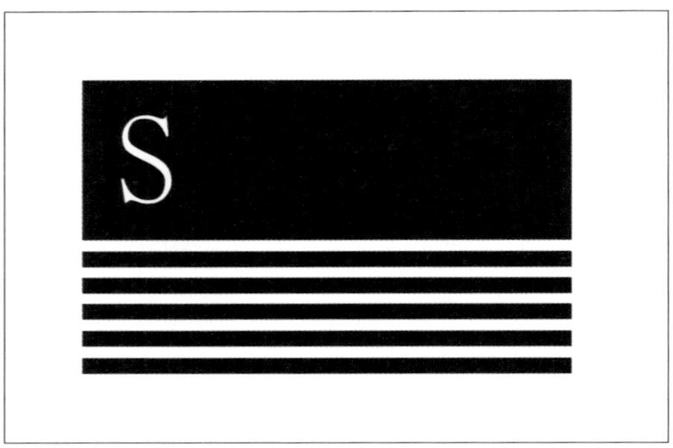

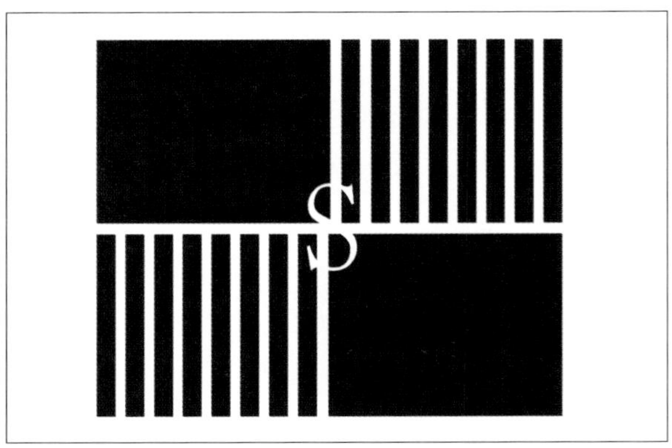

## Asymmetrical Balance

—

An asymmetrical layout can also produce a stable structure as long as the visual relationship between the elements outlines a cluster and does not break the calmness of the background. Although foreground elements are asymmetrical in shape or size, the visual understanding of the elements can bind them in one cluster by contrast with the background. Figure 2-5 is not a symmetrical layout, but it is stable because the vertical lines on the left and the rectangles on the right are balanced in terms of visual weight. Our visual assessment divides this layout into both sides as visual clusters and contrasts them. Asymmetrical balance in visual design means that both halves from the center of the design, both vertically and horizontally, are different yet visually equal.

As Figure 2-6 shows, an asymmetrical balance can produce an attractive and active impression, which a symmetrical balance generally does not. An asymmetrical stable layout is more exciting and energetic than a symmetrical stable layout because the former has a sense of variety.

1 2

1 Figure 2-5. Asymmetrical, but stable
2 Figure 2-6. Asymmetrical layout

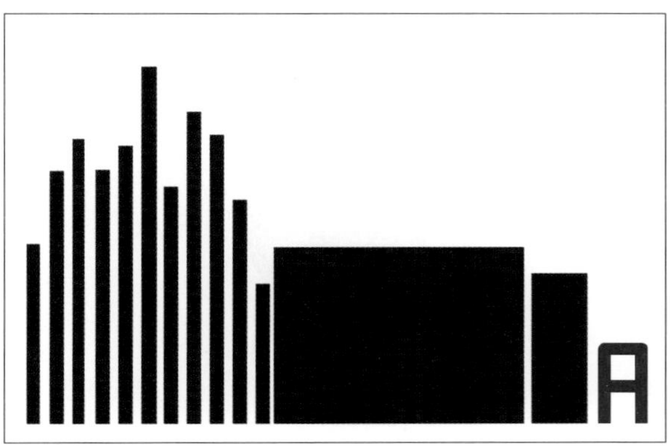

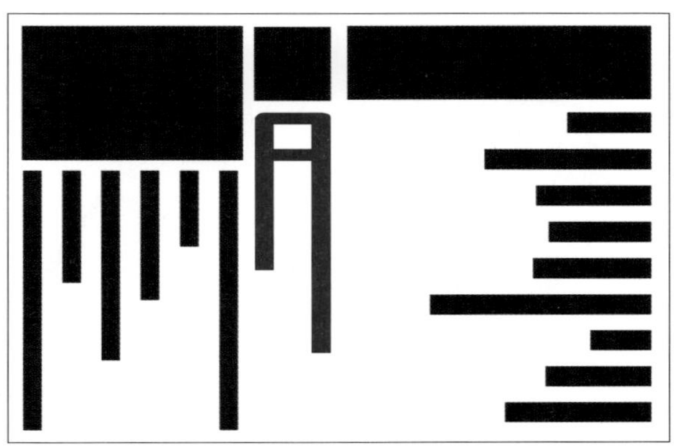

## Stability and the Grid System

—

The grid system brings order and balance to the layout (for details about the grid system, see Chapter 4). In most cases, a stable layout follows the underlying grid structure to maintain balance. By the same token, working against the grid system can create an unstable and unbalanced layout. The most stable and balanced layout is placing a point (a circle) in the middle of an axis (the imaginary lines through the middle of something).

The design elements in Figure 2-7 are positioned with no consideration for the grid lines and rotated at random angles. This produces a disordered and chaotic mood and there is no visual connection among the elements.

In Figure 2-8, however, the circle placed in the middle of the document represents a perfect balance in the bilateral symmetry of the composition.

1 2

1 Figure 2-7. Disorder and the grid
2 Figure 2-8. Stability and balance in the grid

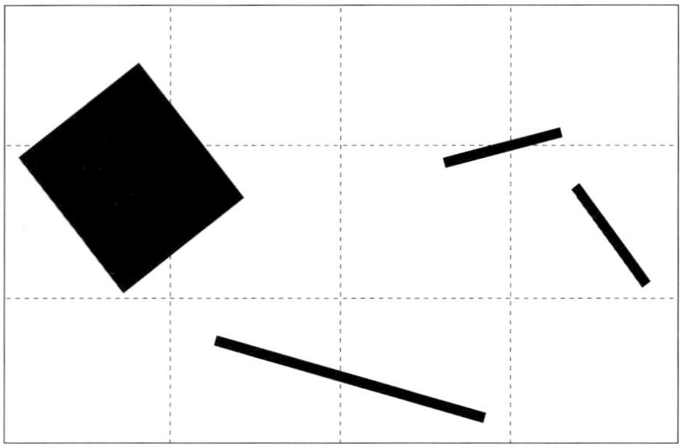

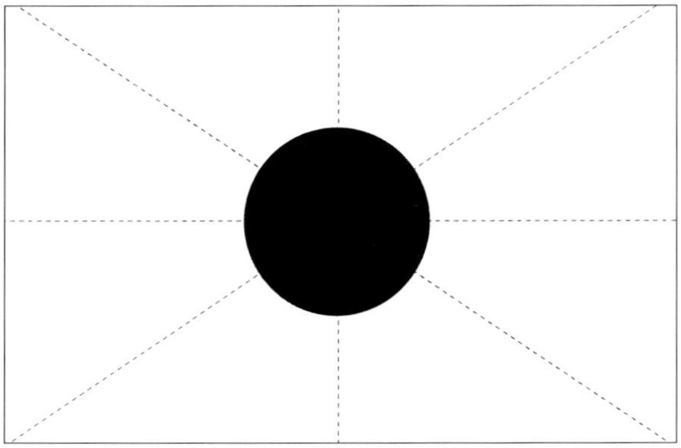

# Proportion and Harmony

The relationship between parts or a part and the whole is defined by a ratio. In other words, proportion is concerned with the relative size of the design objects comparatively. If an object increases or decreases in proportion to another object, it alters the relationship between them. Proportion pursues harmony. A well-proportioned layout is adaptable; the elements in the layout are well harmonized and organized.

1
2

1 Figure 2-9. Direct proportion
2 Figure 2-10. Inverse proportion

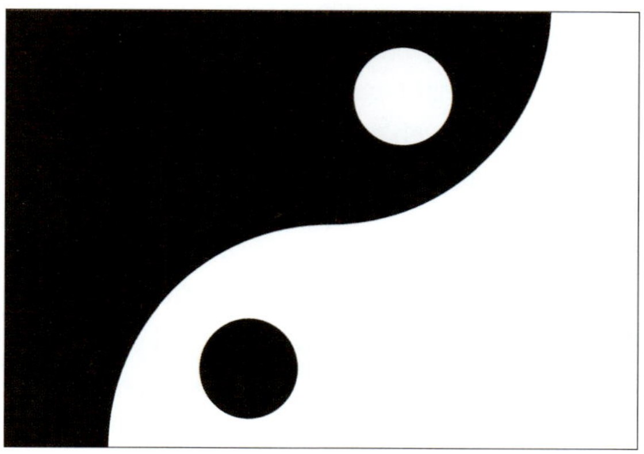

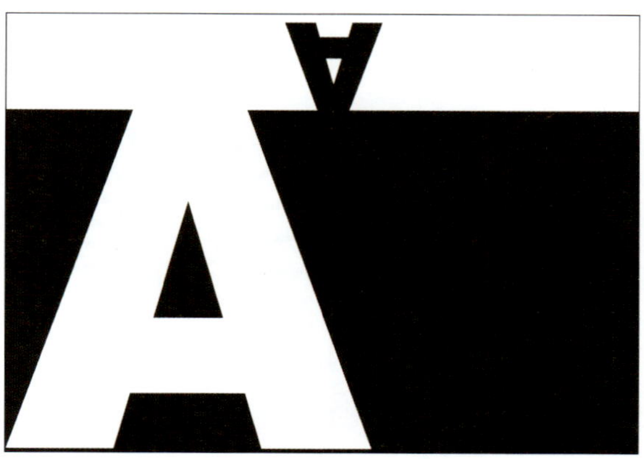


## Direct and Inverse Proportion

Adjusting proportions between objects, including the background, produces various moods and layouts. In most cases, good proportion achieves harmony between design elements.

There are two types of proportions: direct proportion and inverse proportion. If Object A and Object B are in direct proportion, as Object A grows bigger, Object B also grows bigger according to their shared ratio. Figure 2-9 shows you direct proportion between the positive shape (the black areas) and the negative space (the white areas).

If Object A is inversely proportional to Object B, then as Object B gets bigger, Object A becomes smaller by the same factor. Figure 2-10 shows an inverse proportion between the upside down small black letter and the large white letter.

## Golden Proportion

—

Golden proportion (also called the golden ratio or the golden mean) refers to the magical proportion that has been observed to evoke emotion or aesthetic feelings. Artists throughout history and in many different cultures have found that the ratio of 1:1.618 is particularly aesthetically pleasing. This ideal ratio can also be obtained by dividing a line so that the short and long pieces have the same proportion (1:1.618).

### 1 | Fibonacci sequence

The first numbers in Fibonacci's famous sequence are 0 and 1. The next number is the sum of the previous two, resulting in this series: 0, 1, 1, 2, 3, 5, 8, 13, 21, 34, 55, 89, 144, etc. If this series is used to make a new series of the ratios of sequential pairs, the results oscillate around the golden ratio (1.618...): 1/0 = 0, 1/1 = 1, 2/1 = 2, 3/2 = 1.5, 5/3 = 1.6666..., 8/5 = 1.6, 13/8 = 1.625, 21/13 = 1.61538... 34/21 = 1.61904..., and so on.

In Figure 2-11, the shape with eight petals looks more stable and harmonized than the shape with seven petals because the eight petals have well-balanced contrast horizontally and vertically.

In Figure 2-12, the shape of 21 petals looks more stable and well-proportioned than the shape of 22 petals. As demonstrated in Figures 2-11 and 2-12, applying the Fibonacci series to your visual design may give you a harmonious solution because people have already experienced and are familiar with (subconsciously, at least) the aesthetic of the series commonly observed in nature.

1 2

1 Figure 2-11. Compare seven petals (non-Fibonacci) vs. eight petals (Fibonacci)

2 Figure 2-12. Compare 21 petals (Fibonacci) vs. 22 petals (non-Fibonacci)

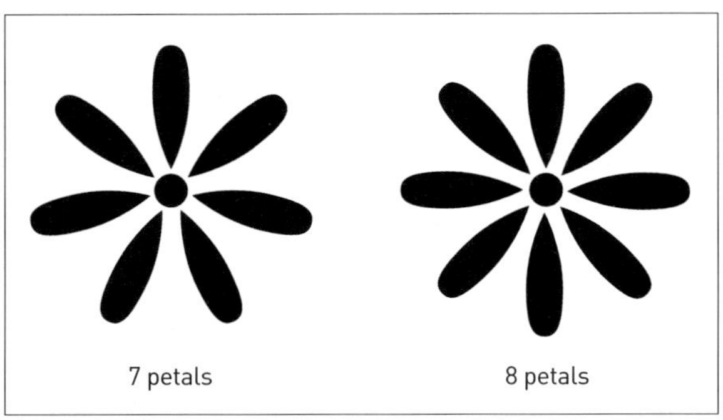


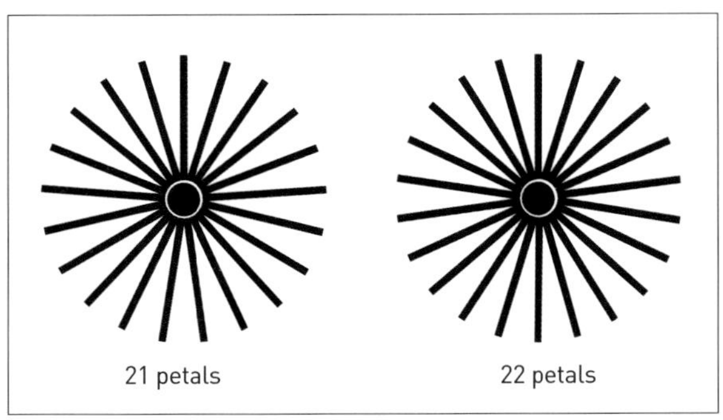

## 2 | Golden Rectangle

Creating a rectangle with two sequential numbers from the Fibonacci series becomes the golden rectangle. As shown in Figure 2-13, it starts with the 1×1 square (a) and rotates to the side (b) to make the next rectangle. The ratio of the sections is the same as the Fibonacci series. As Figure 2-13 shows, the golden rectangle starts with square a (1×1), expands to include b (2×1), then c (3×2), d (5×3), e (8×5), f (13×8), g (21×13) and h (34×21).

Figure 2-14 exemplifies a postage stamp, with the red lines representing the golden rectangle and the swirl graphic applied atop it. Adding the word "swirl" on the bottom right of the plane further completes the design. Like this example, the golden rectangle often suggests a foundation in creating a layout design.

1 2

1 Figure 2-13. The golden rectangle

2 Figure 2-14. A postage stamp design based on the golden rectangle

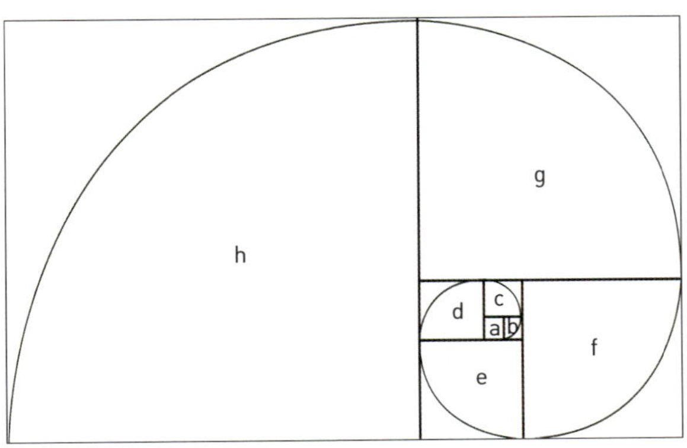


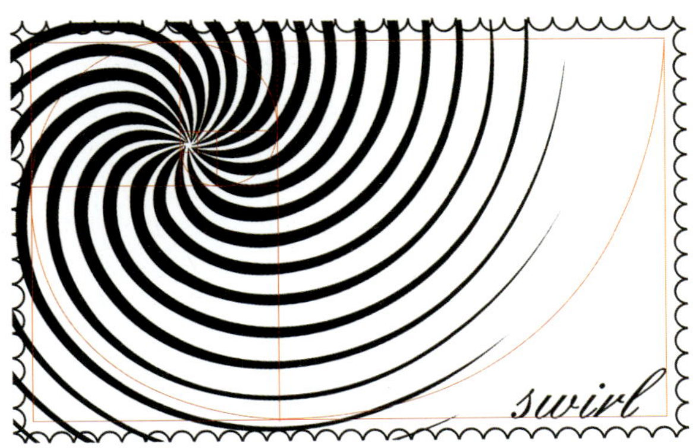

## 3 | Golden Section

The golden section depicts a geometrical harmony. As shown in Figure 2-15, a golden section begins with a perfect square that will be divided into two parts with equal ratio (Line 1). A diagonal line divides up the right half (Line 2). The length of the diagonal line will then be used as the radius. The bottom point of Line 2 will be its pivot point to draw an arc (Line 3) downward until Line 2 is perpendicular to Line 1. Finally, the rectangle (No. 4) has the same height as the perfect square and the same width as the arc from the circle. The perfect square and the new rectangle (which is the combined perfect square plus the added rectangle) have the ratio of 5:8. This is one of the golden ratios in the Fibonacci series (1×1, 2×1, 3×2, 5×3, 8× 5, 13 ×8, 21×13).

As Figure 2-16 shows, the geometric lines in the golden section suggest the possibility of alternating composition. The ratio of 5:8 in the rectangle allows other golden divisions, such that the ratio of a:b and b:c is also the ratio of 5:8. The three sections demonstrate the layout design in terms of proportion and harmony.

1 2

1 Figure 2-15. How a golden section is drawn
2 Figure 2-16. The component triangles of a golden section

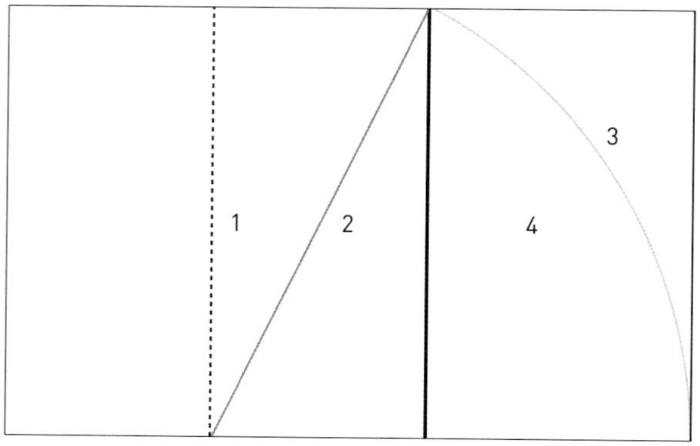


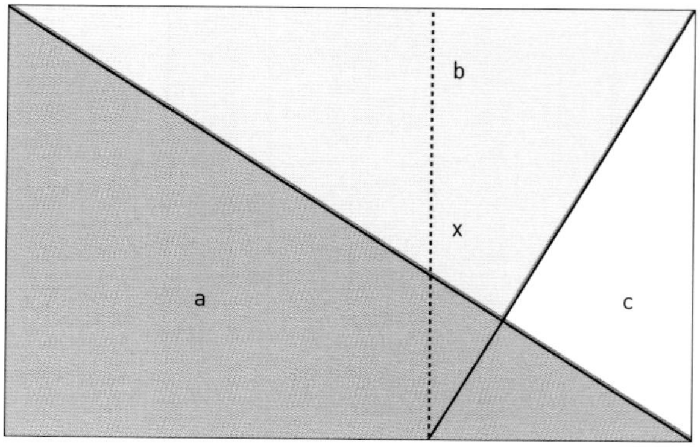

Figure 2-17 shows an example of how the golden section can be used in a layout design. The golden section is simplified with three sections, and the graphic and the shapes are applied. The golden section is a guide for achieving proportion and harmony in layout design.

As Figure 2-18 shows, a golden section can be converted to a grid system. Graphics and design elements can be measured with the golden grid in terms of harmony and beauty. The golden grid can be overlaid on a design to evaluate how well the design aligns with the golden grid.

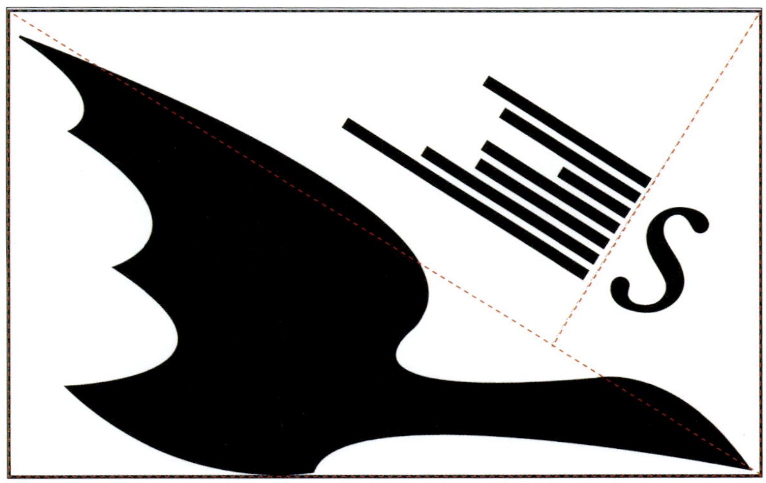

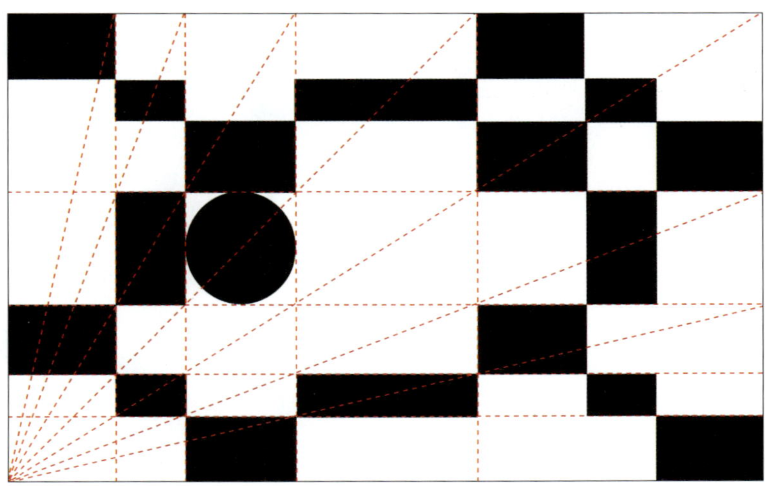

1 Figure 2-17. The golden section suggests a design layout

2 Figure 2-18. The golden section on the golden grid

## Harmony

—

Harmony in visual design refers to all parts of the visual image relating to and complementing each other. Patterns can help achieve harmony. By repeating patterns (see Figure 2-19) in an interesting arrangement, the overall visual image comes together.

Consistent design creates harmony and unity. Using similar typefaces and shapes in a layout and graphics or images within a similar color scheme will produce this effect. All design elements should be arranged in respect to a design theme, producing a harmonized visual identity in a unified design layout.

Harmony refers to the way in which elements are combined into a pleasing arrangement. Objects in harmony are presented as a whole without exclusion or isolation. Both similarity and difference constitute the harmony. Too much similarity among objects can lead to a monotonous mood; likewise, too much difference creates only visual discordance. In other words, harmony requires the expression of unity and variety at the same time.

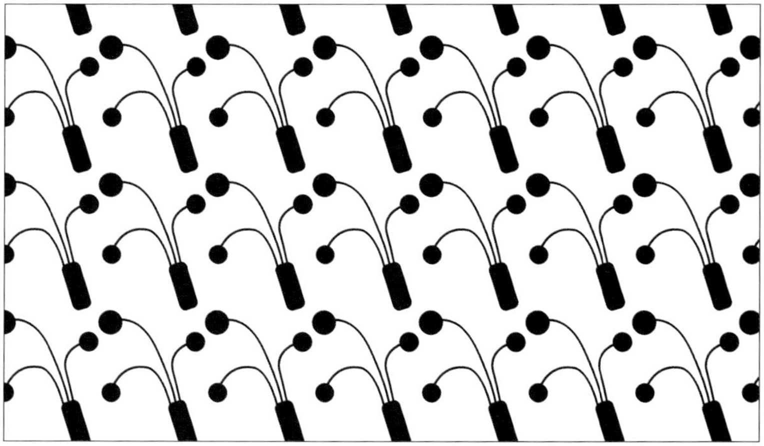

■ Figure 2-19. Harmony through repetition

Similarity in harmony can be expressed through repetition of shape, style, and size. As Figure 2-20 shows, the similarity of shapes and the component ratio constitutes bilateral symmetry, and creates a symmetrical harmony. On the other hand, difference in harmony can be expressed by way of applying different angles, positions, and strong contrasts.

As Figure 2-21 shows, the difference derives from an unbalanced and asymmetrical component ratio and creates a dynamic harmony.

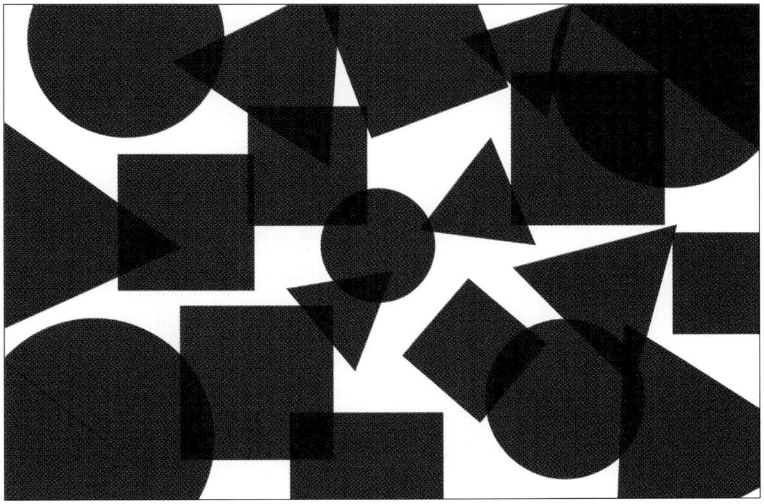

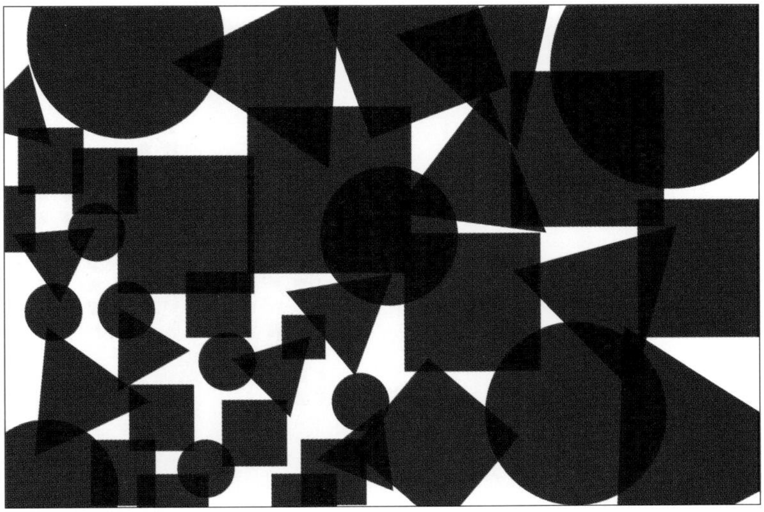

1 Figure 2-20. Similarity and symmetry create harmony

2 Figure 2-21. Variety and asymmetry also produce harmony

# Rhythm and Movement

Rhythm in visual design refers to repetitive movements. A regular series of movements and a regular pattern of changes in a visual flow produce the quality of rhythm in visual composition. Rhythm can animate the design layout with a feeling of vitality and existence, and produce dynamic regularity. (You can read more about movement in Chapter 3.)

## Repetition

Repetition is a key feature in rhythm, visual design, and spatial performance. The distance between the elements and the form of the elements determines the rhythmical expression. Figure 2-22 expresses a feeling of movement with a regular waveform and the repetitive square pattern. Repetition is connecting, parting, and creating an area of attention.

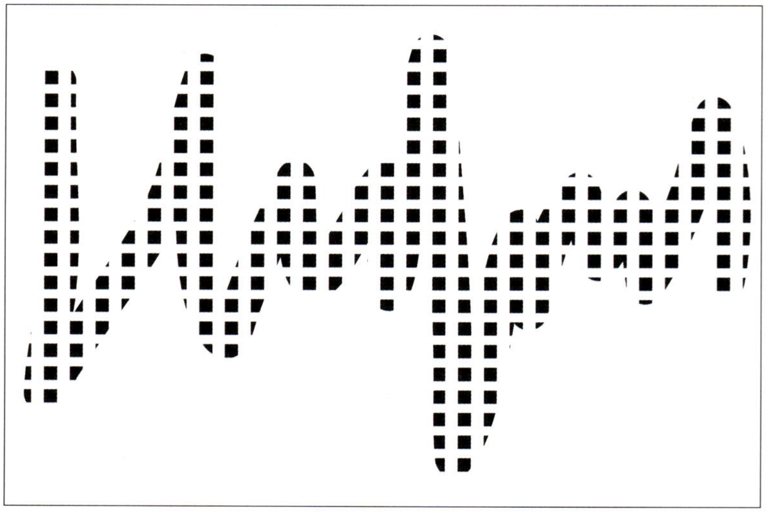

**1** Figure 2-22. Waveform repetition

## Rhythm

—

Rhythm creates a visual flow and helps lead eye movement. As Figure 2-23 shows, the abstract graphics are dominant in the layout and then reused as a background pattern in a smaller size. The repetitive pattern assists and reinforces the main graphic in the layout.

Rhythm is characterized by its own movement, but the repetition can be monotonous. In other words, rhythm can be either dynamic or stable. Within the context of the rhythmical pattern, Figure 2-24 expresses chaotic and energetic qualities. Within the context of the layout, the objects resemble a bunch of grapes, which stabilizes the harmony of the layout.

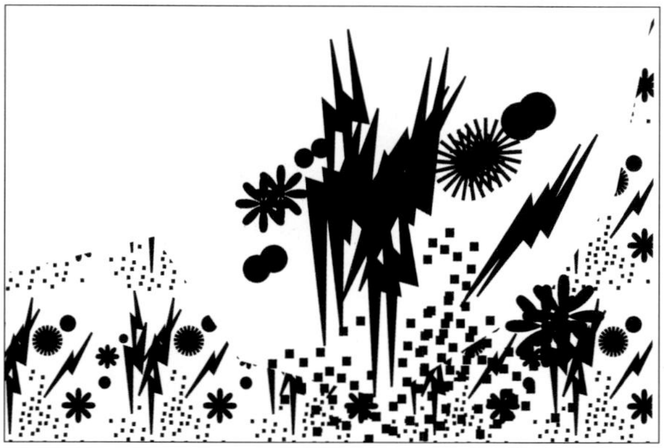

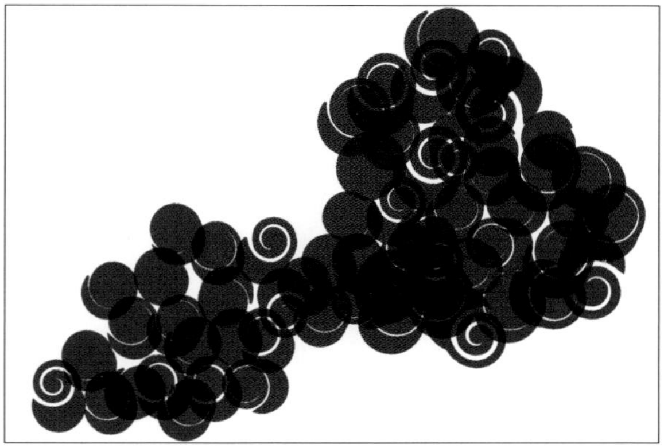

1
2

1 **Figure 2-23.** Abstract repetition
2 **Figure 2-24.** Energetic and chaotic rhythm

## Gradation

Gradation refers to subtle differences or changes in an object's color or shape that gradually blend from one to another. Gradient layouts have variety and movement at the same time, producing a stronger impression (see Figure 2-25).

Gradation can be applied to an object in terms of size and direction, and it produces a linear perspective. Gradation of color, such as from warm to cool and from dark to light, can add interest and movement to objects and layout because the gradation causes the eye to move along. As shown in Figure 2-26, the gradations on each object are used to create a three-dimensional view. The white-blue gradient background in particular creates a spatial mood over the layout.

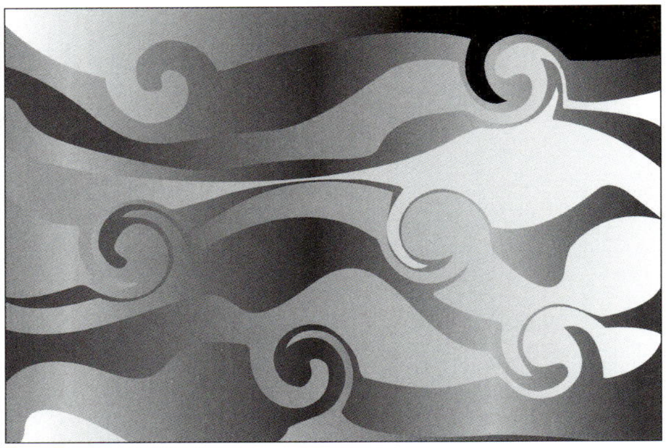

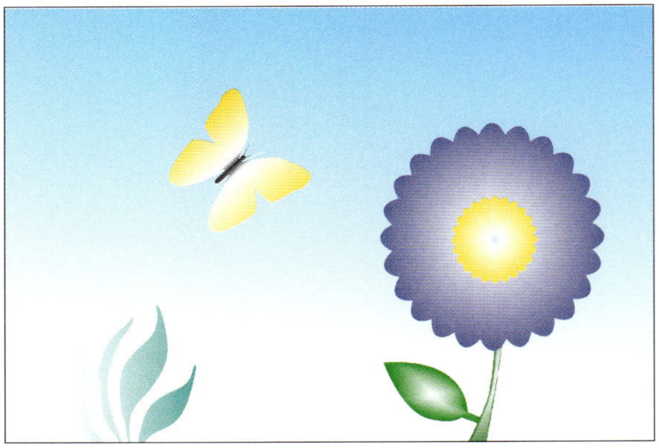

1
2

1 Figure 2-25. Gradation and rhythm promote variety and motion

2 Figure 2-26. Gradient changes in color and temperature lead the eye

# **Design Studio:** Layout Design 1

You are expected to create several layouts with a sense of stability. Stressing again, a stable layout does not mean it should be monotonous and boring. The overall visual structure should be stable or the stability should be dominant in the layout, but you may need to consider adding some visual accent on it in order to arouse the audience's visual interest.

This activity focuses on creating various design compositions with the same elements. In general, design elements must be manipulated to create a layout that meets a certain design theme, such as a stable, dynamic, or scale layout. Commonly, a web page consists of four visual elements: graphics, text, a navigation bar, and web banners. It is important to understand the definition of each element to be able to arrange and manipulate them freely.

- Graphics refer to photos, line drawings, graphics, symbols, or typographical images that support the theme or content of the page.
- Text refers to written material or information that is often partially rearranged or combined with other visual elements for the purpose of attracting visual attention or enhancing the design.
- A navigation bar refers to a series of buttons that represent the structure of a web site. Although a navigation bar usually manifests in the shape of a rectangle, one need not always restrict its shape within a rectangle, because each button (or function) of the navigation could be rearranged within a certain visual composition or a visual metaphor.
- Web banners refer to an area of predominant visual interest or impression in a web page. It is often used as the means of delivering the main theme or mood of an area for advertising. A web banner need not always be in the shape of a rectangle, even though many web sites have a web banner with a rectangle, it could be reshaped in various forms depending on the visual identity or the functional purpose of the site.

## Stable Layout Design

Manipulate and arrange the elements given in Figure 2-27 to create a stable layout. Several stable layouts can be produced with the elements provided within a rectangular space that is 550 pixels wide by 400 pixels high. Give each layout design a descriptive title, such as "symmetrical balance" or "asymmetrical balance." The visual assessments of others will suggest titles. Always show your layout design to others to receive feedback, because the success of the design depends on how people perceive it. While creating a layout, be careful not to lose track of the theme, or you risk losing the initial objectivity of the visual assessment.

There are some rules to remember while creating a layout.

- Do not apply any colors other than black and white or use opacity.
- The color of the shapes can be changed to only black or white.
- Do not use any other shapes other than the shapes provided.

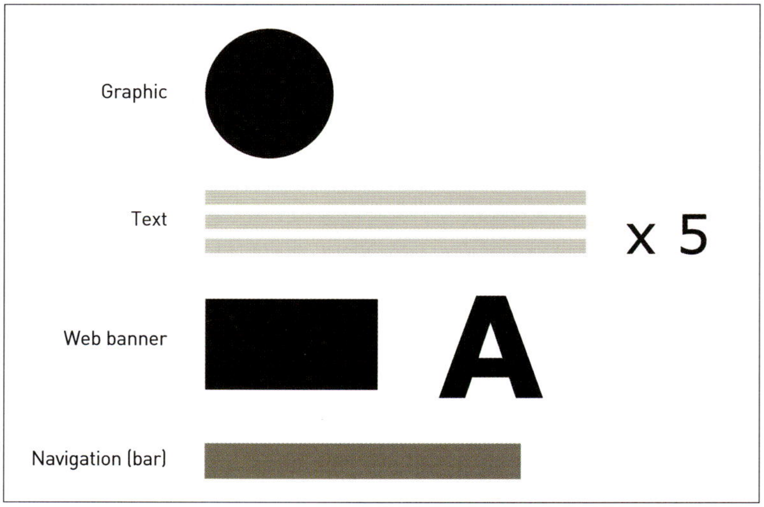


Figure 2-27. Given elements for creating different web site layouts

In the end, a successful layout will be a well-designed work with the correct theme, yet it should also contain creative solutions finalized with professionalism. Lack of experimentation or creativity may result in an uninteresting layout. Figure 2-28 is a rather monotonous layout, but very acceptable in terms of visual stability. The following examples show what is possible with the given elements in terms of stable layouts. Experimental and creative solutions will animate and enrich a layout and, in so doing, will lead more successfully towards a superior stable layout.

Figure 2-29 is a stable layout in which the elements are nested between the web banner at the top and the navigation bar at the bottom. It produces a visual stability overall, but it also contains visual interest by the composition of the letter A, the circle shape, and the text lines. Although the meaning of stability is associated with a calm, peaceful, and static mood, it is important to remember that a stable layout doesn't mean that it should be plain and uninteresting. The three lines near the top connect the shape of the circle and the main text lines visually. Linking the web banner and the main text lines with the letter A creates a similar effect. As a result, all the elements are connected and united visually.

1 2

1 **Figure 2-28.** Basic (but monotonous) stable web site layout

2 **Figure 2-29.** An interesting stable layout achieved through connectedness

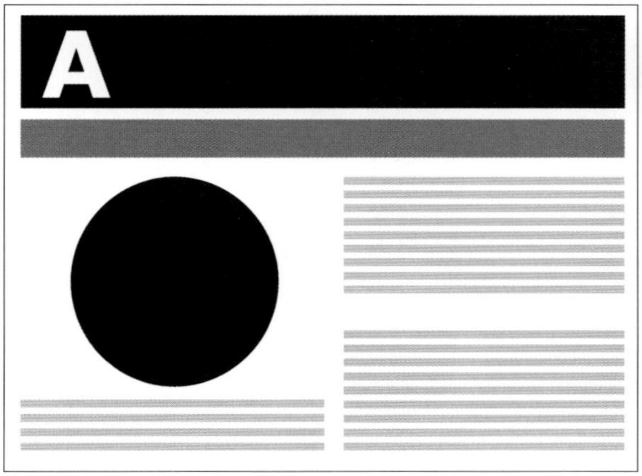


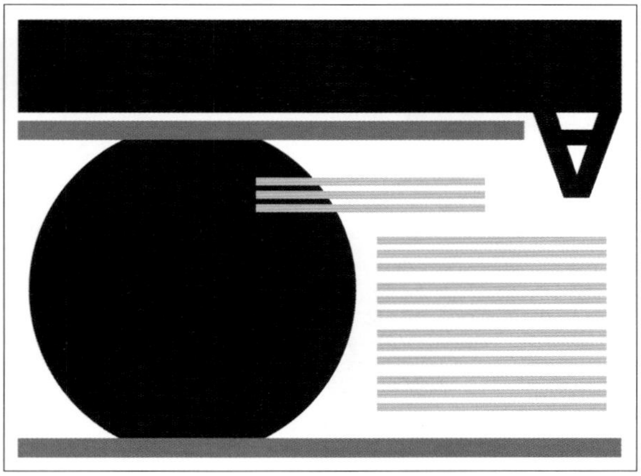

Unlike the previous layout, Figure 2-30 is less stable because there is no single element defining the bottom. Its stability comes from the composition of the web banner, the navigation bar, and the text lines that construct a stable visual structure. A visual interest is added by combining the letter A with the circular shapes that looks like an asymmetrical figure being suspended from the web banner.

Figure 2-31 shows another possible form of the stable layout. It has an asymmetrical contrast between the web banner, navigation bar, and text lines in terms of visual weight. The color of the letter A and the negative circle shape (behind the black circle) were inverted from black to white. The circle assists their visual connection and arouses a visual interest. It breaks the monotonous rectangular shape of the web banner and text lines, and preserves their balance. The letter A, placed in the top left corner of the web banner, suggests a focal point for the user from which to start to read the layout. Although users read the layout from the top left to the bottom by drawing a zigzag, the letter A in this layout clarifies and reconfirms the starting point.

1 2

1 Figure 2-30. A less stable layout enhanced with asymmetry

2 Figure 2-31. An asymmetric layout punctuated by focal points

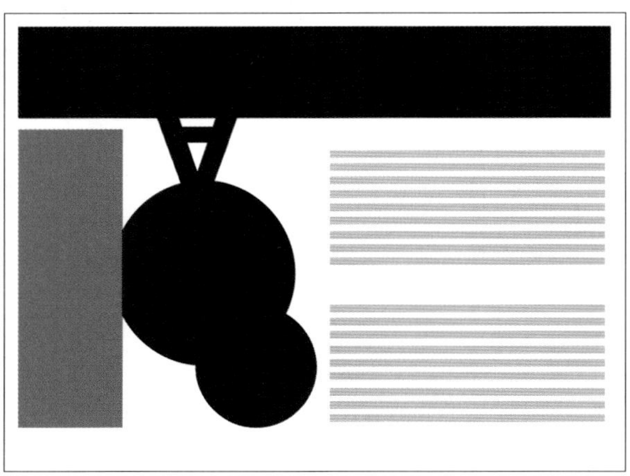


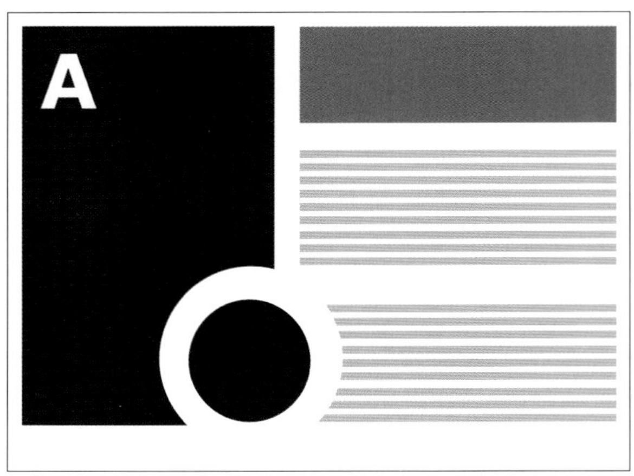

Figure 2-32 generates visual appeal by repeating the circular shape. The letter A connects the rectangular shape of the web banner (an image) with the repetitive circles (a graphic) to balance the text lines and the navigation bar in terms of horizontal length and visual weight. The navigation bar becomes a predominant element in this layout by merging with the web banner. Positioning a design element, such as a web banner or navigation bar, on the edge of the frame (in a web browser) may increase a sense of stability as well as develop visual appeal.

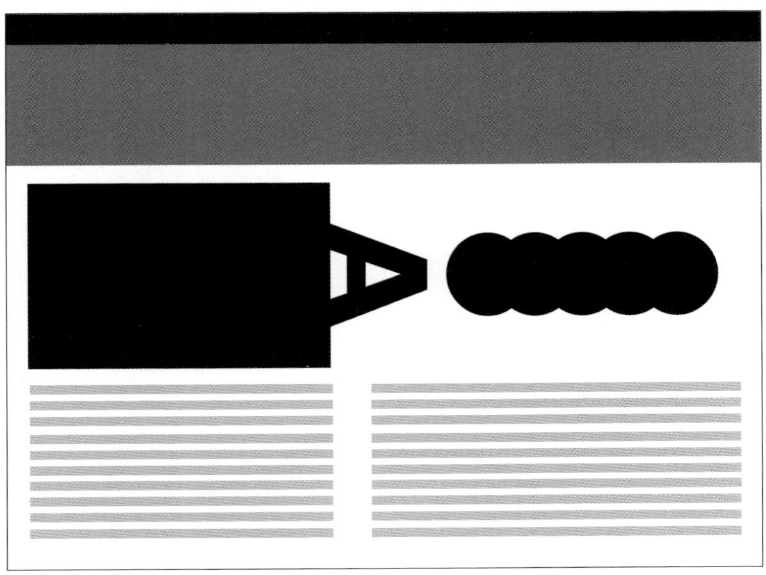

**1** Figure 2-32. Repetition and connectedness stabilize this layout

# **Student Gallery:** Layout Design 1
# Stable Layout

### The Given Elements: Letter C, a Circle, and Lines

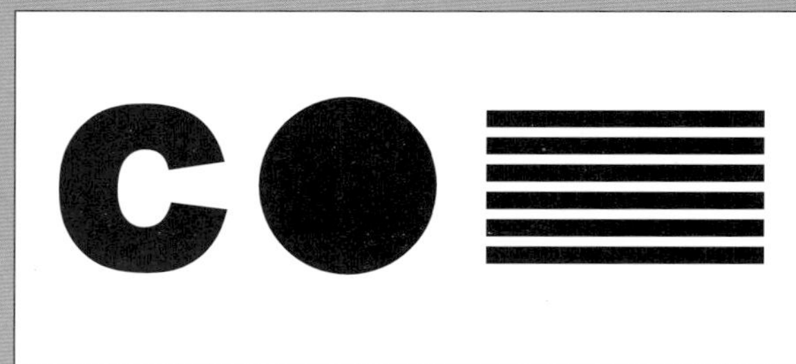


- Activity theme: Stable layout
- Software: Adobe Illustrator CS2
- Dimension:  400 x 400 pixels
- Format: publish a gif format from your work
- You should not apply any colors on the shape and layout.
- You should not use any other shapes.

### Marking Criteria (possible marks: 10)

Student will receive one of the marks in the following:

- 9 – 10: Successful design with creative solutions and professional finish
- 7 – 8: Successful design, but insufficient creativity and finish
- 5 – 6: Adequate, but lack of experiment or creativity
- 3 – 4: Inadequate, partly misunderstanding
- 2 – 0: Wrong theme or no submission

### Student Works

- Bradley John Acutt 2006

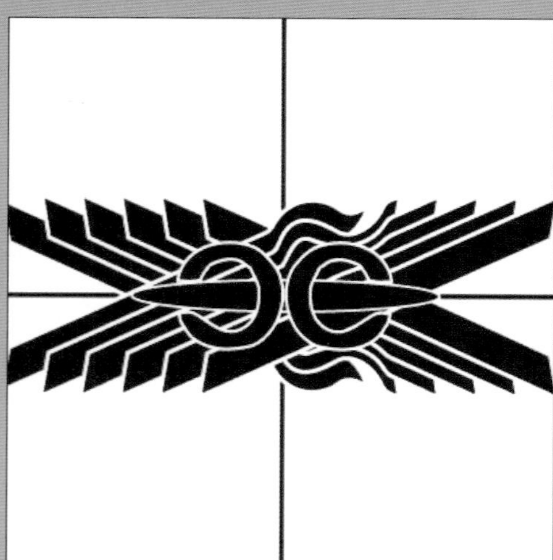

All the students' works presented here are outstanding and innovative. The works are successfully and interestingly addressing a sense of stability from their visual perception and aesthetics. My favorite one is the work to the left. This effectively defines a sense of stability by adding a crosshair in the frame and produces strong visual interest by adding a 3-dimensional tension being placed between stability and dynamic layout.

● Kaylene Court 2006

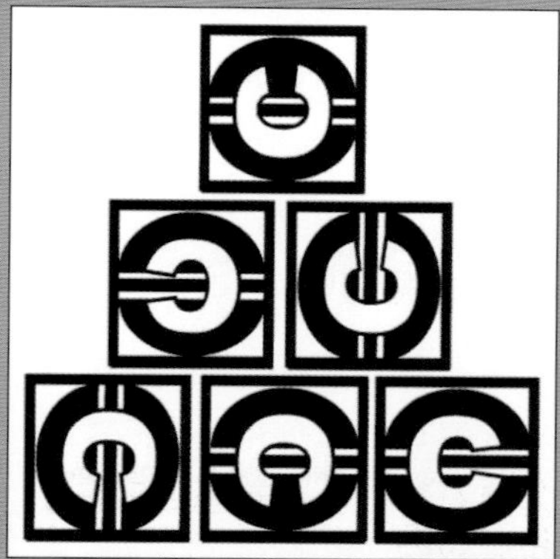

● Joy Reynolds 2006

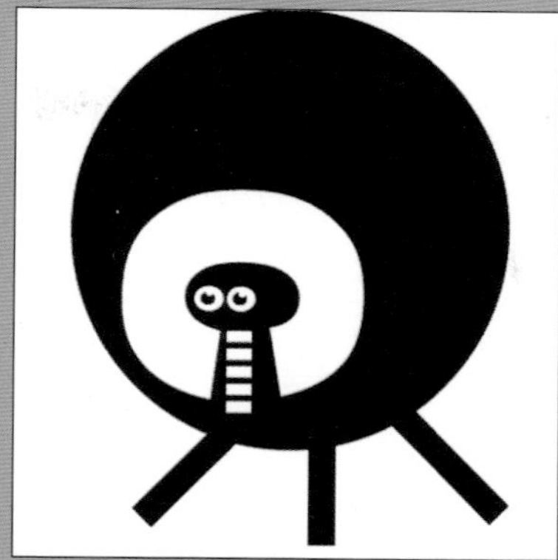

● Sandra Mary Weedon 2006

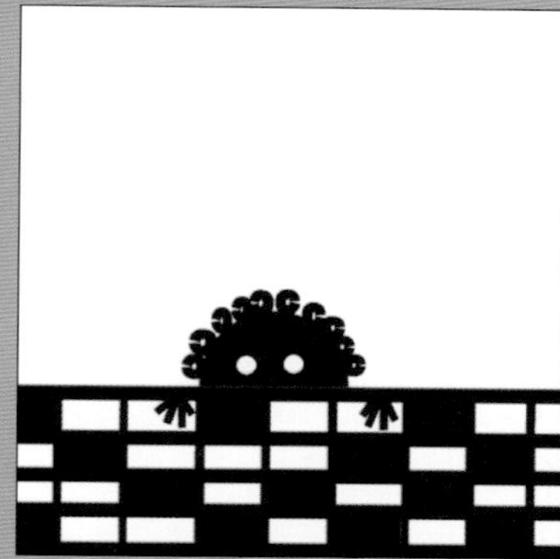

● Elise Sondergeld 2007

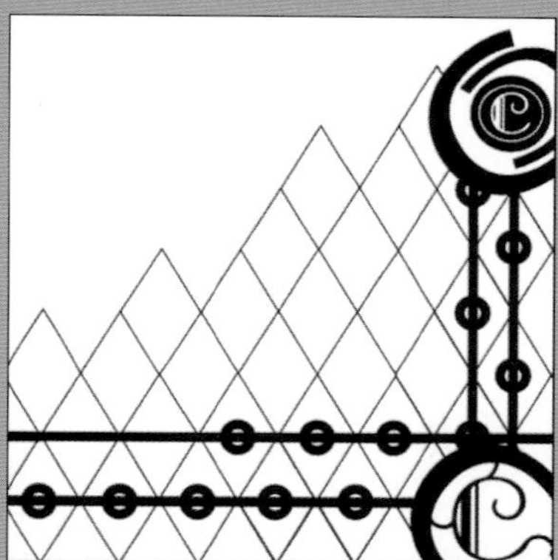

● Justin Andrew Hawley 2007

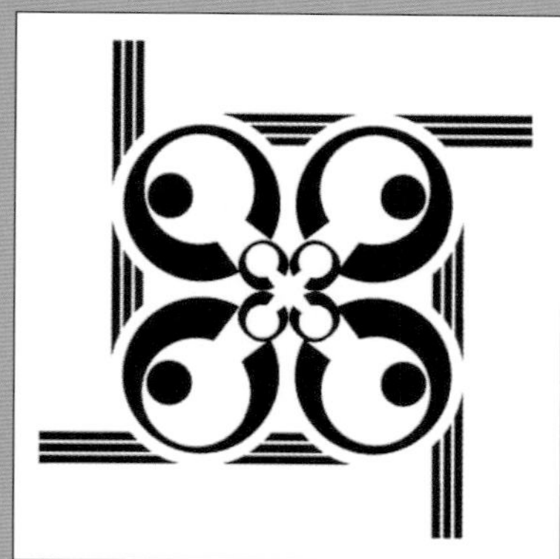

● Karina Maree Voss 2007

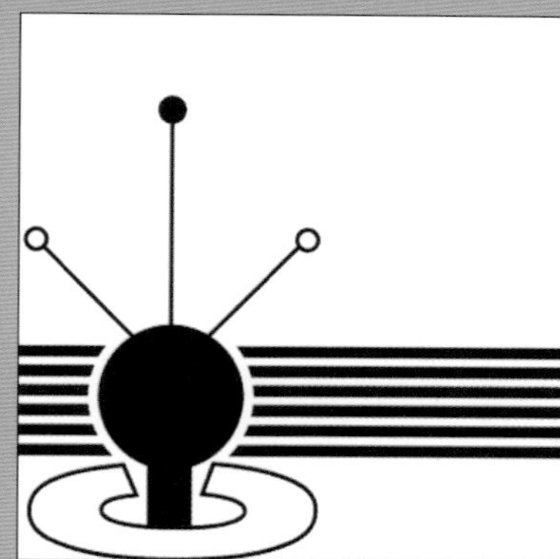

● Krista Avila 2007

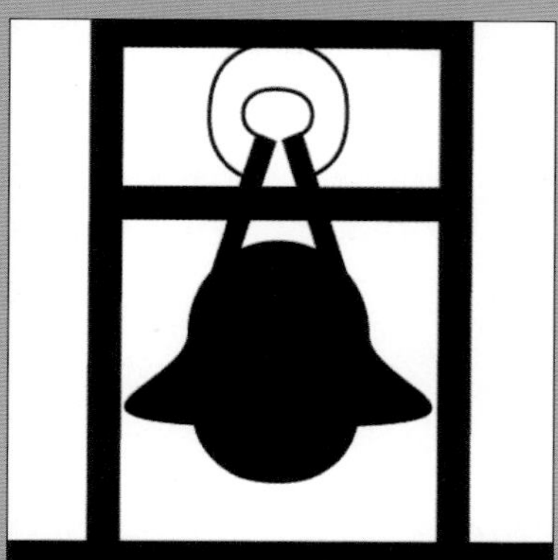

● Natalie Gaye Clarke 2006

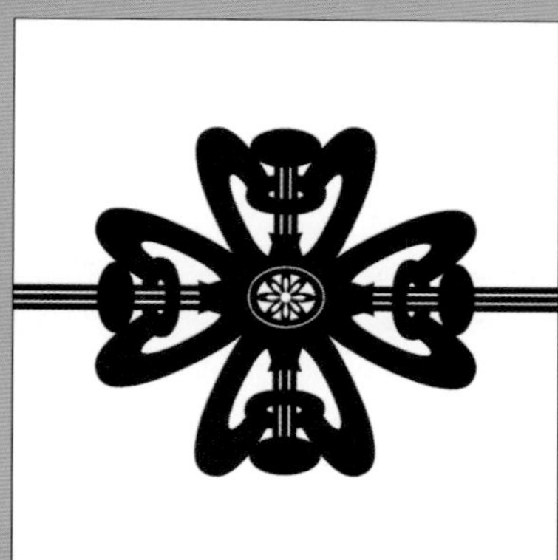

Chapter

# [03]

# Design Principles - Part 2

The chapter will explore the rest principles of layout design; dynamics, variety, emphasis, and movement. In the design studio, you are expected to create several dynamic and scale layouts with given elements. To interpret a visual artwork in a written language is very limited to the extent that it could contain various emotions and expressions. However, it is necessary for designers to understand the visual language (the principles of layout design) in order to appropriately visualize the emotion and expression.

# Dynamics and Variety

A dynamic layout could be full of variety and tensions so that it often presents a process rather than the completion of the work. Dynamic layouts often accompany variety. Variety in visual design means that the layout design contains various attributes and functions. However, you should be aware that dynamic and variety in the layout are not equal to chaos and disorder. The elements should be arranged in a concept of harmony and unity to create a visually balanced layout. Your innovative and creative efforts should be moderated by good visual design that is high quality, appropriate, and relevant for the audience.

A complete layout is static and leaves no space in which the elements can move. This is the opposite of dynamics. Dynamics encompasses the possibility of dramatic movement. A dynamic layout uses design elements that are very active and energetic. Viewers feel a power of movement or a particular energy from the layout design. A dynamic layout makes use of motion.

Dynamics may accompany variety. A variegated design element has attributes that differentiate it from other design elements. A layout contains various features that have diverse design elements. Various attributes, or variety within a particular power or movement, can produce a dynamic layout. When used effectively, dynamics and variety represent the harmony and unity of the elements rather than disjointedness and disorder.

## Dynamics and Movement

—

Figure 3-1 shows only a single square rotated in a frame; yet, the square has energy of movement. The presentation of the square suggests that it is floating in a liquid.

Positioning the square across the edge of the surface, as shown in Figure 3-2, fills the square with energy. It now appears that the square is floating at the surface or moving into or being thrown out of the box.

The floating object is also associated with history of movement. As Figure 3-3 simulates, the mind draws trails that help us perceive floating movement.

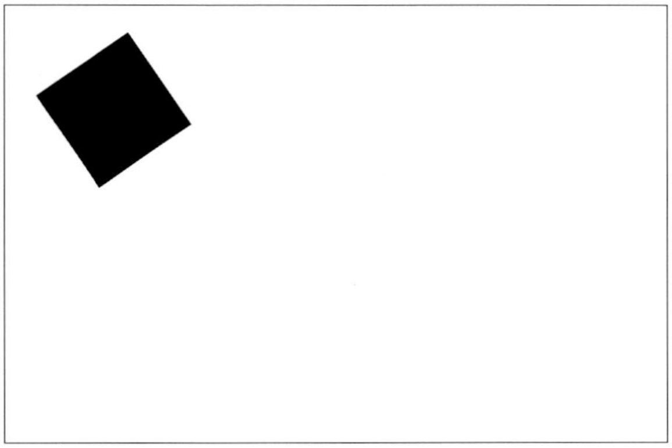

1 Figure 3-1. Rotating an object gives it energy and motion

2 Figure 3-2. Crossing a border line gives an object falling and/or rising energy

3 Figure 3-3. History of movement is supplied by mental interpolation

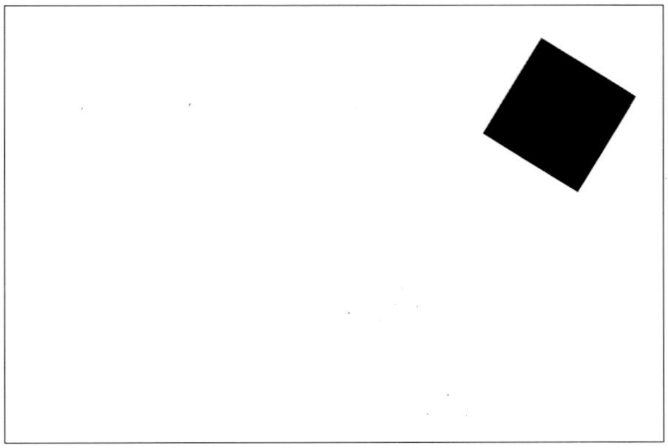

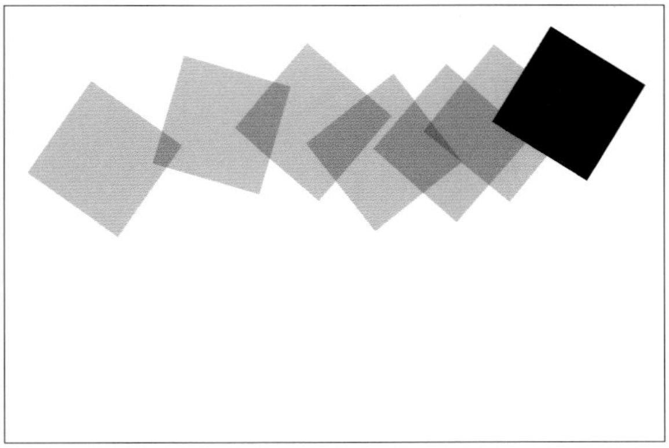

## Dynamics and the Grid System

—

A dynamic layout can be achieved by intentionally positioning the design elements out of the grid system. This will create a disordered and unstable experience containing energy that produces a sense of power or movement. A dynamic design occupies the viewer's eyes and involves the viewer in the sense of activity. In addition, arrangement of the design elements in a particular direction can strengthen the power of dynamics. Figure 3-4 is projecting an explosive energy, whereas Figure 3-5 is progressing with a moving energy in a specific direction. The former has visual discord; the latter has visual concord.

1 2

1 Figure 3-4. A scattered layout projects explosive energy

2 Figure 3-5. Directional energy imbues the design with progress

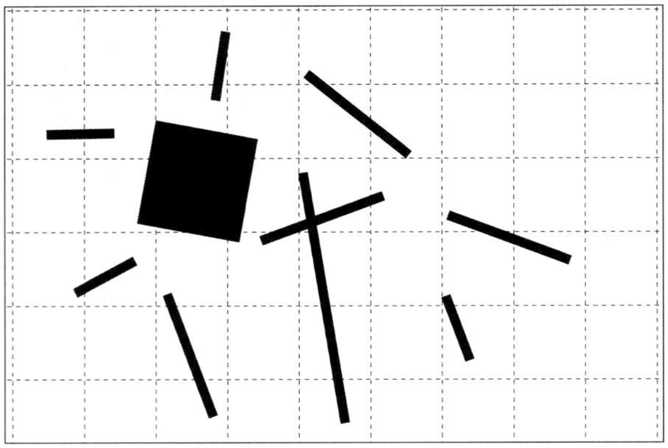

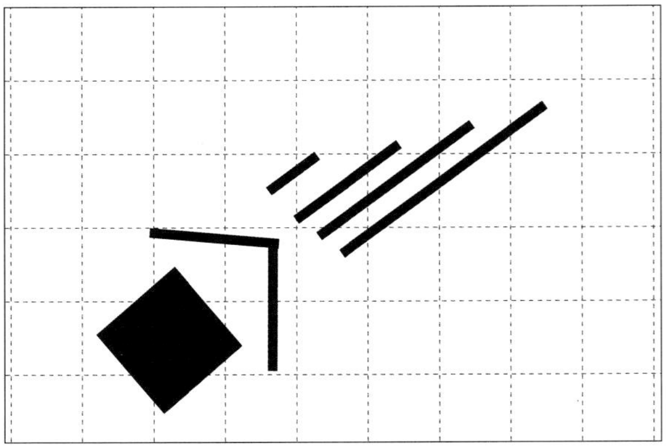

## Variety and Power

—

The variety of design elements, in terms of shape, color, and size, can create a sense of movement and produce an exciting scene. Variety accompanies the feeling of movement. A variety of shapes within a layout produces conflict and disruption among them. As Figure 3-6 shows, the shapes are running in various directions so that their collisions cause power. It is important to understand that elemental disorder and chaos within a particular format, such as direction and/or shape, can produce a very strong impression in a layout design.

A variety of shapes can be organized with a sense of unity. Each shape can be considered an individual variation; otherwise, all shapes can be evaluated as a single unit. Variety forms a group of design elements that link together within a particular layout. Figure 3-7 shows that the variegated shapes can produce dynamics as individuals, but unity as a whole.

1 2

1 Figure 3-6. Variety and disruption lead to energetic disorder

2 Figure 3-7. Variety and unity allow for both individuality and harmony

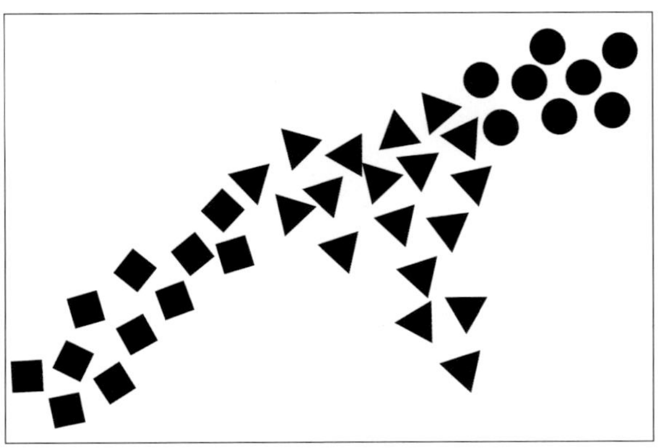

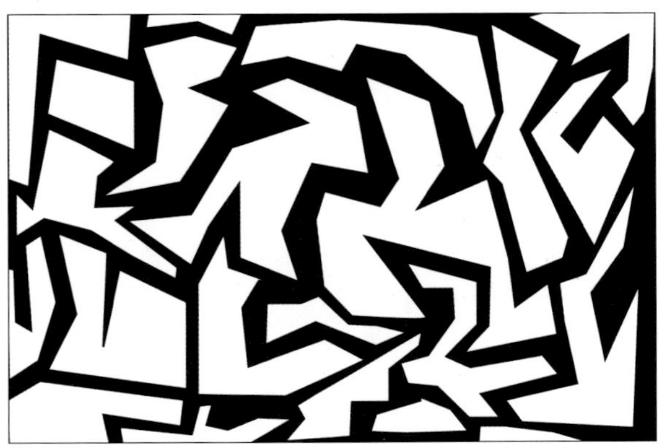

## Kinetic and Potential Energy

—

The concept of kinetic energy is the energy of motion, shown in Figure 3-8 as a ball falling and hitting the ground. A design object that expresses motion usually presents dynamic movement. There are many forms of kinetic energy, including vibrational (the energy due to rapid motion within a minute range), rotational (the energy due to spinning around an axis or pivot point), and translational (the energy due to motion from one location to another). Kinetic energy, in terms of visual design, refers to the expression of that movement.

As shown in Figure 3-9, the concept of potential energy is the untapped energy that is stored in an object (here, the ball). In other words, an object can store energy as the result of its position. The Yo-Yo is a good example. As it begins its fall, it has stored energy due to its position. At the top, it has its maximum potential energy. When it starts to fall, the potential energy is converted into kinetic energy. Conversely, when it is at the bottom, the energy is converted into its maximum kinetic energy which makes it roll back to the top. Potential energy expresses a possibility of motion.

1 2

1 Figure 3-8. Kinetic energy is expressed through dynamic design

2 Figure 3-9. Potential energy is stored in a suspended ball (circle)

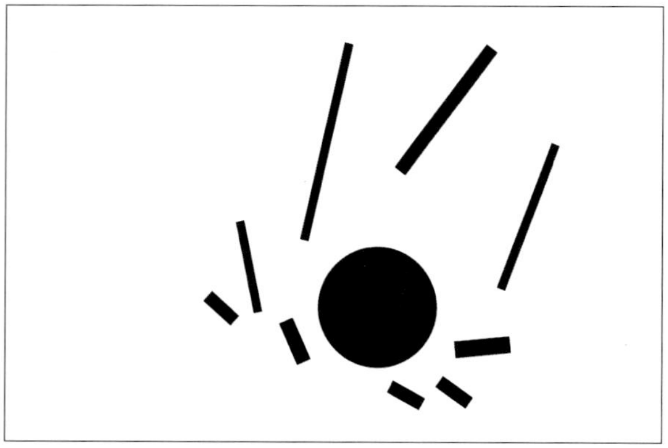

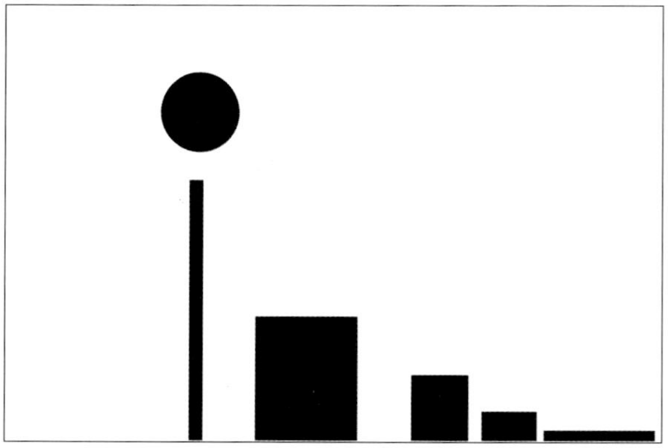

# Emphasis and Scale

Highlighting an object and a specific part in a layout is to visually emphasize and distinguish it from the overall layout. Resizing and moving visible objects may be a very primitive process. Rather you have to pay attention to the relationships between objects from the overall layout structure and, furthermore, the background, regardless of whether it is a negative space or a positive area should be handled as a visible element.

Emphasis is applied to an object or part of an object to differentiate it from others. Scale is a common method in visual emphasis. Scale refers to adjusting an element's size or extent and the spatial relationship between the objects and/or the background. Emphasis and scale pursue variety, differentiation, contradiction, and tension to focus the viewer's concentration and attention (see Figure 3-10).

Adjusting the size of objects in a layout is a way to organize the viewer's attention and create a visual interest. Scale attracts attention through putting a focal point on a particular object (see Figure 3-11). Manipulation of the size of objects, including the amount of visible background, creates various expressions and dramas.

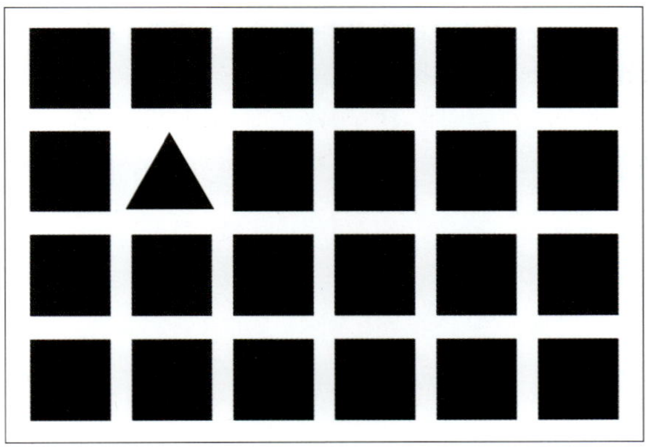

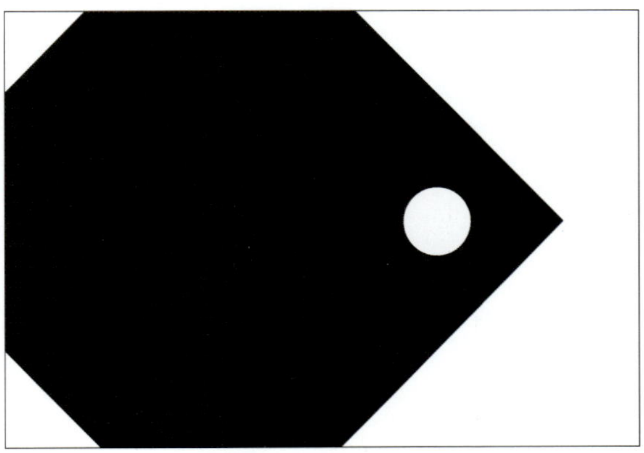

1 Figure 3-10. Differentiation of shape creates a focal point
2 Figure 3-11. Scale and background draw the eye to the circle

## Visual Hierarchy

—

Designing a focal point in a layout is an important process because it is this point that the viewer will be initially drawn to. Determining where or what the focal point will be in the layout requires creating a visual hierarchy or order of priority. In Figure 3-12, the shape of the circle in the middle of the visual structure (focal point) will grab the attention of the viewer initially, and then the viewer will comprehend the rest of the design in a radial pattern.

The most important element in a layout should gain the most attention, and secondary elements should then follow. It also requires an insight into the viewer's process of visual perception in a particular structure. In Figure 3-13, the design objects are organized in the visual hierarchical order represented by the numbers. The target audience's visual assessment (or the designer's experience) will confirm how well the hierarchy structure operates in this layout.

1 2

1 Figure 3-12. Visual hierarchy emphasizes the center

2 Figure 3-13. Enumerated visual hierarchy

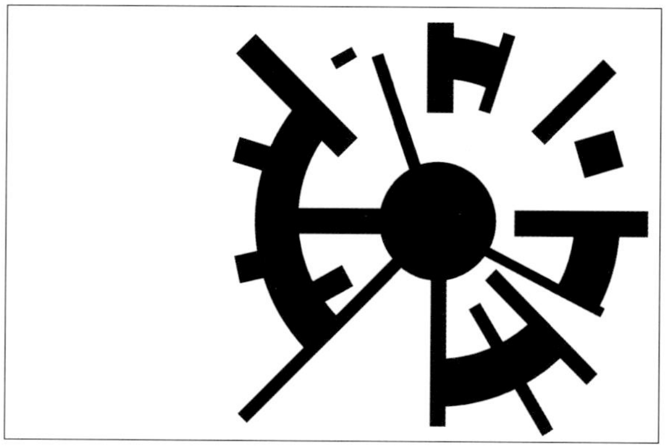

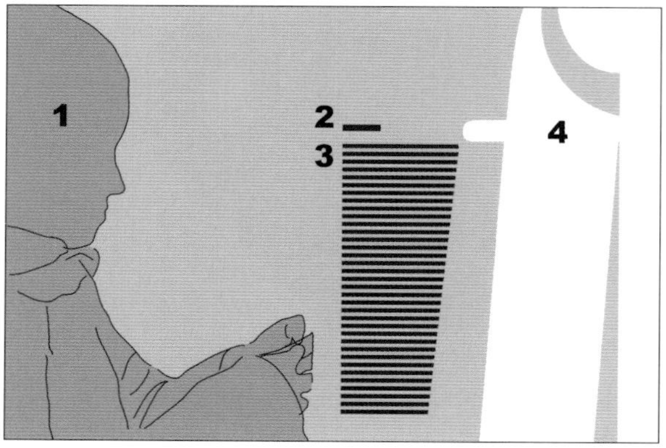

## Background

—

Making use of the background is an effective way to emphasize an important element. Changing the size of design elements affects the amount of visible background. When too much background is visible, it may overwhelm the design elements. In Figure 3-14, the black background is much bigger than other elements and becomes predominant in the layout.

In Figure 3-15, when this white background is given more space relative to the other objects, the design objects (squares) seem very small and the layout displays emptiness. The white space is not perceived to have any dominating quality. Rather, the squares are emphasized.

1 2

1 Figure 3-14. An overwhelming amount of visible background

2 Figure 3-15. Emptiness shrinks the squares, but emphasizes them

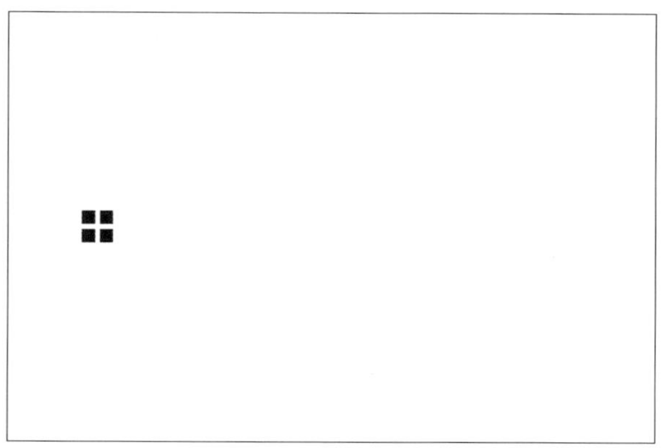

## Contradiction

—

Contradiction in visual design is concerned with the size and scale among the design objects. The visual challenge in contradiction is to break the ordinary visual perception of the size of design objects.

If objects are placed under the same lighting condition, the taller object must have a longer shadow. The object and its shadow will be in direct proportion, but Figure 3-16 uses contradicting shadow sizes to emphasize the figures.

Figure 3-17 shows that a triangle shape given to one of the chromatic keys attracts the viewer's eyes to the key through the contradiction.

1 2

1 Figure 3-16. Contradicting shadow sizes emphasize the design elements

2 Figure 3-17. Contradictive shape draws the eye to the odd piano key

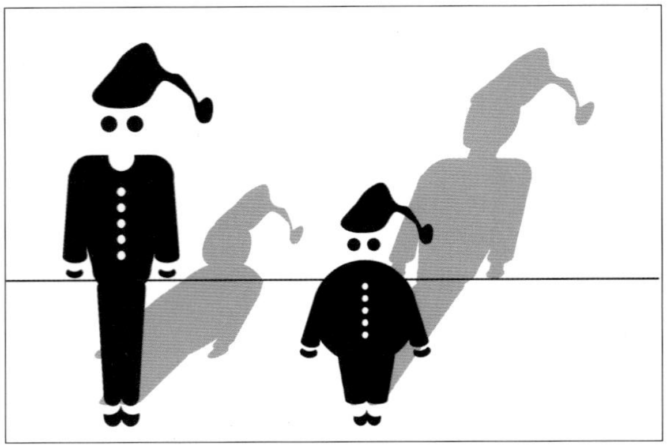

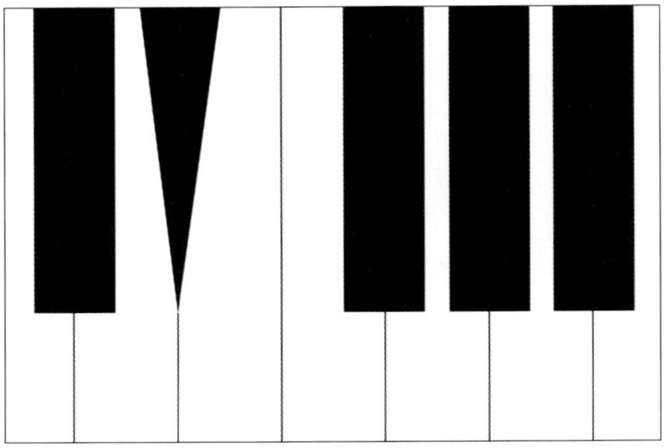

# **Design Studio:** Layout Design 2

This activity will guide you through designing dynamic and scale layouts. The pre-conditions are the same as explained in Chapter 2 Design Studio: Layout Design 1. The four elements are: graphics, text, navigation bar, and web banners.

## Dynamic Layout Design

Using and manipulating the elements given in Figure 3-18, create several dynamic layouts, each within a rectangular space that is 550 pixels wide by 400 pixels high. Give a title to each layout design, such as "rhythmical dynamic" or "kinetic energy in variety." (Review the previous sections if a refresher is needed on what these design principles are.) The visual assessments of others could suggest titles.

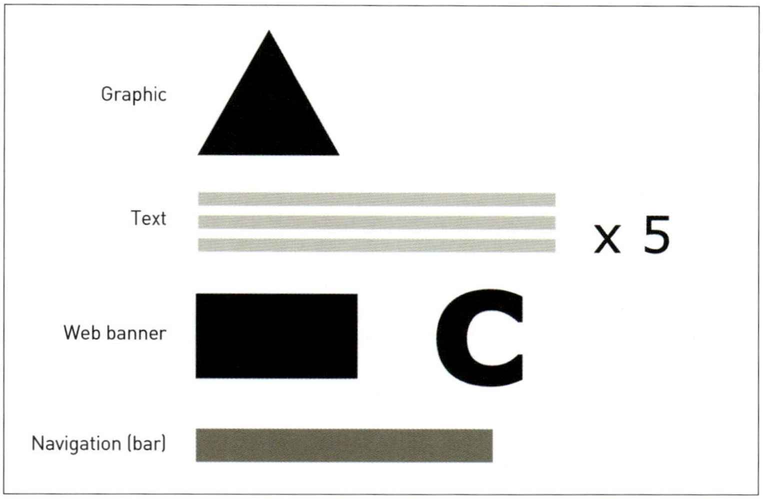


**1 Figure 3-18.** Given elements for dynamic layout design

Try to show the layout design to others to generate feedback about how they perceive the layout. While creating a layout, be careful not to lose track of the theme, or the initial objectivity of your visual assessment may be lost.

There are some rules to remember while creating a layout.

- Do not apply any colors other than black and white or use opacity.
- When changing the color of a shape, use only black or white.
- Do not use any shapes other than the shapes provided.

Creating a dynamic layout requires creativity and extreme experimentation; just remember that a dynamic layout does not mean a disordered and chaotic one. Adding some disorder and chaos can be effective in creating a dynamic mood, but they should be used to achieve overall harmony and unity.

A dynamic layout contains energy and power, therein producing a feeling of movement. It is the opposite of stability. It is visually pleasing when one perceives liveliness and vitality in a layout. A dynamic layout engages the viewer in the layout design. Repetition of a shape, especially, can add a rhythmical property to the layout. As shown in Figure 3-19, the repetition of triangular shapes gives a directional movement from the left to the right, and the letter C's look like chains connecting the web banner and the text lines by following a curved path. There is a large amount of energy and a directional movement that makes this layout dynamic.

As demonstrated in Figure 3-20, element repetition in a layout creates a rhythmic movement or adds a kinetic energy. Further, when the repeating element is combined in a directional arrangement, it adds an organized sense of movement in the layout by leading the viewer along a visual path. The arrow-shaped anchors, made by combining a triangle and a letter C, are placed at the top left and the bottom right to create directional endpoints for the motion of the text lines. This nests all design elements in the unity of the layout

The literal meaning of energy is the ability and strength to do active physical things and the feeling that physical power and life are present. Energy can be illustrated with a disordered and chaotic power akin to water that is simmering just below the boiling point. An explosion depicts a strong energy that is a sudden, violent burst.

1 2

1 Figure 3-19. Dynamic rhythm can be achieved by shape repetition

2 Figure 3-20. Directed repetition gives a sense of movement

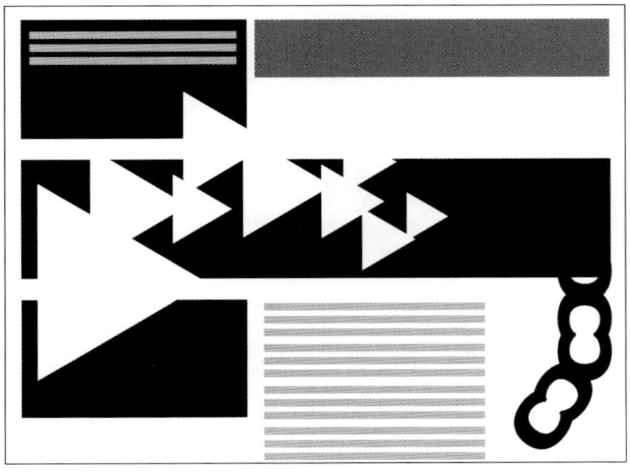

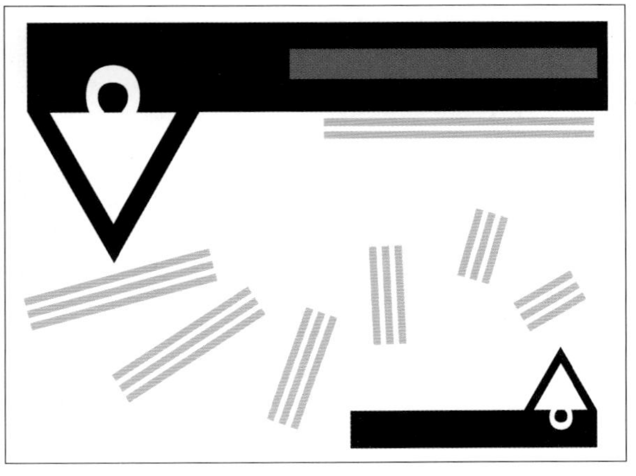

As Figure 3-21 shows, the random arrangement of the triangles at the top gives a visual tension to the layout, and the letter C's seem to be fragments bursting from them. There is another tension that is between the web banner (black background) and the shapes of the white triangles at the bottom of the layout. This is a good example of how the background (negative space) can be used as another design element to create a unique layout.

Normally, text lines in a layout design focus mainly on the delivery of information, remaining largely unchanged because the text is manipulated in terms of its readability only. When text is manipulated graphically and aesthetically, the results can be strong and impressive. As shown in Figure 3-22, text lines are arranged irregularly over the graphic of the chained letter C's. This example demonstrates that there is nothing fixed except change.

Web banners, navigation bars, text, and, in fact, any design element can be edited and transformed within visual design. As the designer creates a layout design with the given elements, the designer's creativity and experimentation are boundless and unlimited. Eventually, the viewer will decide whether it is a successful design.

1 2

1 Figure 3-21. Tension can emerge from projection and repetition

2 Figure 3-22. Irregular text blocking shows a sense of daring

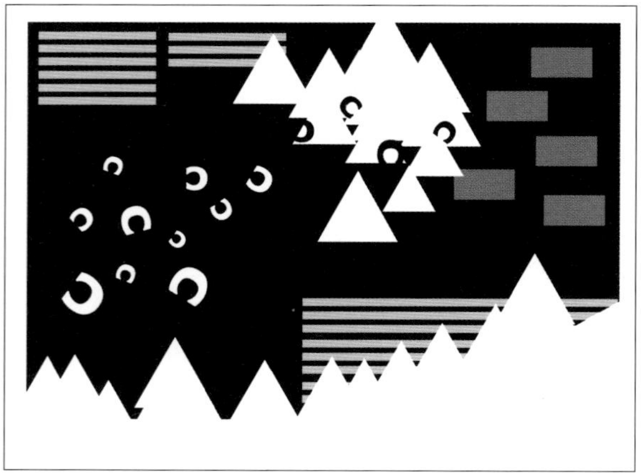

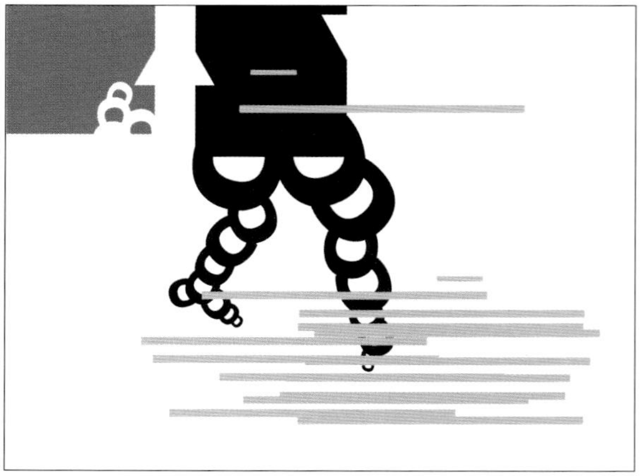

## Scale Layout Design

—

Using and manipulating the elements given in Figure 3-23, create several scale layouts, each within a rectangular space that is 550 pixels wide by 400 pixels high. Title each layout design. (Review the previous sections for a refresher on the relevant design principles.) Try to show the layout design to others for feedback.

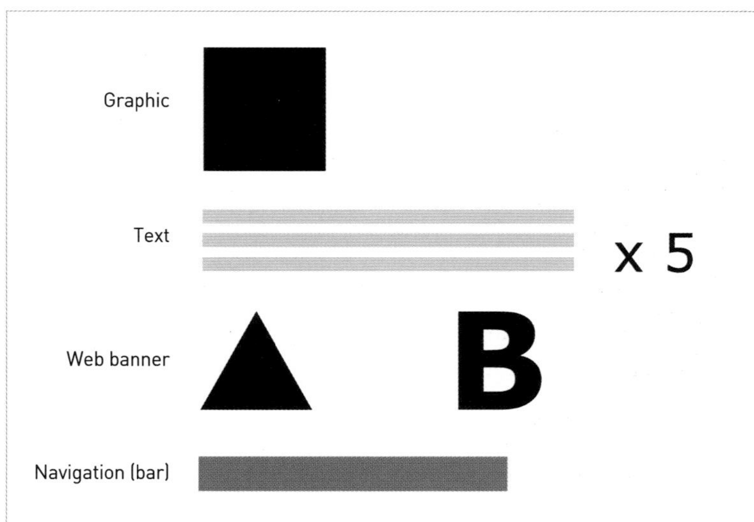


■ Figure 3-23. Given elements for scale layout design

There are some rules to remember while creating a layout.

- Do not apply any colors other than black and white or use opacity.
- When changing the color of a shape, use only black or white.
- Do not use any shapes other than the shapes provided.

Scale layout involves arranging and manipulating the dimensional and spatial relationships between the elements (including the background). Both the dimensional and the spatial relationships can be applied to the design elements and to the whole layout.

Plenty of blank background leads the viewer's attention to the elements. Figure 3-24 shows how lots of white space can perceptually reduce all of the elements dimensionally. The layout lets the viewer concentrate on the elements from top to bottom.

In Figure 3-25, the graphic (black rectangle) is enlarged prominently. The shape created by the web banners (triangles) and the text lines is relatively smaller than the graphic. The navigation bar and web banner overlay the graphic. While the shapes of the navigation bar and the web banner stand out, the predominant graphic maintains the solid and firm mood of the layout. Therefore, the dynamics are used as additional and supportive visual interests in this layout.

1 2

1 **Figure 3-24.** Vast white space reduces visual impact

2 **Figure 3-25.** Large graphics shift dynamic elements to a supportive role

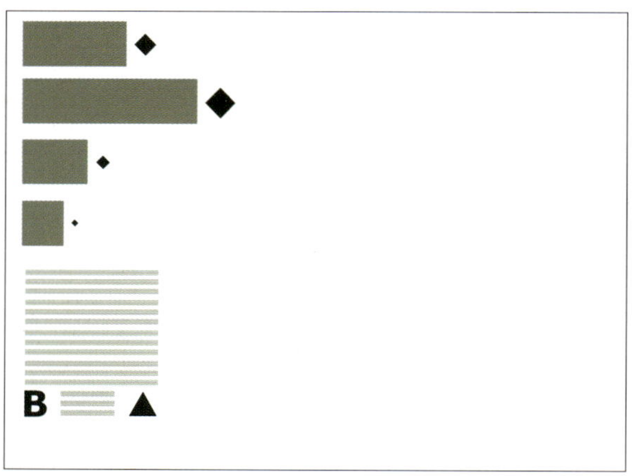


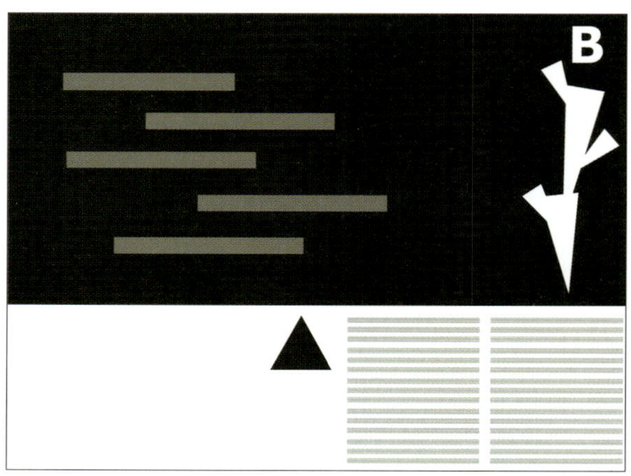

In Figure 3-26, the web banner (double-triangle) overwhelms the other elements. Obviously, scaling one of the design elements prominently emphasizes that element. The other elements look relatively small, but they are contrasted with the large web banners asymmetrically. The web banner emits an irresistible force because of its scale and irregular shape. As the dynamic principle in layout design is to create a sense of movement and a powerful energy, the scale principle is to create an interesting and unique layout design.

The goal of scale in visual design is to create a mood and support either a stable or a dynamic layout. In Figure 3-27, the letter B is enlarged to span the frame vertically and become a predominant object in this layout. As this is a scale layout, it can also be a stable layout that looks firm and balanced.

1 2

1 Figure 3-26. Power can be achieved through enlarging an element

2 Figure 3-27. Scaling up the letter B applies a firm, stable mood

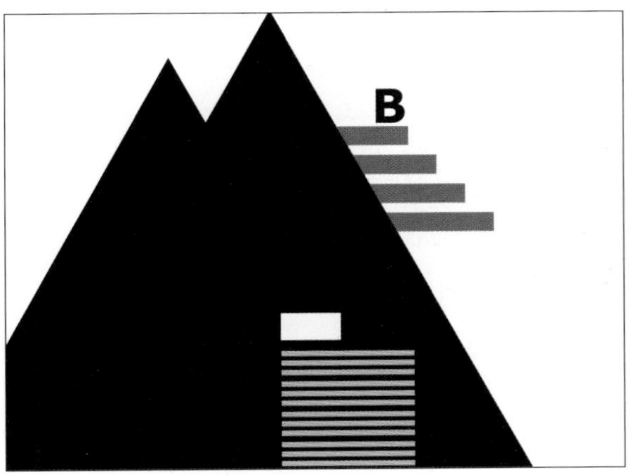


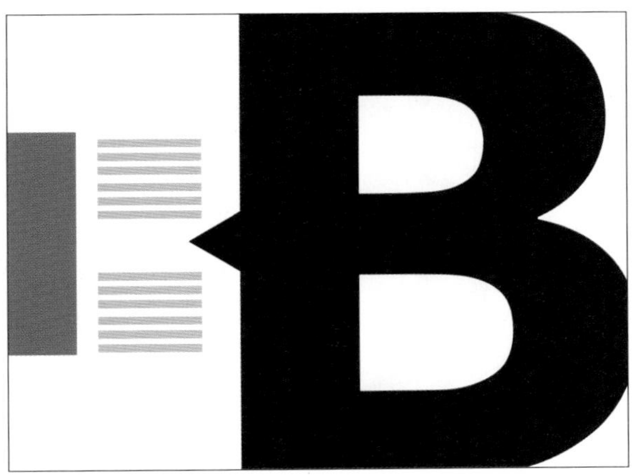

# **Student Gallery:** Layout Design 2
# Dynamic and Stable Layout

### The Given Elements for Dynamic Layout: a Letter C, a Star Shape, and Lines

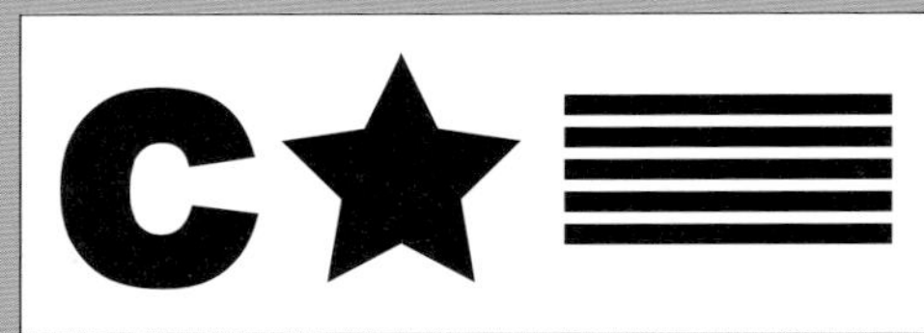


### The Given Elements for Stable Layout: a Letter B, a Square, and Lines

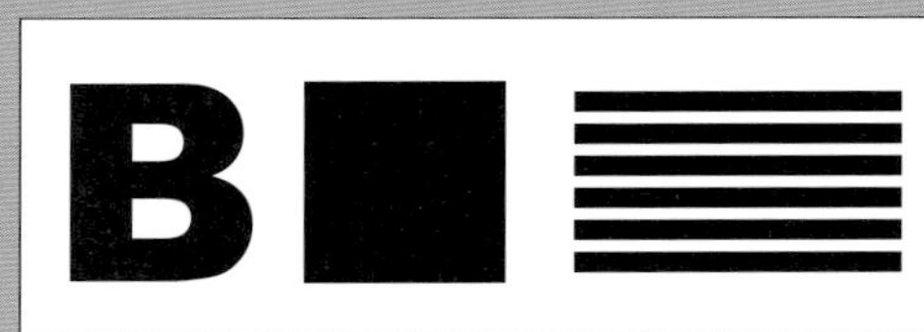


- Activity theme: Dynamic and scale layout
- Software: Adobe Illustrator CS2, Dimension: 400×400 pixels
- Format: publish a gif format from your work
- You should not apply any colors on the shape and layout.
- You should not use any other shapes.

### Marking Criteria (possible marks: 10)

Student will receive one of the marks in the following:

- 9 – 10: Successful design with creative solutions and professional finish
- 7 – 8: Successful design, but insufficient creativity and finish
- 5 – 6: Adequate, but lack of experiment or creativity
- 3 – 4: Inadequate, partly misunderstanding
- 2 – 0: Wrong theme or no submission

### Student Works - Dynamic Layout

- Douglas (Chak Cheung) Tsang 2006

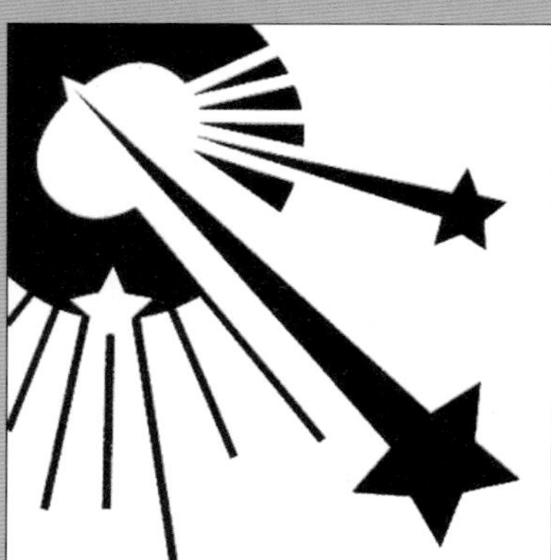

- Krista Avila 2007

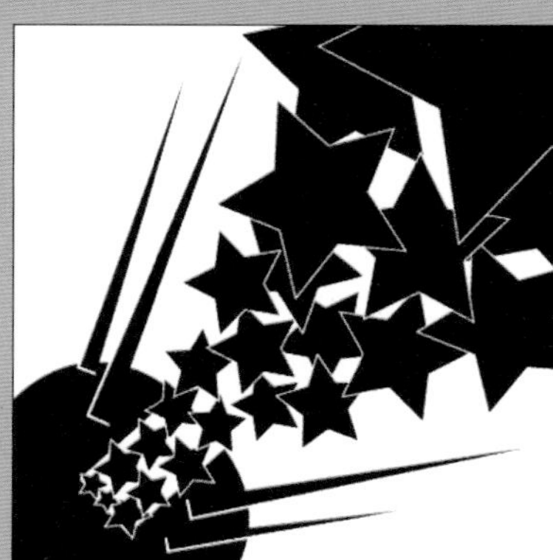

- Justin Andrew Hawley 2007

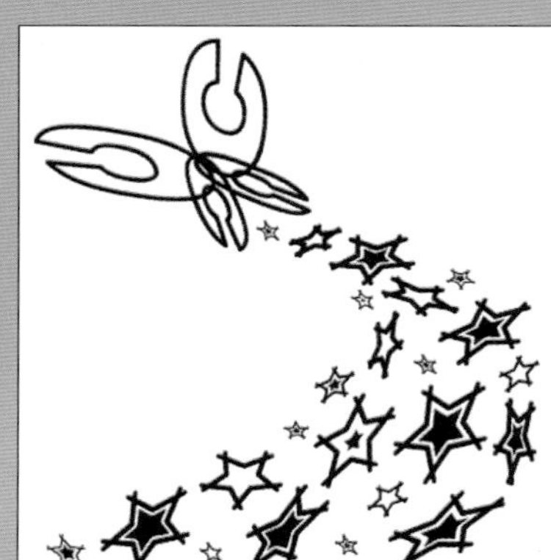

Kaylene Court 2006

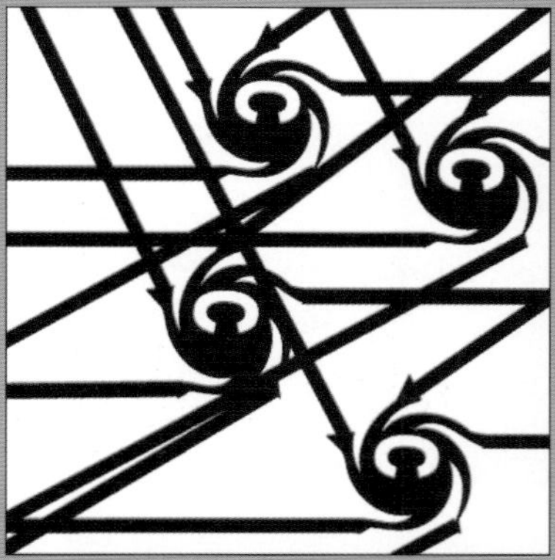

Joy Reynolds 2006

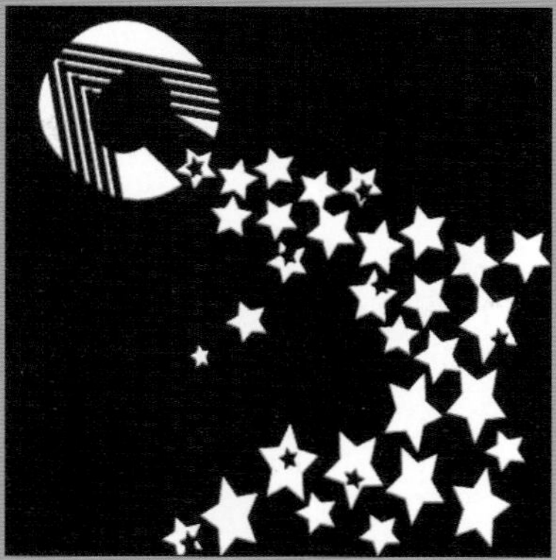

Sandra Mary Weedon 2006

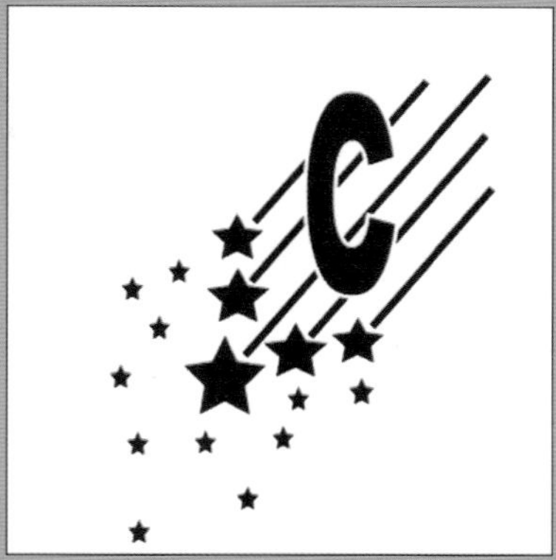

Natalie Gaye Clarke 2006

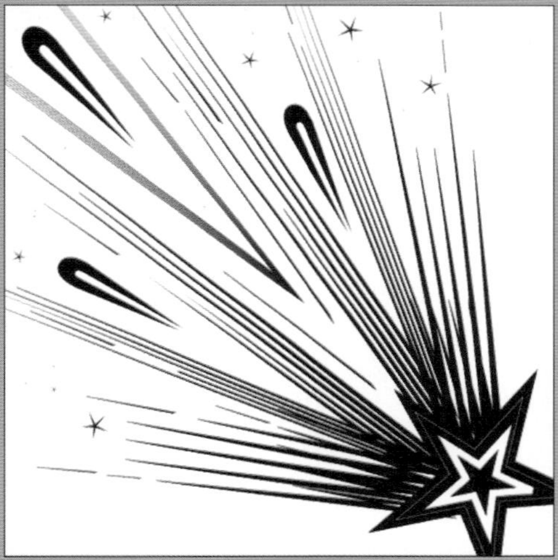

The activity asked students to create a dynamic layout with the given elements; a letter C, a star shape, and lines. Many students illustrated a comet flying or dropping because the star shape is easily associated with stars in the universe and a flying comet undoubtedly represents strong kinetic energy. Natalie's work was the most successful work to the extent that it visualizes well the energy of the comet as a layout design.

## Student Works - Scale Layout

Bradley John Acutt 2006

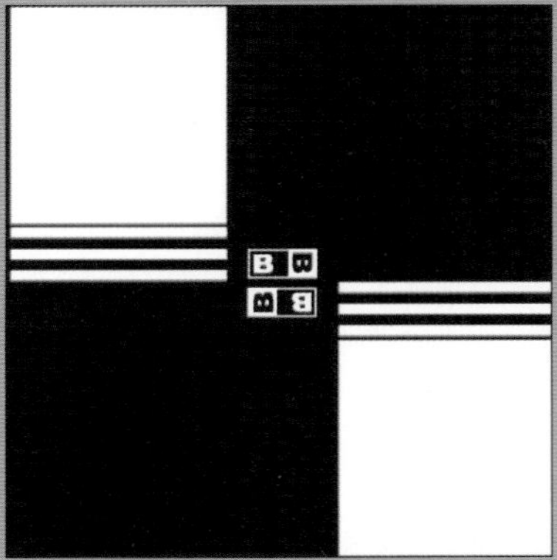

Kaylene Court 2006

Douglas (Chak Cheung) Tsang 2006

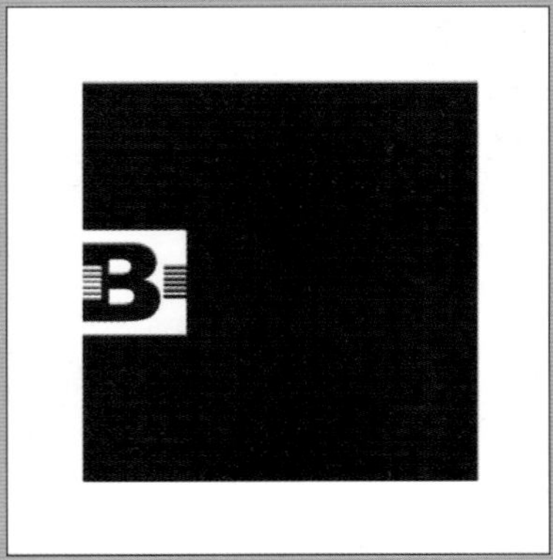

Natalie Gaye Clarke 2007

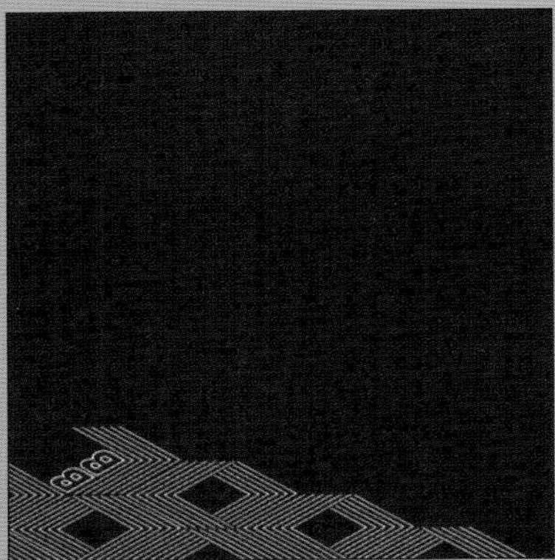

Justin Andrew Hawley 2007

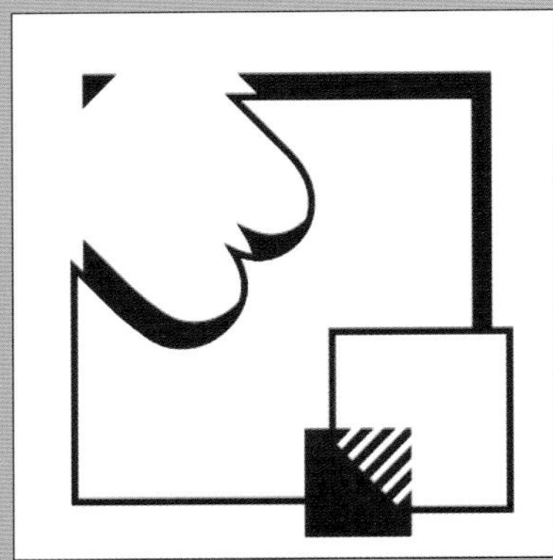

Elise Sondergeld 2007

Karina Maree Voss 2007

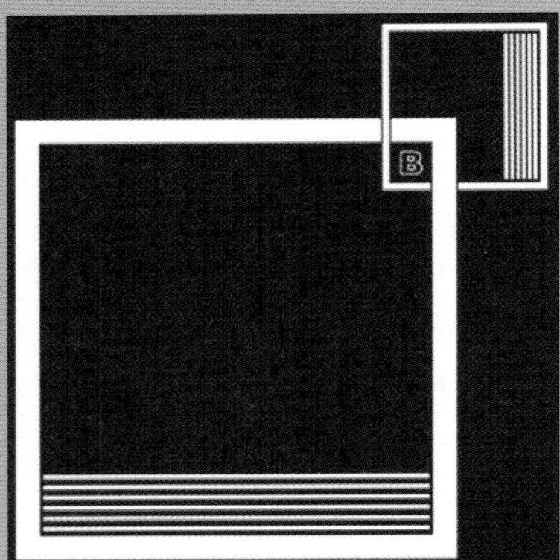

Joy Reynolds 2006

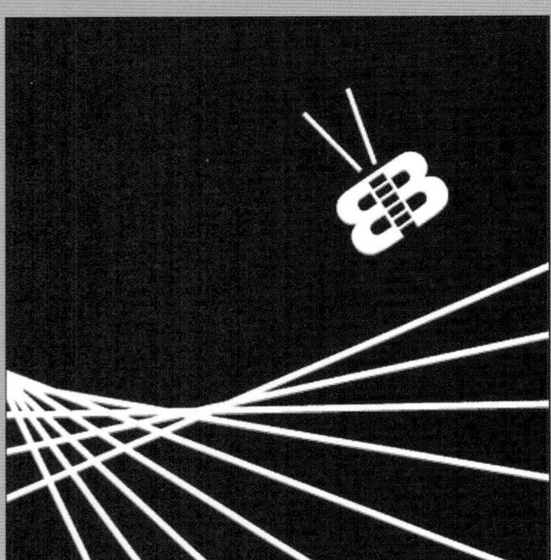

Creating a scale layout design with the given elements, a letter B, a square, and lines was a task in this activity. The key point is to define a spatial relationship including background (or negative areas) in terms of a layout design. Many students defined a scale layout within fundamental plane relations of the elements. Therefore, those students who used the square for creating a negative space in the frame were given high marks. Joy Reynolds' work to the left was the most outstanding in that it creates a 3-dimensional mood by arranging the lines in the negative area.

Chapter

# [ 04 ]

# The Grid System and Visual Elements

Well-designed visual works have a common feature in that the design elements in the layout are consistently organized and structured. Designers use a grid system to develop a consistent layout. Use of a grid in visual design not only improves a layout structure but also saves time.

A grid is an essential tool in arranging text information. It provides readability and is given priority over other functions. A grid is most suitable for positioning text. An ill-organized and inconsistent design interferes with the viewer's visual perception. A consistent layout involves arranging the elements in terms of an ordered and structured visual map. A grid helps the designer arrange the design elements from the audience's point of view and makes the layout consistent and predictable. As a result, it improves the design's functionality and aesthetic quality.

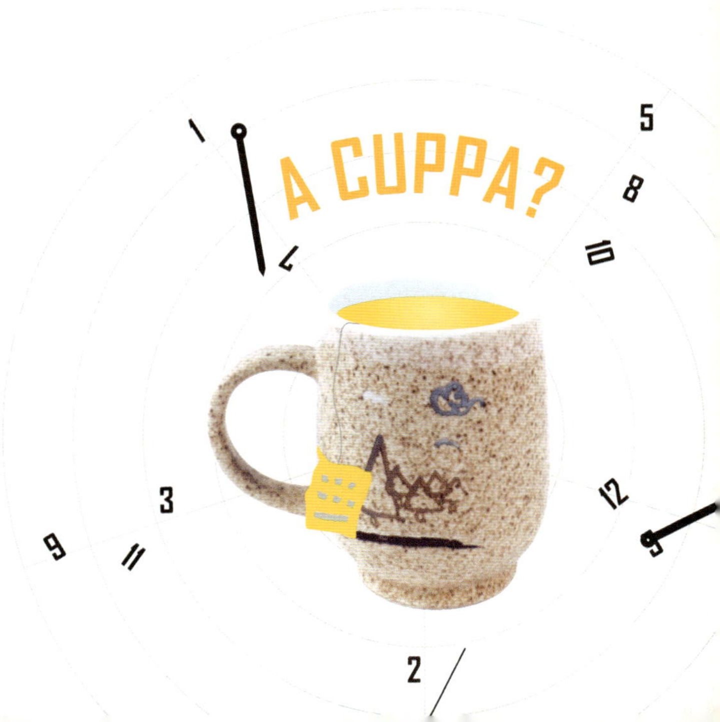

# The Grid System

A grid is technically a pattern of straight lines that cross over each other horizontally and vertically. A grid in terms of visual design refers to a system supporting the arrangement of the design elements in a layout. Gestalt theories assist the importance of a grid system in visual design to the extent that people experience beauty from consistently and systematically organized information.

## Gestalt Principles

Gestalt is a German word literally meaning shape or form. Gestalt theory, founded by Max Wertheimer in 1910, discusses how we perceive objects in our environment. It suggests the difference between figure (foreground) and ground (background) and examines how various principles help us to decide which one is figure and which one is ground. The idea is simply that "the whole is more than the sum of its parts." Each of the individual parts has its own meaning. As a whole, however, they may have a different meaning. In Figure 4-1, some viewers may see a bird pattern. Others may see pointing fingers. No matter what is seen as the ground or the figure, birds and pointing fingers coexist together.

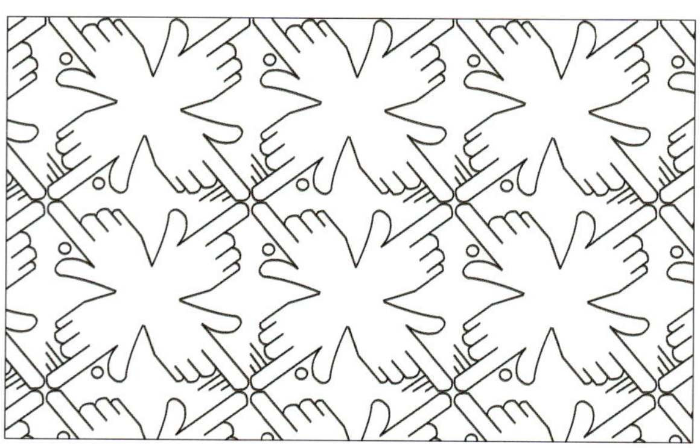

**1** **Figure 4-1.** Birds and hands coexist as both figure and ground

Gestalt theory provides the idea of grouping objects that we perceive as more structured and united rather than fractional parts in disorder. Gestalt theory refers to the visual interpretation and perception of design elements in a layout. In this point, Gestalt theory assists the layout design and the grid system helps the viewer understand the visual design.

There are factors that determine grouping:

- Proximity: Elements tend to be grouped according to their nearness
- Similarity: Items similar in some respect tend to be grouped together
- Closure: Items are grouped together if they tend to complete some entity
- Simplicity: Items will be organized into simple figures according to symmetry, regularity, and smoothness

An assessment of Figure 4-2 shows that there is a single star in the top left corner and a group of stars on the right side. Proximity principle in Gestalt theory refers to how the elements in close proximity tend to be grouped. It suggests that arranging design objects together requires the designer to judge how they are meant to be shown or how the audience will perceive what they represent.

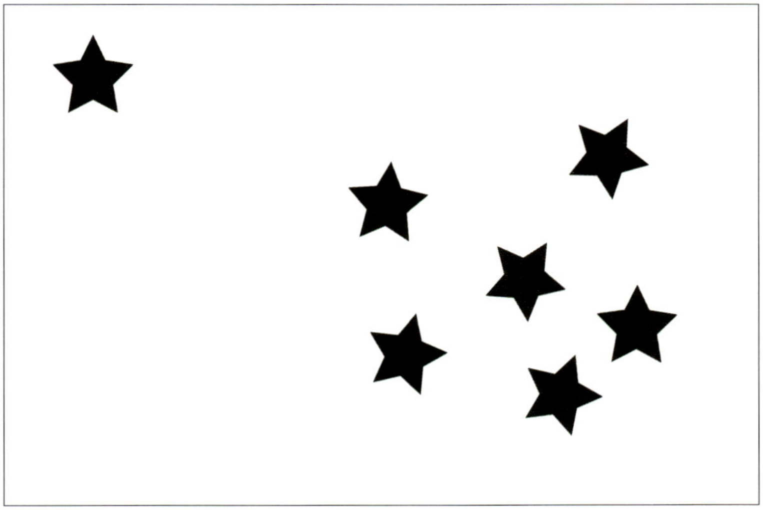

■ Figure 4-2. Proximity groups the six stars on the right side

Figure 4-3 is an example of the similarity principle in Gestalt theory. Most viewers will count two groups of shapes: stars and circles. Although the layout of the stars divides the circles into two groups, visual assessment combines them as one group because similar items tend to be grouped. This illustrates the similarity principle in Gestalt theory. Arranging multi-designed objects in a page may require being aware of their similarities and differences from the audience's grouping point of view.

When people see an unfinished or incomplete work, their minds try to complete it. In Figure 4-4, visual assessment connects the dots and forms a star. This demonstrates the closure principle of Gestalt theory, as items are grouped together if they tend to complete some entity. This principle is useful when the designer wishes to present an object indirectly using the rough information of an object to suggest its presence to the viewer.

For most people, visual assessment tends to simplify a complex shape. As Figure 4-5 demonstrates, the simple shapes in the bottom row are the average viewer's assessment of the irregular shapes on the top row. The simplicity principle refers to objects being organized into simple figures according to symmetry, regularity, and smoothness. Conversely, it also suggests that a simple shape can be grouped with other forms and keep its individuality because of its simplicity.

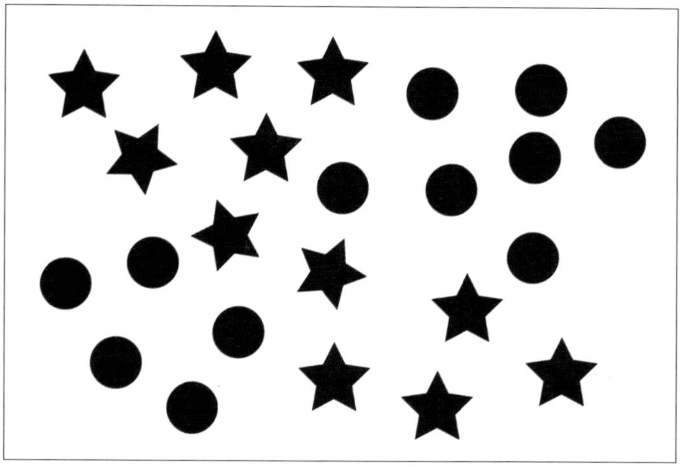

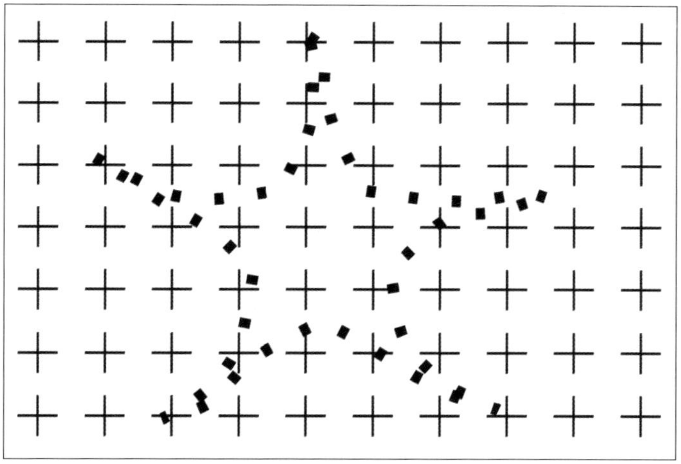

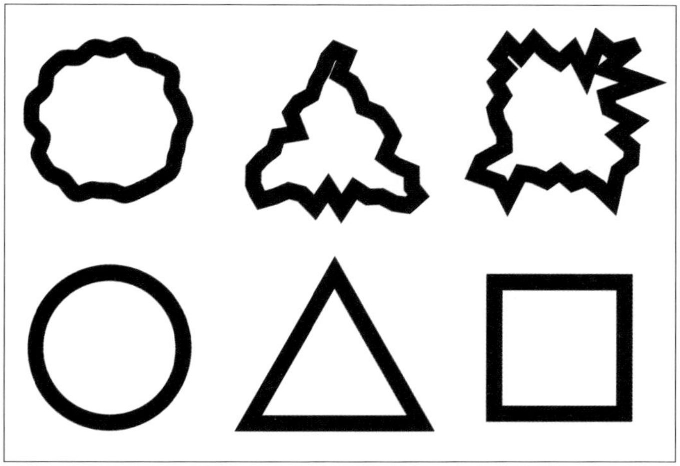

■1 Figure 4-3. Similarity of shape creates two groups instead of three

■2 Figure 4-4. Closure connects the dots into a star shape

■3 Figure 4-5. Assessment of complex shapes simplifies them into familiar ones

## The Grid System

To organize the design elements with a particular purpose or with consistency, guidelines are required that can define their spatial relationships to each other. In general, a grid is a pattern in which straight, vertical and horizontal lines cross over each other forming squares. A grid system organizes the design elements in a systematic structure in order to deliver information more efficiently or arouse a visual interest and attention.

Figure 4-6 shows a well-structured layout in the left-hand figure and an ill-structured one on the right-hand. When both are overlaid with the rectangular grid (Figure 4-7), it shows how they differ in terms of visual balance and composition.

1
2

1 Figure 4-6. Well-structured (left-hand) and ill-structured (right-hand) layouts

2 Figure 4-7. Well-structured and ill-structured layouts on the grid

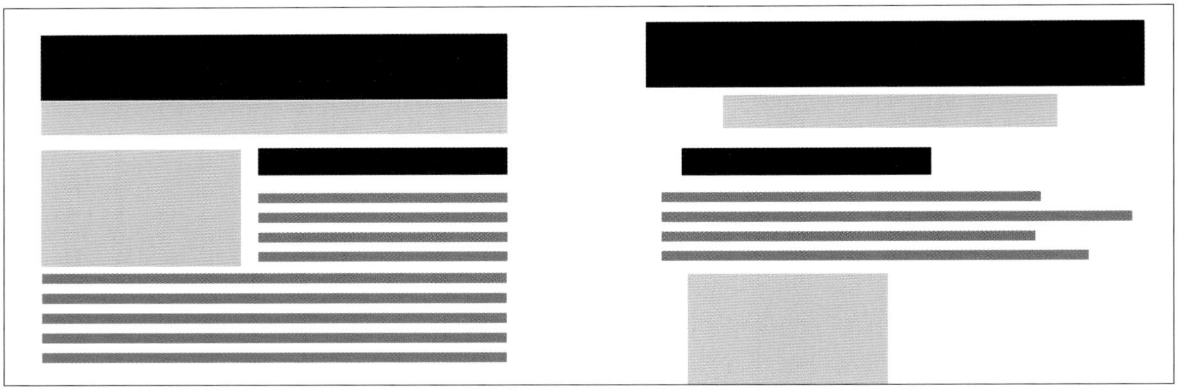

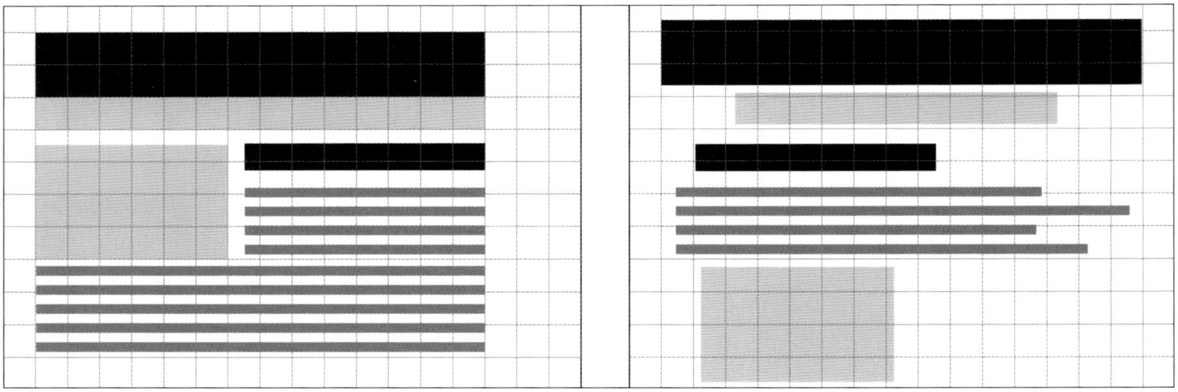

Originally, the grid system was designed as a drawing aid and made by drawing small squares on transparent plastic. The grid system assists with drawing an object in proportion to the real object (see Figure 4-8).

To achieve a consistent layout design, the grid system is necessary. The grid system does not confine an idea to a limited area, but assists in creating a new style. Integrating the grid means throwing away a sense of boredom and cliche and introducing a cadence and tension into the layout. A music sheet is to the musical scales what a grid is to the design elements.

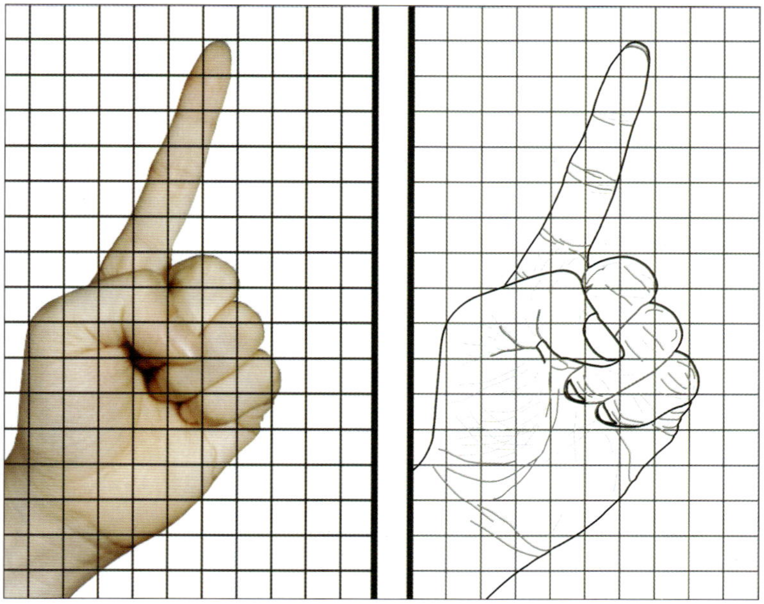

■ **Figure 4-8.** Drawing with a grid helps with subject accuracy

# Invisible Lines and Layout

A grid creates visual paths in a layout and determines where the elements should be placed. From the viewer's point of view, grids help their visual understanding of the work and enable them to communicate information visually.

From the viewer's perspective, the grid lines invisibly and subconsciously help them grasp the points of information at a glance in an orderly way for evaluation. Carelessly compiled web pages prevent the user from readily recognizing the outline of information. When the user opens the web page, a glance is all that is needed to realize if the page is a well-structured layout or not. As shown in Figures 4-9 and 4-10, the orange line indicates the invisible path the viewer's eyes will follow from top to bottom in a second. Therefore, an ill-structured layout may be rejected without having an opportunity to explain the real information. The layout is the result of the implementation of the grid combining functionality and aesthetics.

The grid increases the reliability and security of information in terms of well-structured, intellectual, and clarified layout, allowing the user not only to integrate design elements quickly and easily within a united visual structure but also to retain information in long term memory. However, remember that the grid is nothing but a tool that helps layout design. How easy it would be if layout design were simply arranging design elements in the grid.

There are some variables that affect layout design:

- Visual hierarchy of design elements
- User experience (e.g., cultural background, nationality)
- Design concept (e.g., avant-garde style, minimalism)
- Designer's creativity (e.g., creative solutions, designer's style)
- Functional limitations (e.g., browser compatibility, platform (PC or Mac))

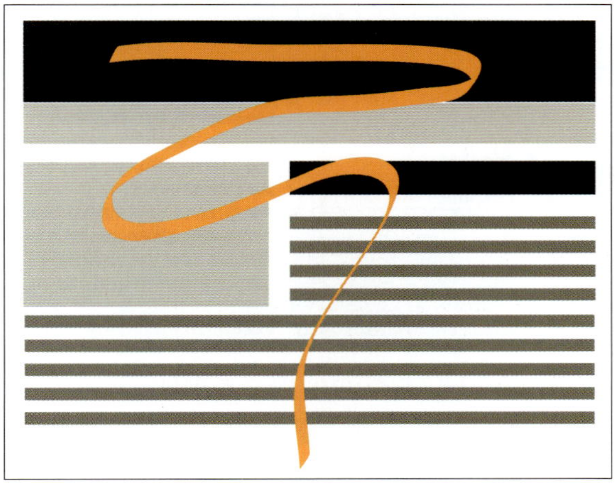

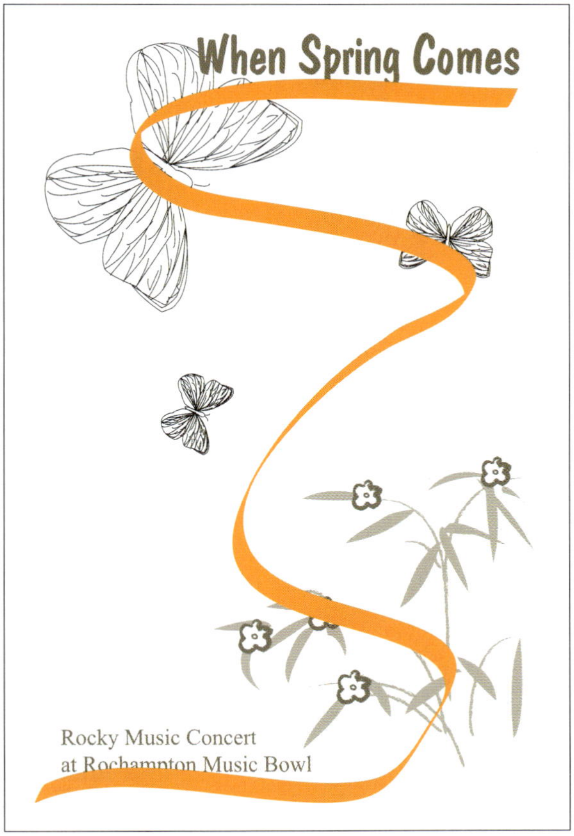


1 2

1 Figure 4-9. The orange line follows the average scan path

2 Figure 4-10. Again, the orange line traces the average scan path

The variables above imply that the grid format may vary as content and design concepts change. In other words, the grid is not an unchangeable and immutable rule. Rather, it is a designable object. Figures 4-11 and 4-12 show how layout designs can be varied depending on the grid structure. Using the same design objects, flower graphics and text lines, a three-column design produces a different mood than a four-column one. The first layout focuses visual attention on the flower graphics; the second makes the text information readable and adds visual interest by using flower graphics. Grid structure adds flexibility to the layout rather than fencing in the designer's creativity.

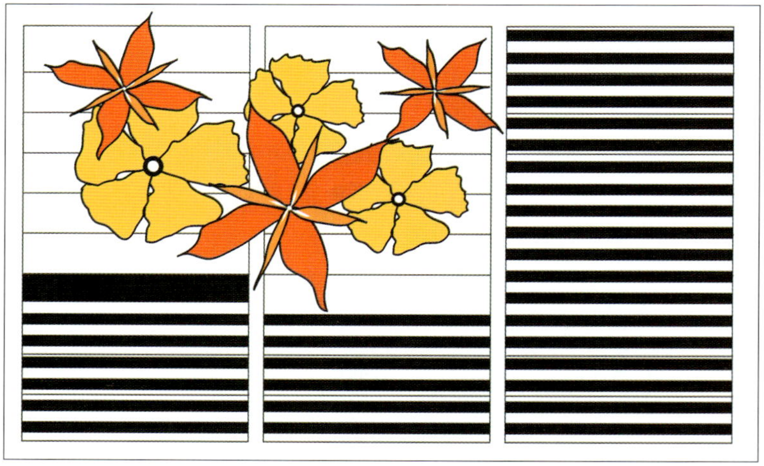

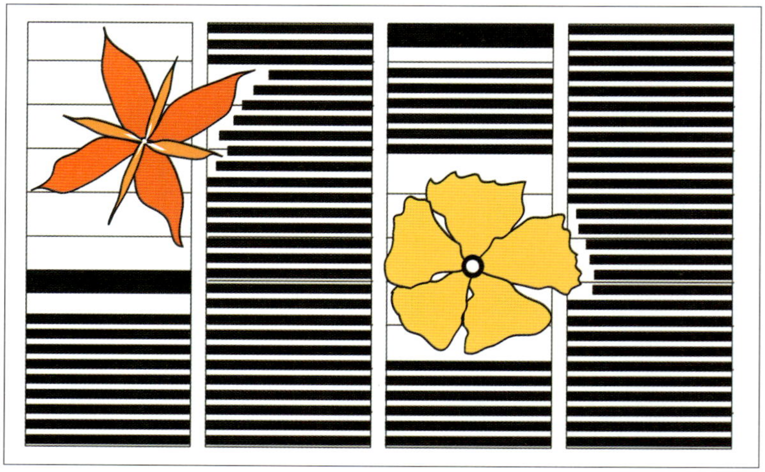

1
2

1 **Figure 4-11.** A three-column layout emphasizes the flower graphics

2 **Figure 4-12.** A four-column layout enhanced by the flower graphics

Grids do not always have to be a pattern of straight lines that intersect to form squares. Figure 4-13 uses a rectangular grid as the background pattern as well as the visual structure, and it is harmonized with the tea break concept design. The grid in this design represents the time schedule of work, and time (numbers and clock hands) disappears like steam off the tea while the break is taken.

However, this layout design can be changed totally by using a different type of grid. Figure 4-14 shows a polar grid applied to the same design concept. Figure 4-13 presents the theme within a stable layout, while Figure 4-14 presents it with a dynamic one.

As shown in these examples, different grids can produce different types of layouts and moods and help the designer find creative solutions.

1 2

1 **Figure 4-13.** Break time evaporates like steam from a cup of tea

2 **Figure 4-14.** Applying a polar grid energizes the design

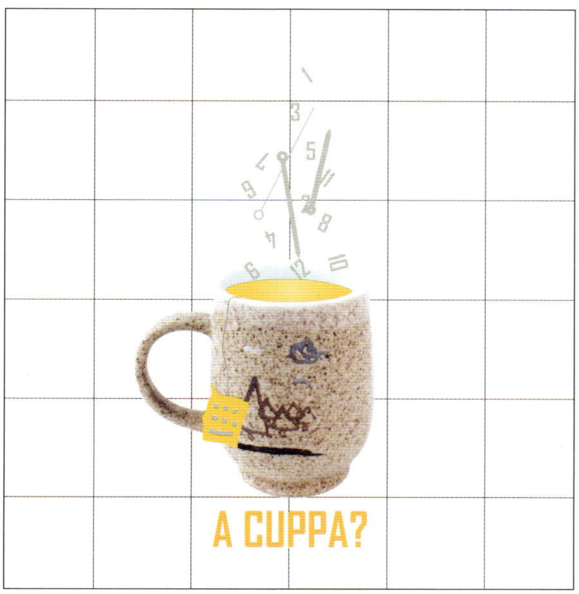


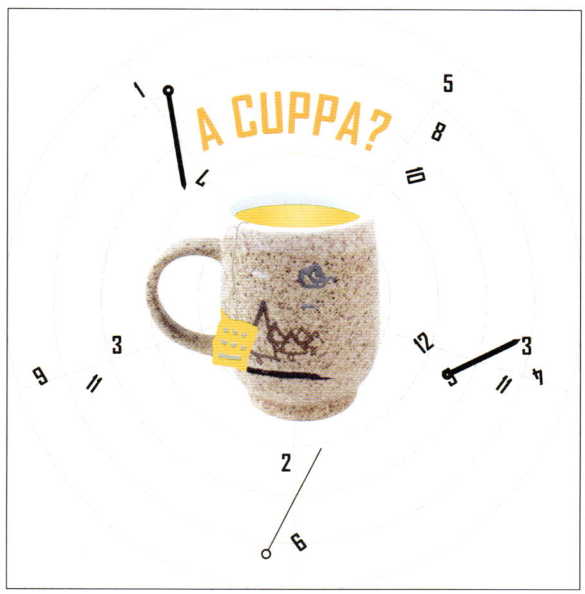

# Grid Elements

A grid system in visual design concerns the following elements: grid units, column width, column number, margins, and field number.

The grid is a network of uniformly placed horizontal and vertical lines for locating points by means of coordinates. In general, the vertical lines are used for dividing columns and the horizontal lines for determining the size of images. To determine the grid most appropriate for the design, consider the following grid aspects:

- **Grid units**: In general, a grid division of $72 \times 72$ pixels is suitable for screen design, and subdivisions may be applied if necessary. In the case of a 72 pixels grid, $9 \times 9$ pixel units are suitable for the subdivisions.
- **Column width**: Column width is determined by various elements such as font size, image size, and screen size. In general, the column width can be determined by the readability of text cells no wider than about 365 pixels based on 12-point Times New Roman.
- **Number of columns**: The correct number of columns to use depends on screen size, design elements, and content. For example, many portal and newspaper sites use three or four columns. This is an effective way to accommodate large amounts of different information.
- **Margins (top, left, right, bottom)**: Margins define the blank outside boundary of the page. There are different default values for margins among Internet browsers and their versions. Thus,

designers have to consider accessibility issues in terms of usability.

- **Fields**: Fields are divided horizontally into columns and are used for distinguishing visual units of information from the contents. Fields can be produced according to content sub-topics.

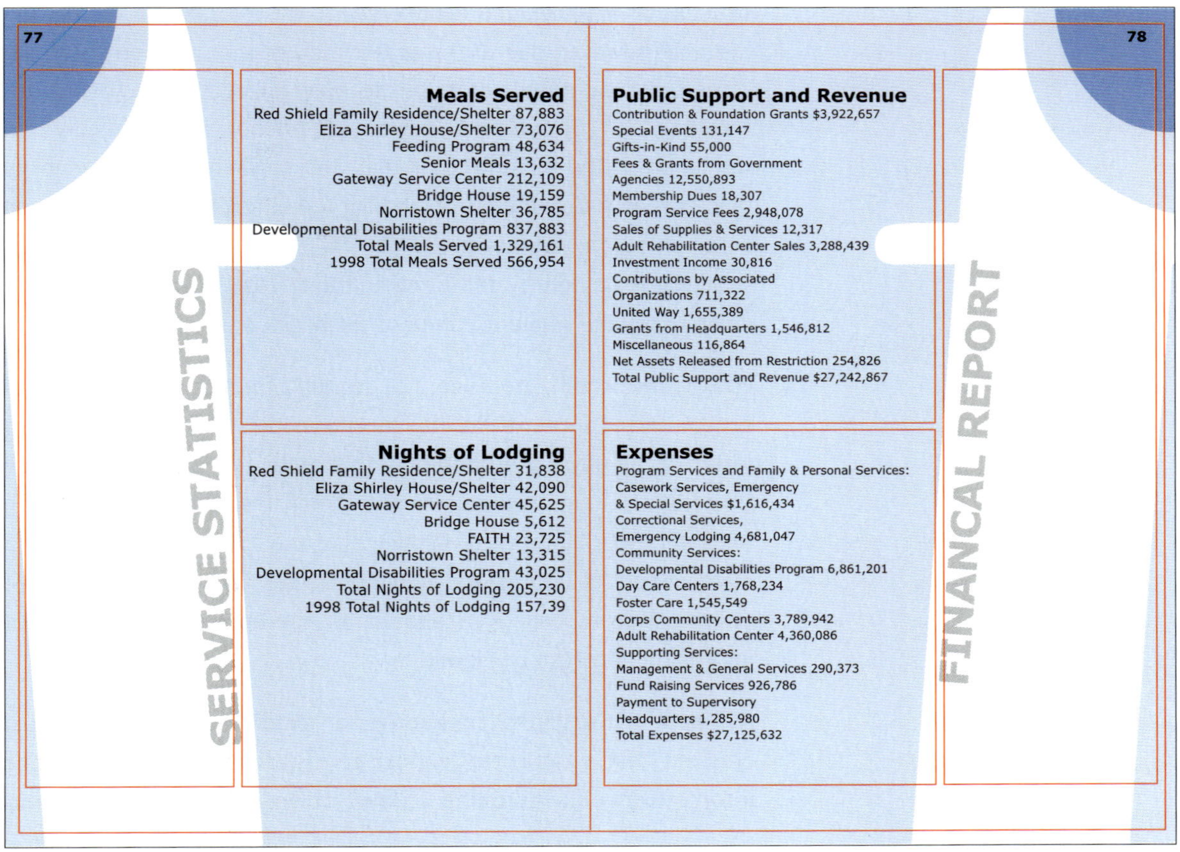

# The Grid in Web Pages

Scrolling function is very often required for web page design to present a large amount of information, although it is very uncomfortable, both functionally and aesthetically.

In print, a reader can see the whole page, recognize the information structure as a whole, and easily organize the information visually. On the web, however, due to the aspect ratio of the common computer screen, it may not be possible to view the entire page without scrolling. To compound the problem further, the relatively low resolution of the screen means that web pages have less readability than printed pages, thereby increasing the difficulty of effective visual communication. As shown in Figure 4-15, the entirety of the page structure is limited by the browser frame. The viewer has to scroll down to see the whole structure of the page.

Putting the screen size aside, the scrolling function breaks the grid system and reduces readability of information. The screen size is a factor of the physical environment that requires preparatory research to determine the average viewer's screen resolution. The scrolling function, especially vertical scrolling, has the advantage of allowing a huge amount of information within one page. Conversely, it is a huge disadvantage to have no standard for the appropriate amount of information that can be viewed.

As Figure 4-16 suggests, the information should be divided into visual clusters that enable the viewer to clearly perceive groups of information while scrolling up and down. Grouping information matches the original grid system and helps to access the information quickly and easily while scrolling. Groups of information should be organized into blocks that fit the height of the browser.

With large amounts of written information, as Figure 4-17 suggests, page-based displays are more readable and accessible than vertically-scrolled pages. In addition, providing a printable version of a page will increase its usability.

1 2
3

1 Figure 4-15. Browser size limits the viewing window
2 Figure 4-16. Visual clusters in a scrolling web page
3 Figure 4-17. Page-based web pages are the most usable

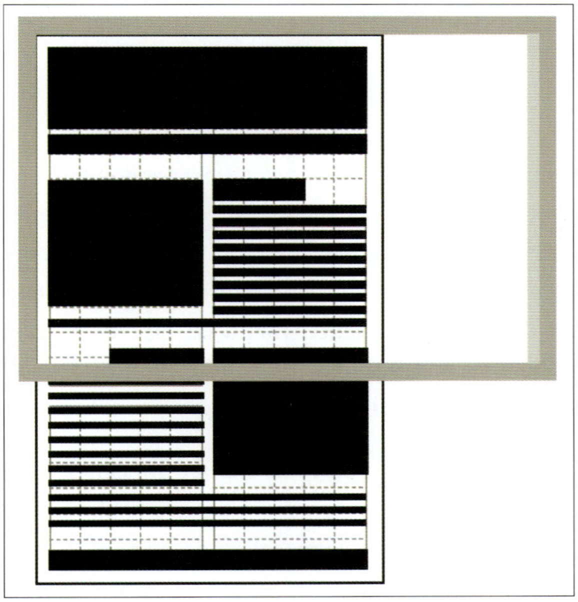

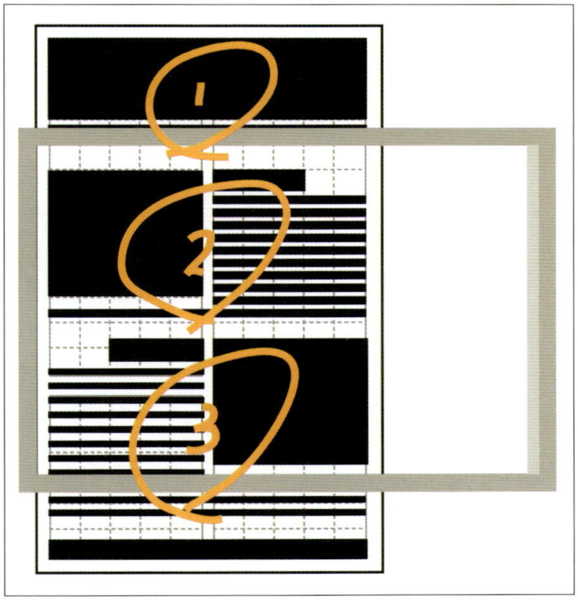

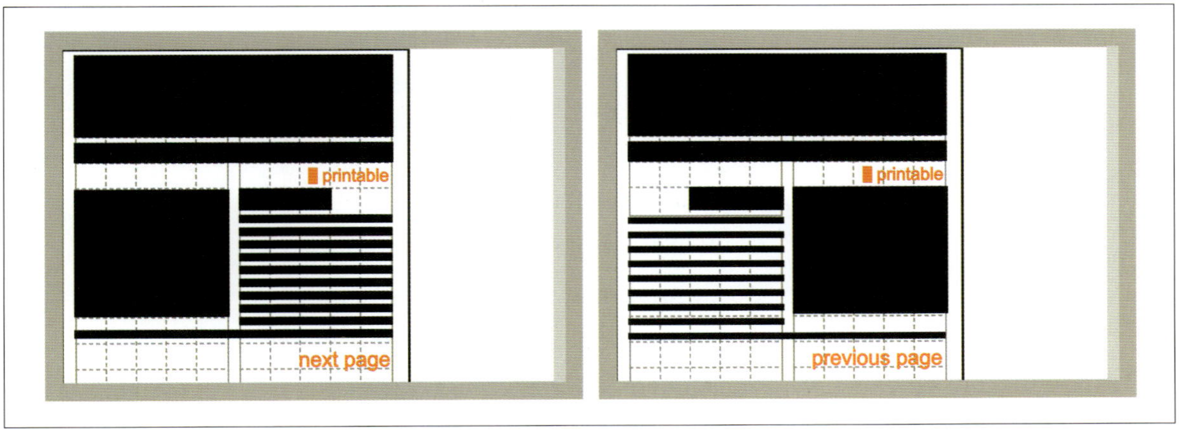

# **Design Studio:**
# Grid and Layout Design

This activity expects you to create a layout design using an image on the basis of the design principles covered in Chapter 2 and 3. A grid system will help you to create appropriate visual paths and determine where the elements should be placed in your layout. A good layout will be produced by a good combination of the grid system and designer's creativity.

The grid is a collection of invisible lines that attracts and guides the viewer's eye. The grid structure guides the viewer to the starting point and ending point in a layout like a map. The grid structure helps the designer to create a particular visual journey in a layout and determines where the design elements should be placed. A good layout design can be achieved through the combination of a good grid structure and the designer's creativity.

The purpose of this activity is to apply the design principles from Chapters 2 and 3 to actual design elements. Prepare a black-and-white product image like the following kettle or phone designs. Create a poster with any theme using the chosen image. It should contain one letter of the alphabet and a short sentence describing what it is. Remember the following rules:

- Alter the scale of the image.
- Use supportive graphics such as lines or shapes.
- Employ a grid system.
- Be experimental and find creative solutions.
- The work must be done in grayscale only.
- The size in pixels must be one of the following:
  760 × 420, 420 × 760, or 500 × 500

## Kettle

—

In Figure 4-18, the dotted lines represent the visual guidelines. The design elements are a square, the letter K, and lines. Arrange them on the visual guidelines. All elements are connected according to the visual guidelines.

As shown in Figure 4-19, the shape is converted to the kettle image, the lines to texts, and the letter K remains as before. Finally, the positions of the elements may be fine-tuned.

The final step is to stimulate the viewer's interest or add a visually pleasing element such as the wavy shape in Figure 4-20. This element visually suggests that water will come out of the kettle and splash on the ground. It breathes new life into the layout. The water being poured into the letter K overflows and harmonizes with the text information.

1 2 3

1 Figure 4-18. Position elements using the same visual guidelines
2 Figure 4-19. The actual elements are inserted
3 Figure 4-20. The design is finished with a splash

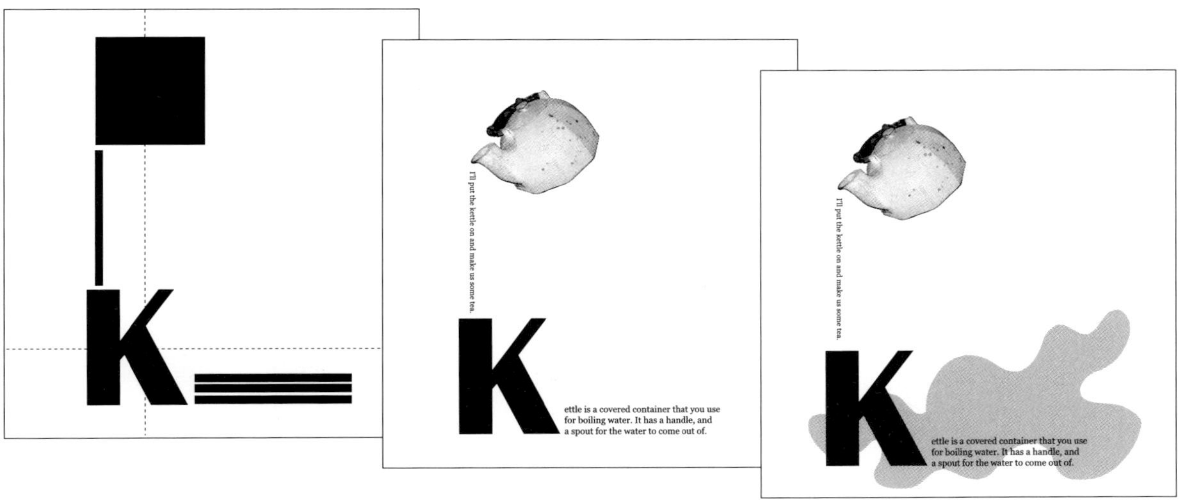

## Phone

A grid structure as a visual guide is an important factor that determines the success of layout design. Figure 4-21 is not visually exciting because the grid seems to restrict the connection between the design elements. It looks stable and symmetrical, but uninteresting. It doesn't catch the viewer's eye. Applying a different grid structure will produce a different result.

The new grid, rotating around the center of the layout, animates the whole layout (see Figure 4-22). It looks as though the speech is coming out of the phone, or that the phone is broadcasting messages in every direction. In this case, the grid is used as another design element that not only integrates all elements into the layout but also enhances visual appeal.

1 2

1 Figure 4-21. A well structured and uninteresting layout on a square grid

2 Figure 4-22. An exciting design achieved with a radial grid

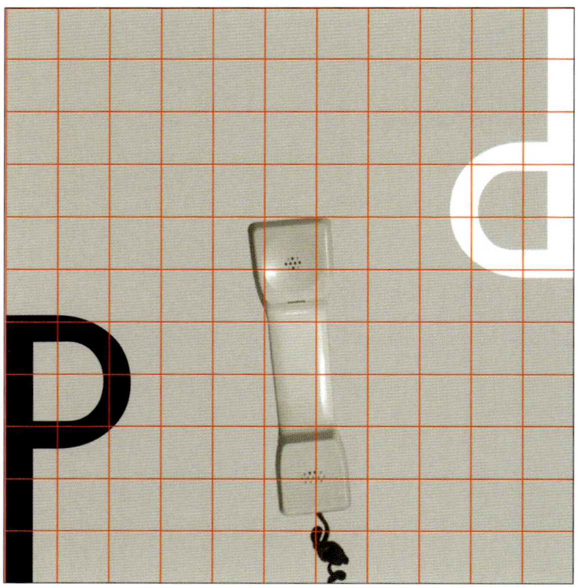

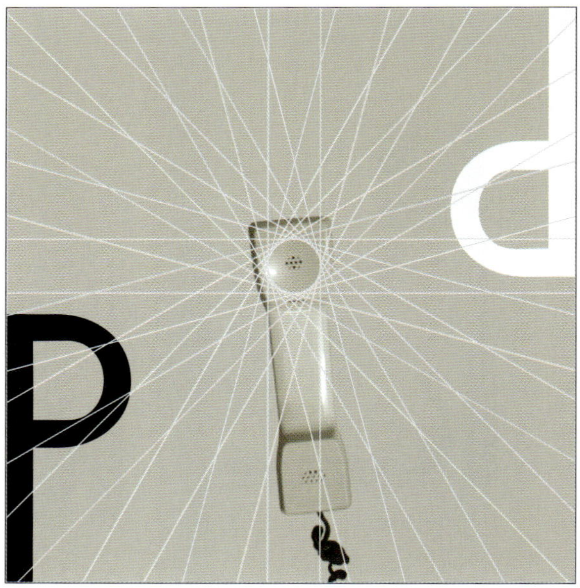

# Student Gallery
## Grid and Layout Design

You are required to create a poster with any theme using a mug image supplied. It must contain one letter (from A to Z) and a short sentence describing what it is.

- Alter the scale of the image or duplicate it.
- Use graphics such as lines or shape
- Employ a grid system
- Software: Adobe Illustrator CS2
- Dimension: 500 x 500 pixels
- Format: publish a gif or a jpg format (depending on the image quality and file size) from your work

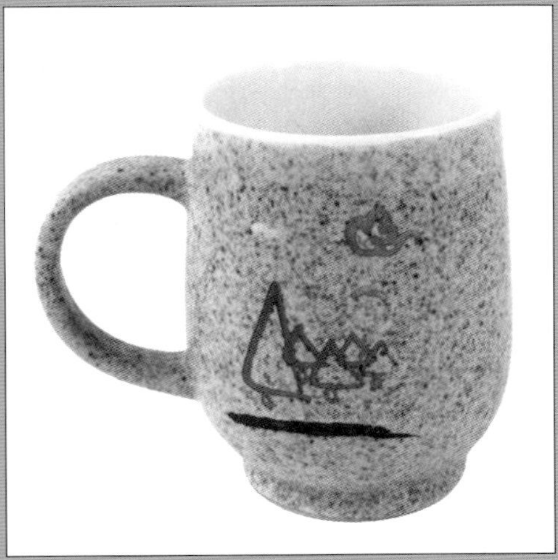

### Marking Criteria (possible marks: 10)

Student will receive one of the marks in the following:

- 9 – 10: Successful design with creative solutions and professional finish
- 7 – 8: Successful design, but insufficient creativity and finish
- 5 – 6: Adequate, but lack of experiment or creativity
- 3 – 4: Inadequate, partly misunderstanding
- 2 – 0: Wrong theme or no submission

## Student Works - Dynamic Layout

- Karina Maree Voss 2007

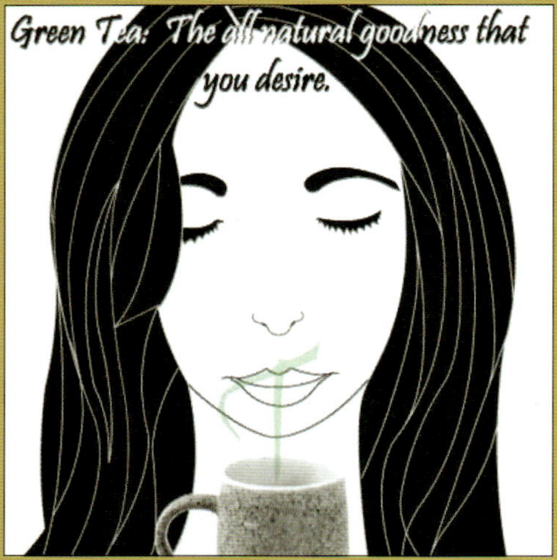


The activity asked students to create a poster design by using a mug image and a letter (A - Z) for the purpose of practicing using a grid system in the layout design. Karina's work to the left was chosen as the best work in that the elements are arranged in a stable layout that is well matched with its subject and overall mood. The letter T undoubtedly represents green tea that is visually in harmony with the female character appreciating its fragrance.

- Douglas (Chak Cheung) Tsang 2006

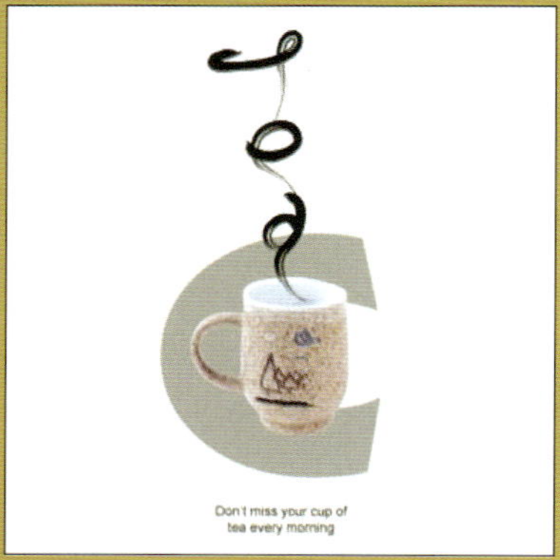


- Natalie Gaye Clarke 2007

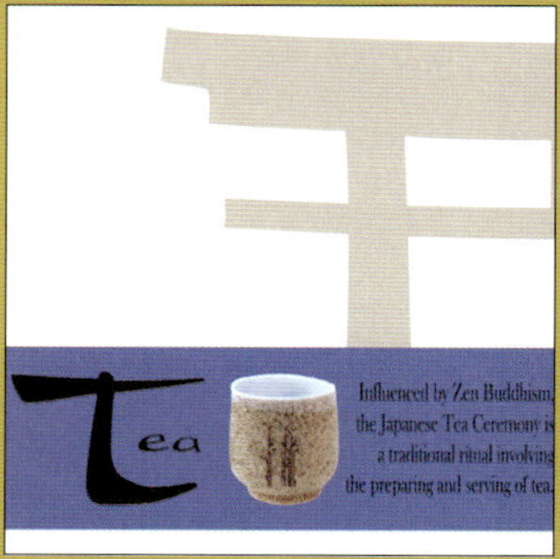


- Justin Andrew Hawley 2007

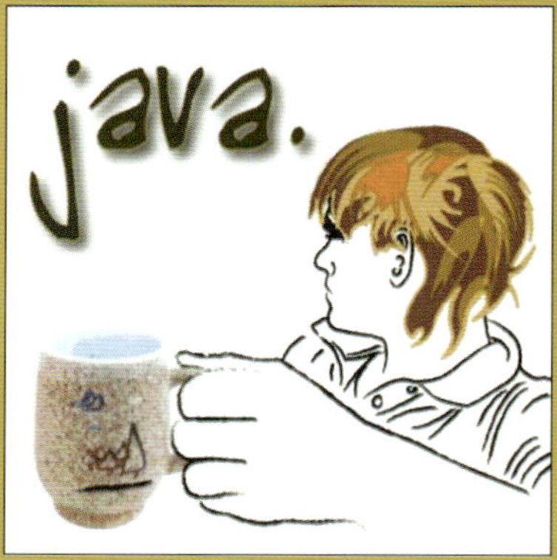


- Chelsea Sutherland 2007

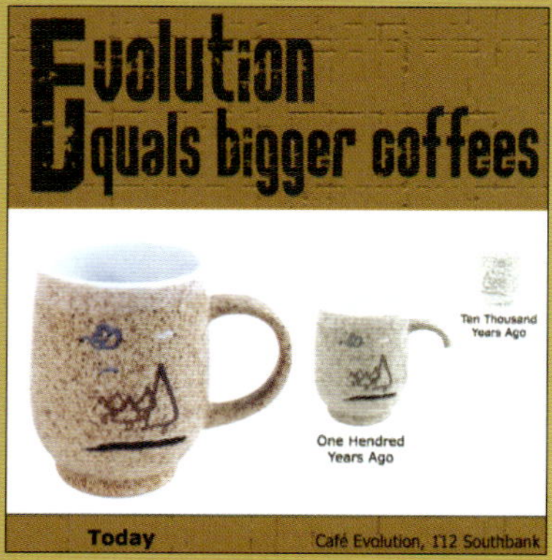


- Karina Maree Voss 2007

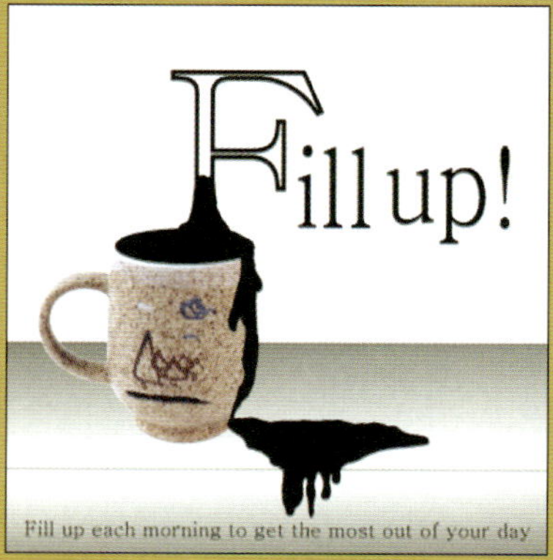

Chapter

# [05]

# Color

Most people have visited a multimedia web site that uses sound or background music. How would it compare if the background music or moving graphics were removed? Removing these multimedia elements may make the site feel less dynamic and eliminate the feeling of movement. The use of sound in multimedia animates a design and enriches its emotional experience. Color is to visual design what sound is to multimedia. Color adds liveliness and interest to a visual design and often determines its identity.

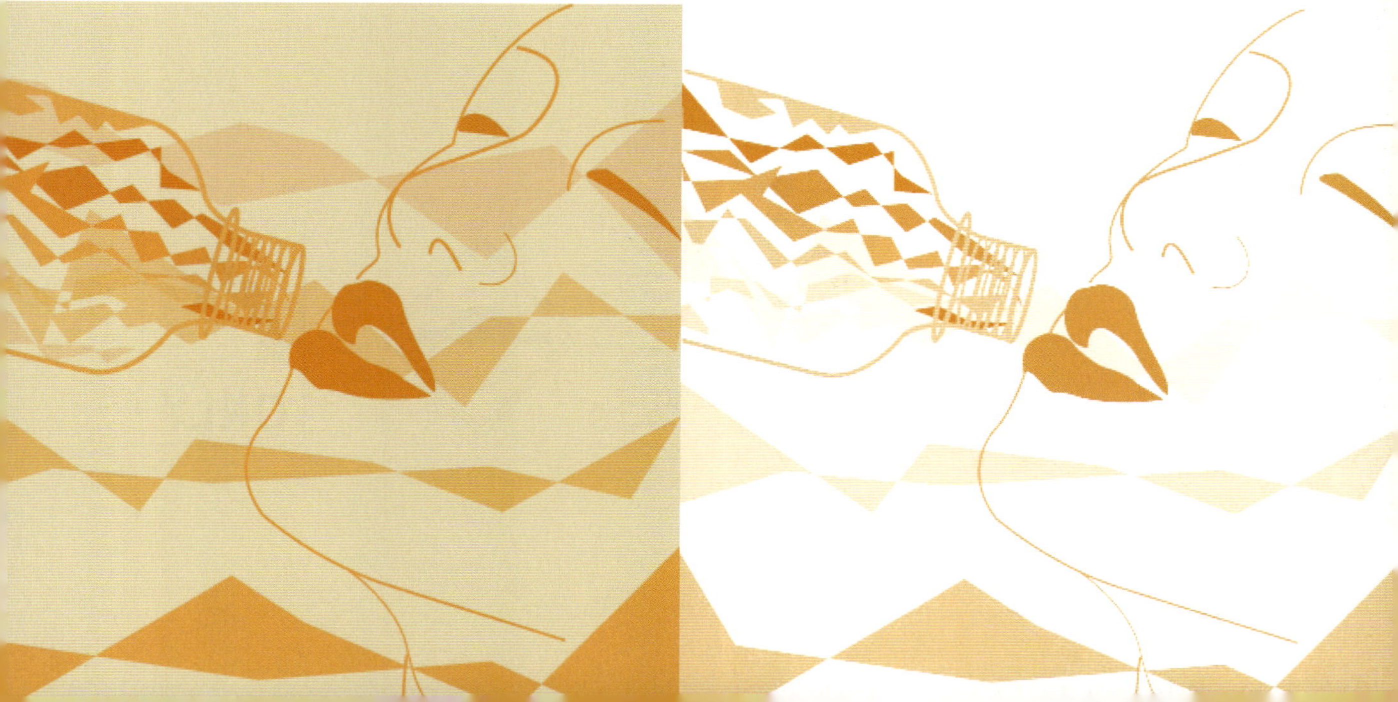

# Defining Color

Color is one of the most important factors of success in visual communication. Selecting and applying an appropriate color in the design process requires a lot of time and effort. Color is a very influential factor as it can affect the whole design process and may even change the layout design in many ways. Color alone can alter the mood and message of the design. The designer may decide to adapt a layout to fit the mood of a color rather than the main concept or the original purpose of the design. Therefore, color is usually applied later in the design process. Selecting a color scheme is a process of exploring and defining the visual experience in relation to the design's objective and the viewer's experience.

## Color and Message

Separating colors from an object is analogous to taking the soul from its body. Color can contain the critical identity of an object, and colors deliver messages of their own. As shown in Figure 5-1, each Australian road sign indicates its message clearly, such as directions, warnings, and speed limits. Because of the use of color, the driver can distinguish the sign's message at first glance. In this case, yellow gives a warning, white tells directions or instructions, and red shows limits; the colors of the road signs are a social norm and are a means of delivering a normative message.

**1** **Figure 5-1.** Traffic signs are designed to relate information quickly

## Color and Emotions

Colors can reflect social feelings, such as wealth and poverty or urban and rural, as well as personal feelings, such as warmth and cold, strength and weakness, delight, gloom, excitement, boredom, passion, neutrality, aggression, and peace. What colors do you associate with the sun, for example? The sun is sometimes illustrated as a generous father figure, and Figure 5-2 shows one potential color visualization of the sun.

Regardless of whether color reflects social or personal feelings, people interpret messages from a particular color or color scheme. Color is a way of tapping into a person's emotions rather than logic. This is true regardless of whether the color-emotion is learned through education, experience, or is an instinctual reaction. People don't think about color; they feel it. What color-emotion do you associate with the moon? The crescent moon is often illustrated as a charming lady. She is attractive, beautiful, and glamorous. Figure 5-3 is an example of how the moon can be visualized with red, yellow, pink, and purple.

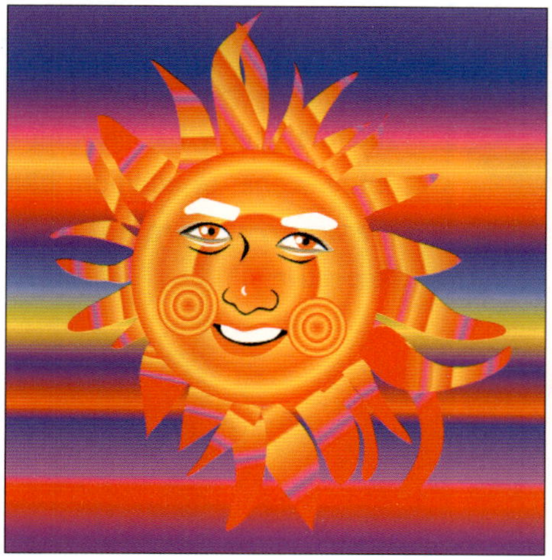

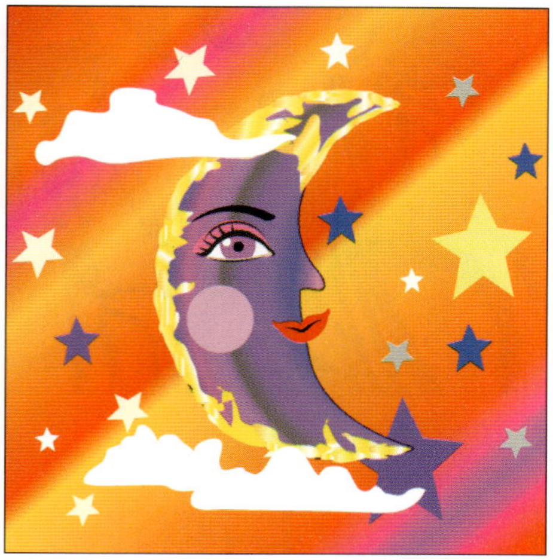

1 2

1 Figure 5-2. Benevolent colors make the sun seem fatherly

2 Figure 5-3. The moon illustrated as a charming lady

Understanding the audience's preference or experience in relation to color is an important step in determining the right color scheme for a design. The emotion triggered by a color is influenced by culture, nationality, personal preference, age, education level, and gender. Color is communicated emotionally, but choosing colors should be done scientifically.

## Color and Statistics

In general, the majority of people in one culture share common feelings and opinions about a color through social and personal experience. For instance:

- Red: power, anger, violence, revenge, sexuality
- Yellow: warmth, joy, lightheartedness, warning
- Blue: cold, patience, tranquility, peace
- Orange: courage, youth, friendliness, cheerfulness
- Green: growth, freshness, envy, greed, jealousy, responsibility

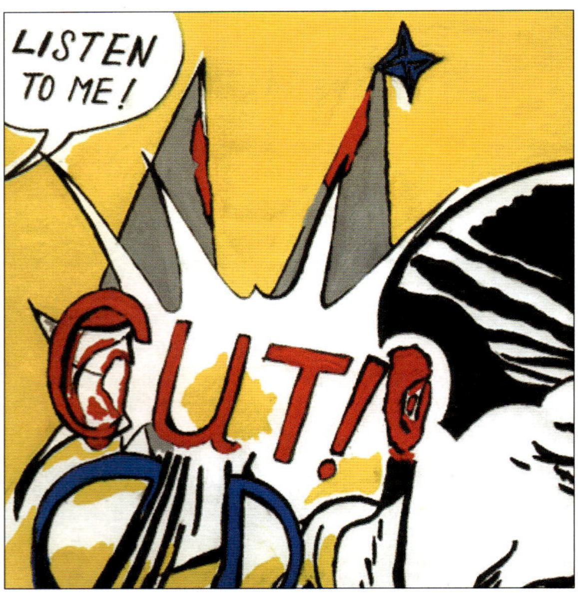


Figure 5-4 shows how colors are used to convey the theme of an image. The image illustrates a cruel and bizarre scene that depicts a person whose ear has been cut off with scissors. Considering the command "Listen to me!" in this illustration, someone (a third person) may have cut off the ear because the victim had not been listening to the speaker carefully. The image uses mainly red and yellow shades. Red represents violence and anger, and the yellow background calls attention to the entire scene. In addition, blue and gray colors on the scissors represent coolness and neutrality, respectively.

Figure 5-4. Color is used to great effect in a violent scene

# Color Theory

Many designers and scientists have discovered certain principles and facts about colors. The following sections introduce some basic color theories for visual design.

## The Color Wheel and Hue

The most basic but important part of color theory is the color wheel, which consists of twelve colors (see Figure 5-5). There are three groups in the color wheel: primary, secondary, and tertiary. The primary colors–red, yellow, and blue–are the foundation of the color wheel. Their importance was identified by Isaac Newton in 1666. The twelve colors on the outer ring of the color wheel are the more common organization of hues.

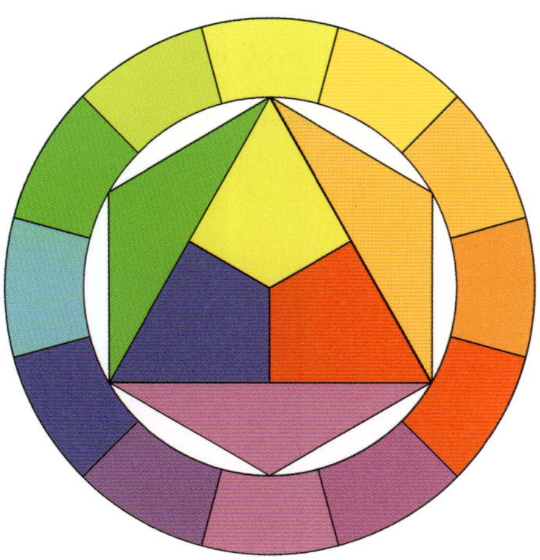

**Figure 5-5.** The 12-hue color wheel

## 1 | Primary colors

Red, yellow, and blue are the three primary colors of the subtractive color model (see Figure 5-6). A subtractive color model uses pigments, like paints, to create colors, as opposed to the additive color model used in televisions and computer screens that mix colored light. The three primary colors cannot be formed by mixing any other colors. They form the central basis of the color wheel and all other colors are derived from these three colors.

## 2 | Secondary colors

The secondary colors are equal mixtures of any two primaries: orange, green, and violet (see Figure 5-7).

- Red+Yellow ▢ Orange
- Yellow+Blue ▢ Green
- Blue+Red ▢ Violet

## 3 | Tertiary colors

The tertiary colors are created by mixing one primary and one secondary color (see Figure 5-8).

- Blue+Green ▢ Blue-Green: BG
- Blue+Violet ▢ Blue-Violet: BV
- Red+Violet ▢ Red-Violet: RV
- Red+Orange ▢ Red-Orange: RO
- Yellow+Orange ▢ Yellow-Orange : YO
- Yellow+Green ▢ Yellow-Green : YG

**Note** | These color-mixing properties refer only to pigment. Colored light can produce very different effects.

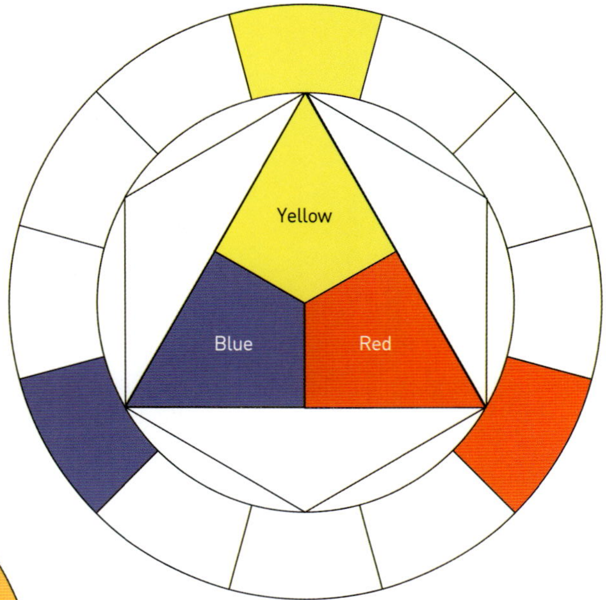


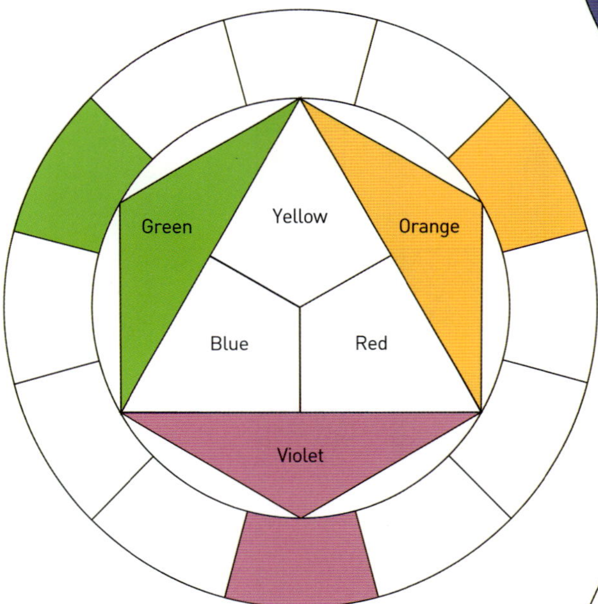


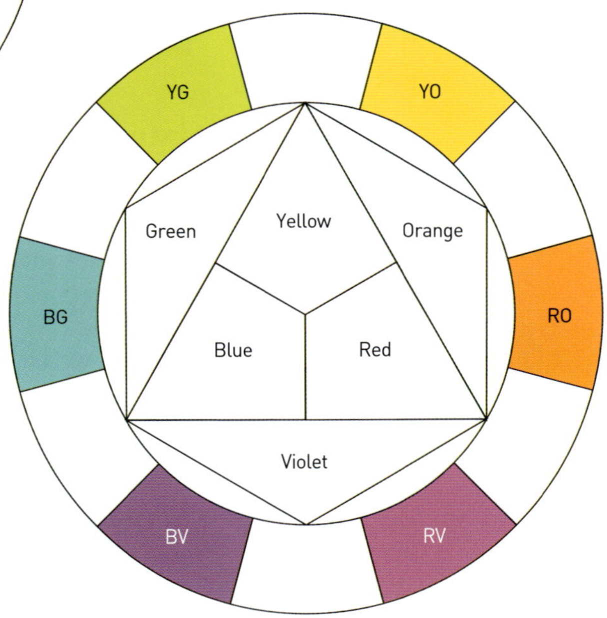


1 Figure 5-6. Primary colors in the color wheel
2 Figure 5-7. Secondary colors in the color wheel
3 Figure 5-8. Tertiary colors in the color wheel

## Value

Value refers to the lightness or darkness of a color. Contrasting values separate objects in space. The value order of the primary and secondary colors is, from lightest to darkest: yellow, orange, red, green, violet, blue. The lighter the color, the closer it is to white. This is often called a tint. The darker the color, the closer it is to black. This is often called a shade (see Figure 5-9). Controlling the level of value allows for expressing richer and more subtle variations of color. In addition, gradation of value suggests depth and contour of an object.

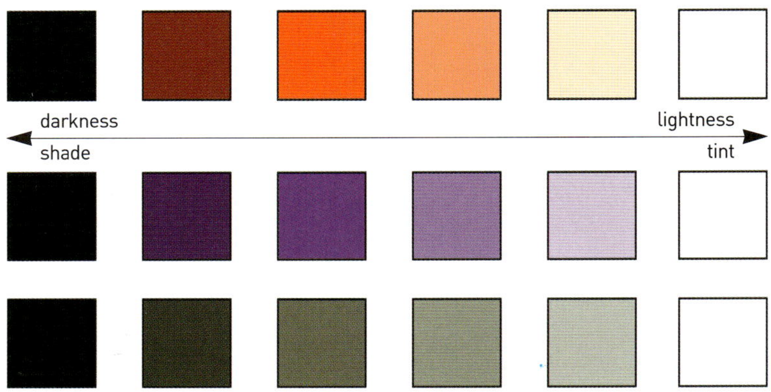


**1** Figure 5-9. Value is the darkness or lightness level of a color

## Intensity

Intensity, also called chroma or saturation, refers to the brightness of a color. The primary colors are at full intensity because they have not been mixed.

Intensity can be manipulated in two ways.

First, as Figure 5-10 demonstrates, you can dull a color by adding gray to it.

As Figure 5-11 demonstrates, the intensity of a color can also be changed by mixing it with its complementary. (This is the color found directly opposite on the color wheel.)

Mixing complementary colors together produces a dull tone. However, placing a color with its complementary color side by side can increase its intensity (see Figure 5-12). This effect is called simultaneous contrast and causes each color to be intensified by the other. This creates visual tension.

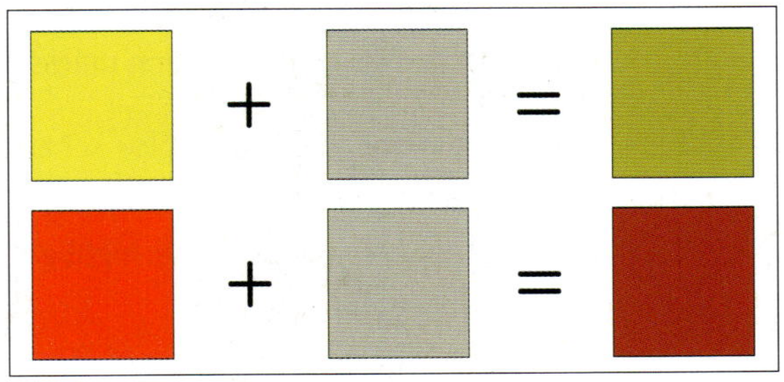

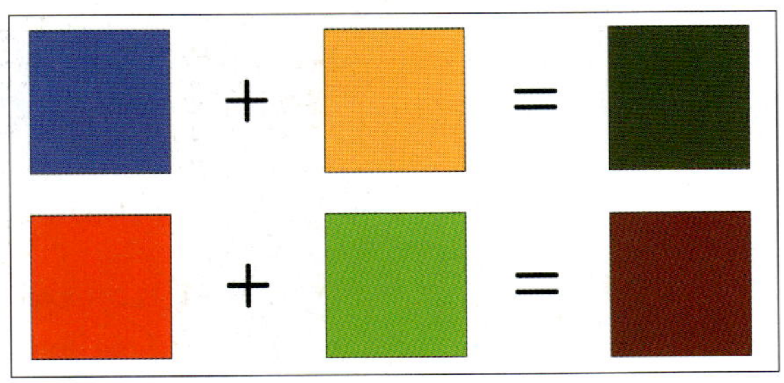

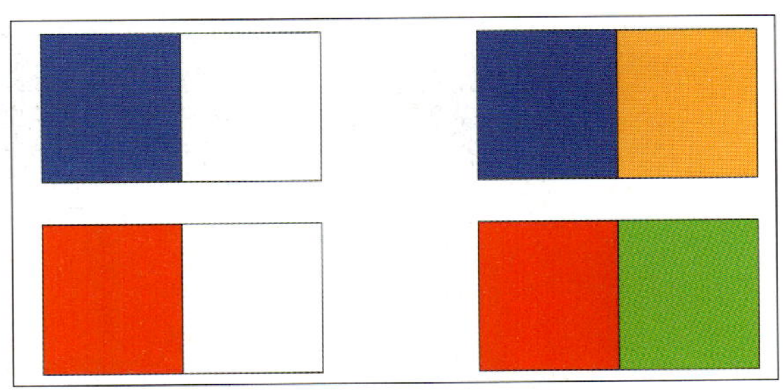

1 Figure 5-10. Color intensity is dulled by adding gray

2 Figure 5-11. Colors mixed with their complements

3 Figure 5-12. Color intensity is increased when adjacent to its complement

## Color Harmonies

Color harmony is an arrangement of colors that is pleasing to the eye. Non-harmonious colors increase eyestrain and cause boredom. Color harmony delivers visual interest and a sense of order.

There are four basic color harmonies: monochromatic, analogous, complementary, and triadic.

### 1 | Monochromatic harmony

Monochromatic colors use a single hue and vary only by value. In other words, any individual color (hue) from the color wheel (Figure 5-13) can be the foundation of a monochromatic color scheme with its different tints and shades. These hues create a subtle and elegant atmosphere due to the lack of color contrast. Monochromatic schemes may be boring unless there is diversity within the design.

A monochromatic color scheme can produce a soothing effect with varying saturation to look clean and peaceful. It is also very gentle on the eyes, yet can be highlighted by adding a different hue on an important element.

A monochromatic scheme applied to a design will more easily achieve visual balance, simplicity, and harmony. But, because of a lack of contrast, it may produce a boring and dull mood. As Figure 5-14 shows, this monochromatic in purple looks very subtle and has very little contrast. However, it looks clean and elegant and is easy on the eyes.

Figure 5-15 is an example of a monochromatic image in purple that casts a lonesome and gloomy mood over the image.

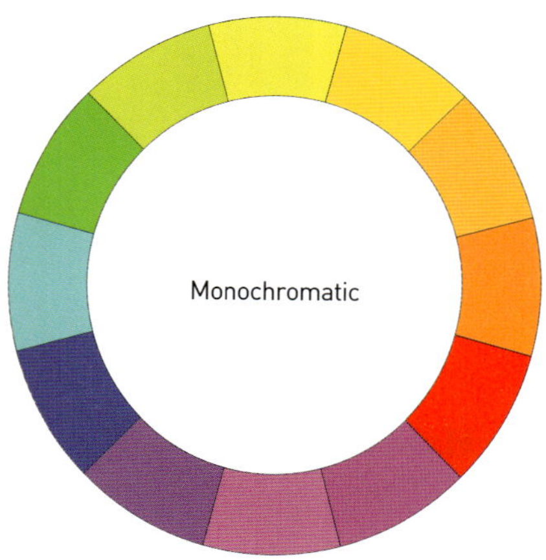


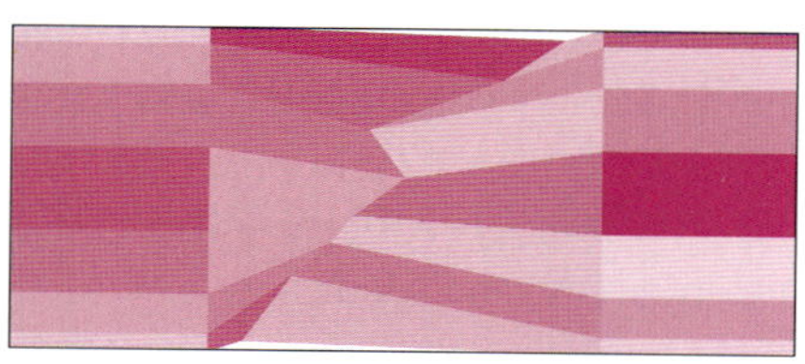

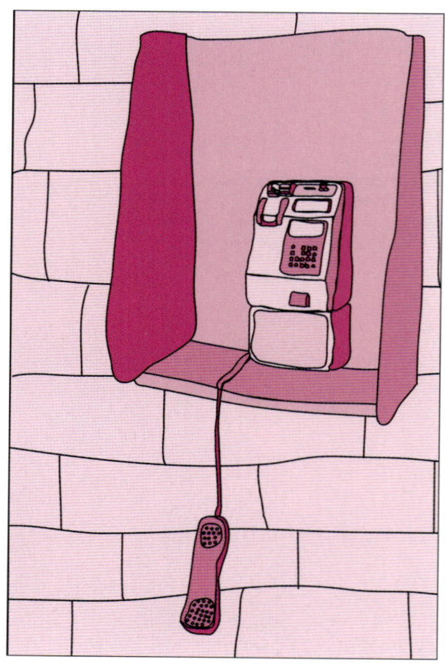

1 3
2

1 Figure 5-13. The monochromatic colors are the 12 hues of the color wheel

2 Figure 5-14. A monochromatic color scheme is simple but well balanced

3 Figure 5-15. A purple monochromatic scheme applied to a public phone

## 2 | Analogous harmony

The analogous color scheme combines three to five colors adjacent to each other on the color wheel (see Figure 5-16).

One color is used as the dominant color, while others are used to enrich the scheme. The analogous scheme is similar to the monochromatic one in terms of visual effect, but it offers more nuances. Therefore, the analogous color scheme looks richer than the monochromatic color scheme but still has little contrast like a monochromatic. In addition, combining warm and cool colors can break the color harmony.

Figure 5-17 lacks vividness and looks a little bit desaturated due to less contrast in the analogous color scheme. But it looks well-blended and harmonious.

The image in Figure 5-18 demonstrates how analogous colors are harmonized and are pleasing to the eye. The color combinations bring about unusual but fascinating moods in an exotic atmosphere.

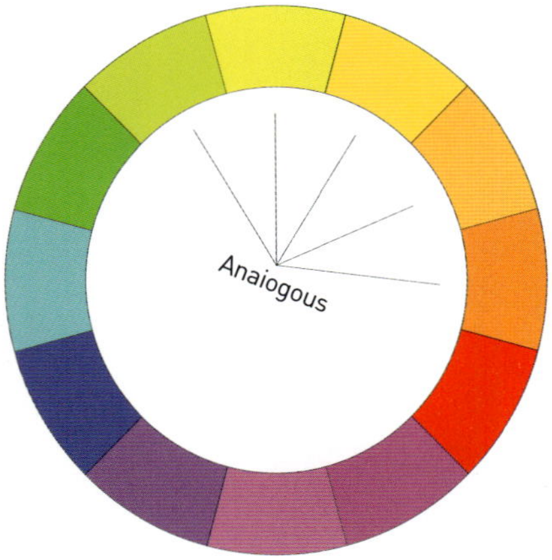


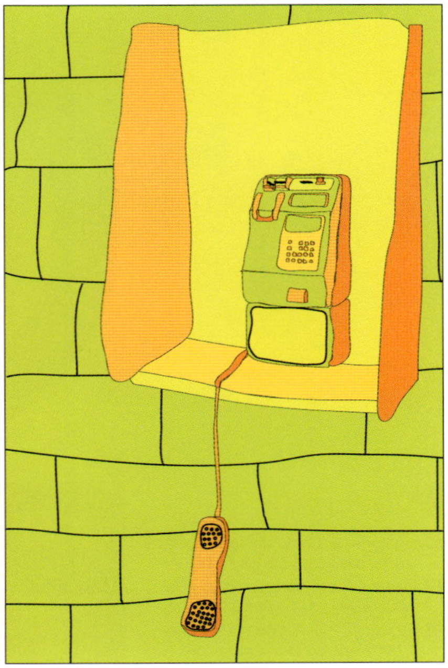

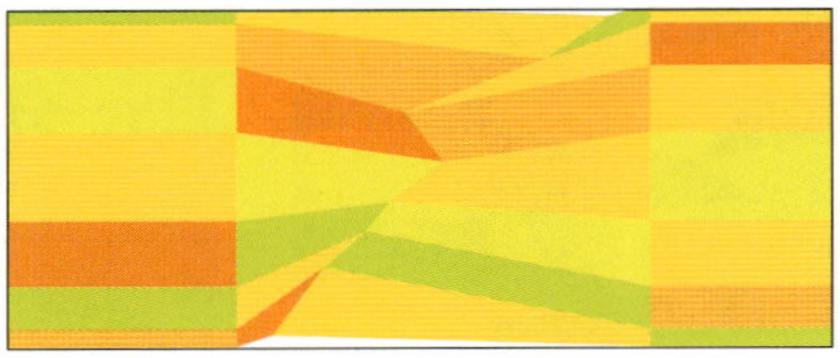

1 3
2

1 Figure 5-16. Analogous colors are adjacent on the color wheel

2 Figure 5-17. An analogous scheme lacks vividness but looks harmonious

3 Figure 5-18. An analogous scheme applied to a public phone

## 3 | Complementary harmony

Complementary harmonies link colors opposite one another on the color wheel (see Figure 5-19). The effect is lively and more dynamic than monochromatic and analogous color schemes due to the high contrast.

When using the complementary scheme, choose one color as a dominant color and use its complementary color for accents. For example, using one color for the background and its complementary color to highlight important elements produces color dominance combined with sharp color contrast. However, complementary schemes are harder to balance than the preceding schemes. To emphasize one element with a complementary scheme, it is a good idea to apply the analogous colors of the opposite color to other elements (see Figure 5-20). This provides good contrast without the strong tension of the complementary scheme.

In Figure 5-21, the yellow wall and the blue and purple phone contrast. The difference in hue draws the viewer's attention and creates visual tension.

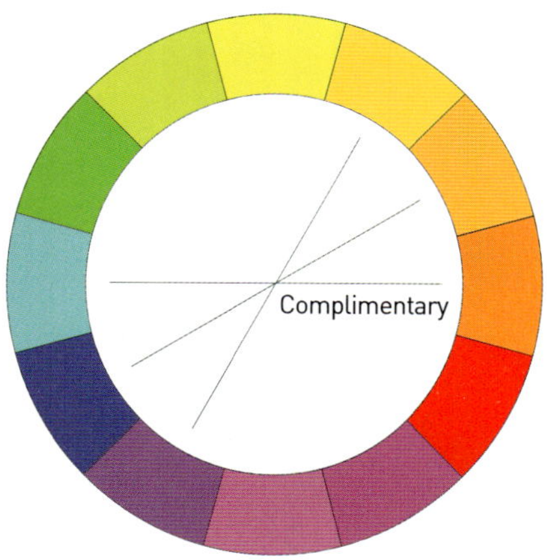


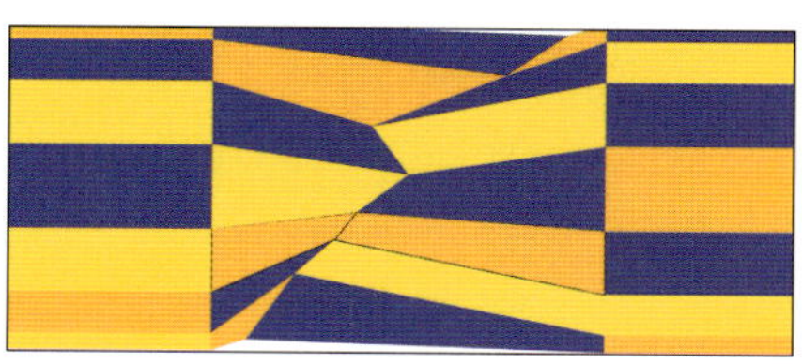

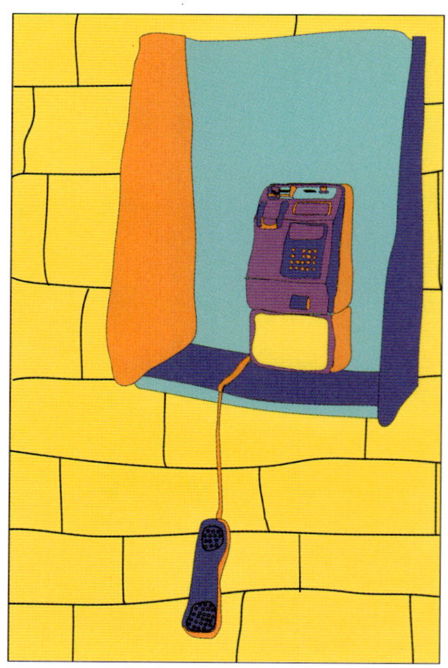

1 Figure 5-19. Complementary colors are the pairs opposite each other

2 Figure 5-20. A complementary color scheme with good contrast

3 Figure 5-21. A complementary scheme applied to a public phone

## 4 | Triadic harmony

Triadic harmony involves a set three hues that are separated by 120 degrees (see Figure 5-22). The primary (red, blue, and yellow) and secondary (violet, orange, and green) color sets are examples of triadic colors. This combination provides high energy, contrast, and liveliness.

Triadic color schemes are the most common because they offer strong visual contrast while retaining balance and color richness. However, the contrast is not as strong as the complementary color scheme, but it looks more balanced and harmonious.

Triadic colors in Figures 5-23 and 5-24 emit high energy and are very vibrant. A successful triadic color combination is used when one color is used in larger amounts, but the other two colors become the dominant ones.

Traditionally, the four basic color harmonies, monochromatic, complementary, analogous, and triadic, are used separately, but they can be mixed with one another to create a unique color scheme.

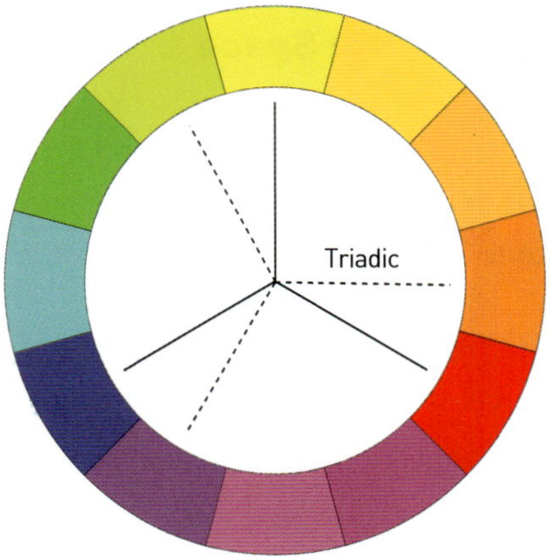


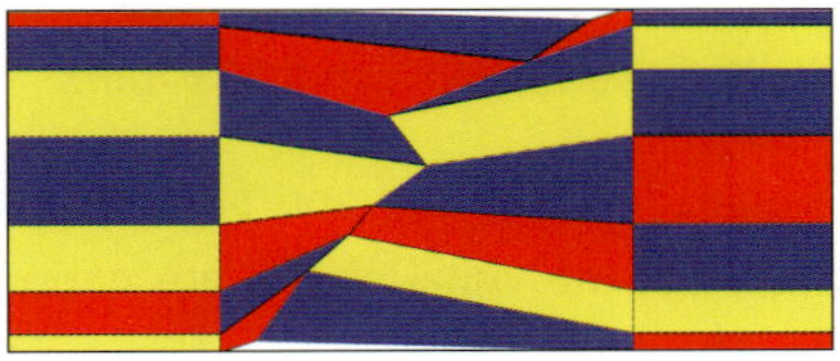

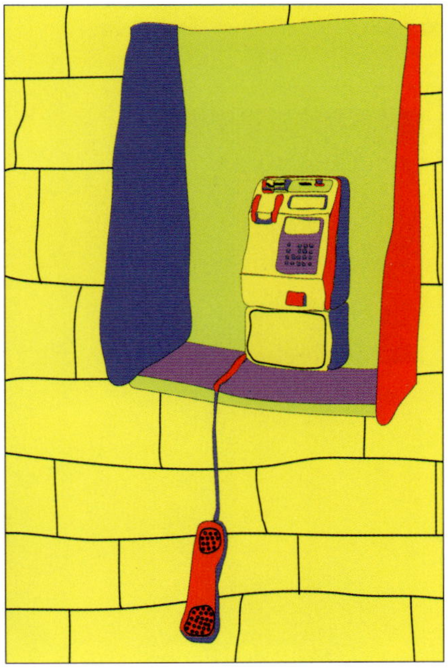

1 3
2

1 Figure 5-22. The triadic colors are separated by 120 degrees

2 Figure 5-23. A triadic color scheme has strong contrast and richness

3 Figure 5-24. A triadic scheme applied to a public phone

# Color Effects

Color is so powerful when determining the structure of layout design, that choosing a color scheme should be done after finishing the layout design. Otherwise, color may break down the underlying design concept.

Color is critical in determining the overall design process, and it may even change the design concept and layout design. Color affects moods, emotions, styles, and business. Designers are also affected by color. Therefore designers may attempt to remove their color preferences in order to meet the customer needs.

**1** Figure 5-25. Color depth achieved with specific color choices

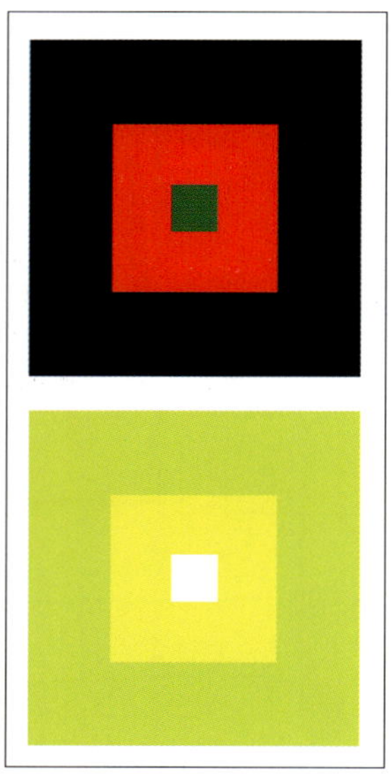

## Perception of Space

The use of color plays an important role in the representation of space or depth in design. The following list is an example of using color to manipulate space.

- Expand space: cool, light, or dull colors; minimal contrasts
- Shrink space: warm, dark, or bright colors; maximum contrasts
- Forward: intense warm colors, such as red, yellow, and orange
- Recede: cool colors, such as blue and green
- Deep: cool colors and light tints
- Shallow: warm colors and dark tones

In Figure 5-25, the top and bottom images are the same size and format, but the visual effects are entirely different. The top image moves forward, while the bottom image recedes.

Tonal ranges also imply a sense of depth. Colors tend to lose their clarity as they recede. Figure 5-26 shows a series of red squares increasing in color intensity from 5% to 100%. This causes them to appear to move from far to near.

Figure 5-27 is an example of applying tonal range in color and shape at the same time.

1
2

1 Figure 5-26. Tonal range provides depth
2 Figure 5-27. Tonal change in color as shape also changes

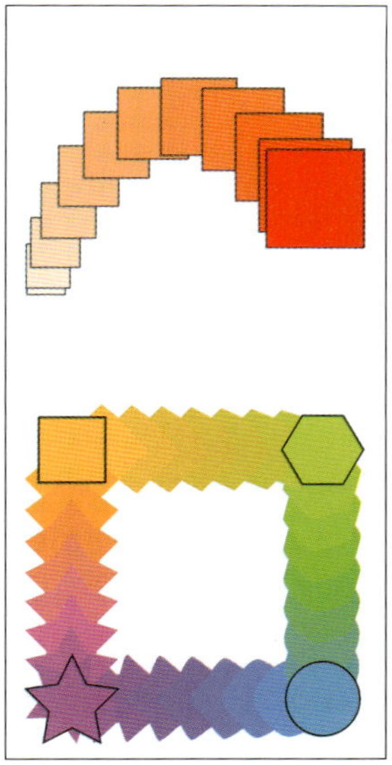

## Simultaneous Contrast

Certain color combinations can cause intense muscular reactions in the eye due to simultaneous contrast. The circular area in each quadrant in Figure 5-28 is exactly the same color. However, they appear different due to the surrounding color and the lateral interactions that occur.

Figure 5-29 shows the blinking effect within a static image. Our eyes make this image dynamic; the twinkle effect is the eyes' attempt to fill in the white circle intersections with the black of the background.

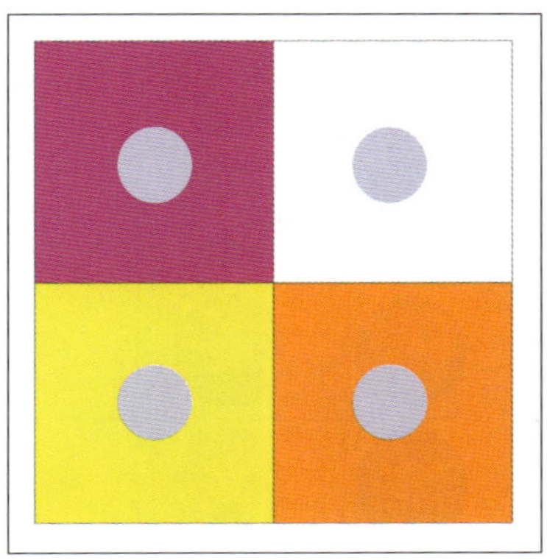

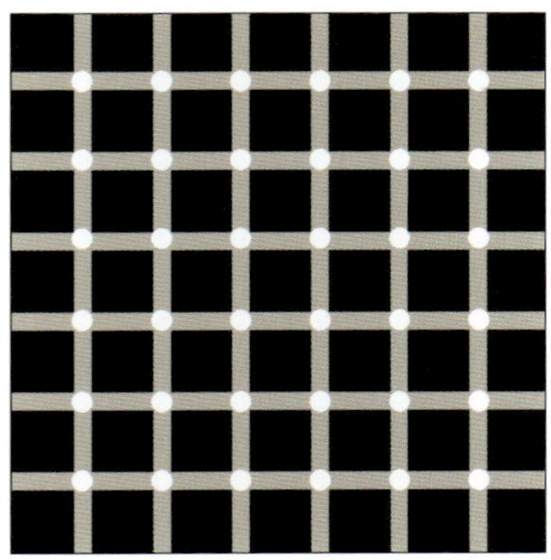

1 2

1 Figure 5-28. Varying color contrast affects appearance
2 Figure 5-29. High contrast creates the illusion of blinking lights

## Color and Expressions

Color in English metaphors help clarify emotional states:

- I feel blue.
- He turned red with anger.
- I try to stay in the red.
- She looks green around the gills.
- I am green with envy.
- He turned purple with rage.
- He turned yellow with fear.
- The future looks gray.
- She talked until she was blue in the face.

These color references can often be used for intensifying visual communication. Finding the meaning of a color in people's communication and culture can suggest effective methods for using color schemes to involve the viewer emotionally. Figure 5-30 presents the relationship between color and emotion with an illustration of facial expressions. It shows some different facial expressions using the correct color and an incorrect color. The correct color indicates what the majority of native English-speakers accept as traditional for that emotional state.

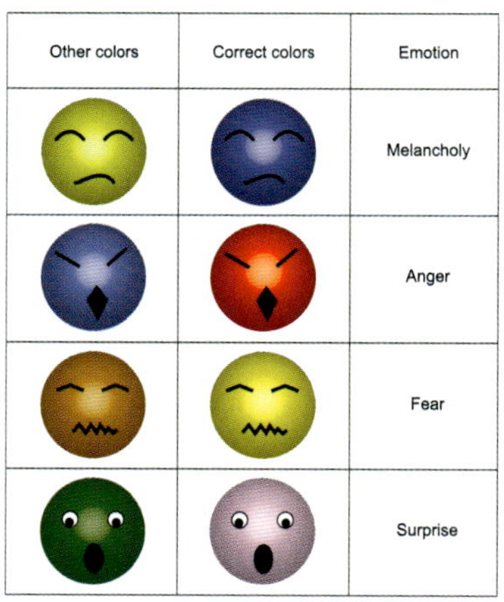


**Figure 5-30.** Colors relate to emotions

## Colors in Nature

Nature provides many perfect color harmonies. You can extract the color scheme from a nature scene and apply it to your design. Regardless of whether or not the design elements follow the same shapes and composition of the nature scene, a color harmony scheme extracted from a view of nature should be a good source for the color scheme of your design.

Figure 5-31 extracts eight colors from a flower photo and applies them to a cute little girl image. As the pink colored flower is small and pretty, so too is the girl shown as young and cute.

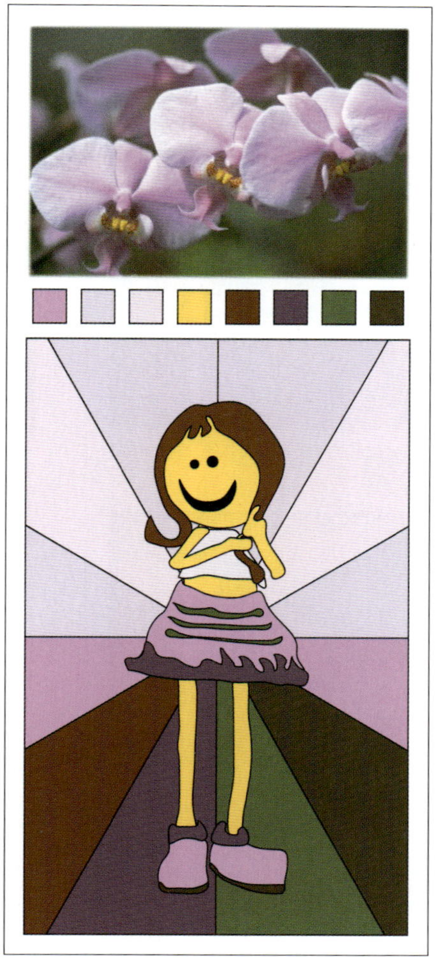

■ Figure 5-31. Flowers provide a good color scheme for a little girl

Figure 5-32 is another example of extracting a color scheme. Seven colors from the photo are applied to an image of a dark woman carrying something on her head. The color combinations of the image are simple and produce an ethnic style.

Extracting a color range is not limited to natural environments. We can find a perfect color harmony in a man-made environment. As Figure 5-33 shows, colors are extracted from a photo of a candy shop in a cinema. Then, the color scheme is applied to the image of the woman from Figure 5-32, produces the effect of a woman standing underneath a blazing sun.

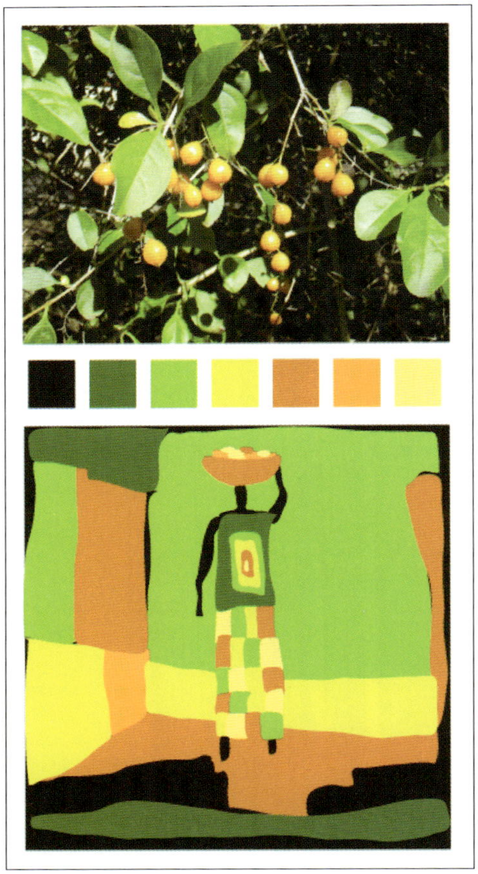

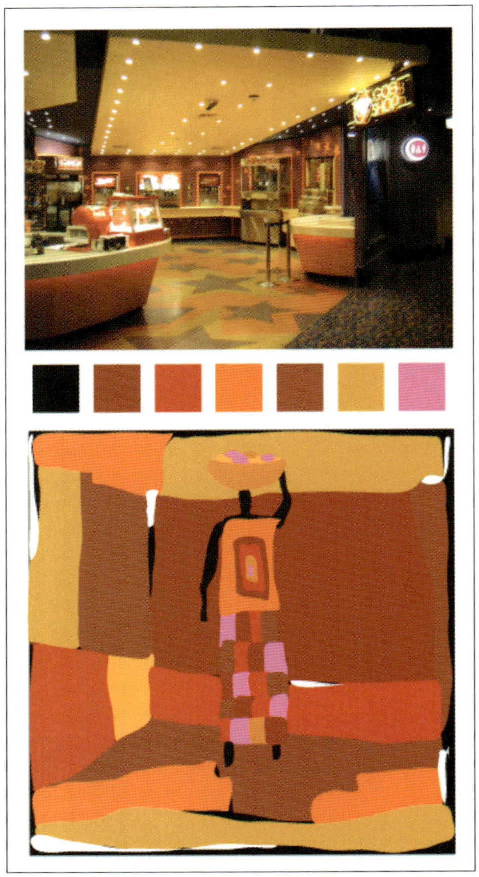

1 2

1 Figure 5-32. A natural scheme is applied to cool a woman

2 Figure 5-33. A modern scene produces a hot color scheme

# **Design Studio:**
# A Sequence with Colors

This activity allows you to experience how color works as a determinant in design.

This activity allows you to experience how color works as a determinant in design. Create (or choose) a sequence of events or a story using the four basic color harmony schemes. The event or story should incorporate four frames and use each of the color harmony schemes once, in this order:

- Frame 1 — Monochrome
- Frame 2 — Analogous
- Frame 3 — Complementary
- Frame 4 — Triadic

The color wheel should be referenced to choose the right colors for each color harmony. The size of the artwork should be a 320 pixel square for each frame, making the finished work 1280 pixels wide by 320 pixels high.

### Thirsty

The following event has been illustrated with four sequential designs. There is a woman who feels thirsty. She is drinking a beverage to quench her thirst. The color harmonies will be applied in each sequential design as defined above.

Figure 5-34 illustrates that the thirsty woman starts to drink a beverage. The color scheme should represent her thirst. Warm colors are best for describing thirst visually. Monochrome emphasizes the characteristics of a hot environment as boring and monotonous. A dull orange color with different hue values suggests thirst and hot weather. The many corners of the angular shapes suggest intolerable heat.

In this second sequence (Figure 5-35), the woman starts to drink. The thirst is being quenched. The analogous color scheme enriches the quenching sequence. Green is chosen as the dominant color. The colors do not harmonize perfectly because warm and cool colors are combined. They break the color harmony. The curves and corners of the shapes suggest that the thirst and its relief coexist.

The third sequence (Figure 5-36) represents a moment right before the perfect relief from thirst. Many curved shapes describe the relief. The woman is back to life as the contrast of the complementary color suggests. To enhance the contrast, blue is used as the background color, and orange colors are used for the accent of the beverage running down her throat. Another complementary color scheme, yellow and red, is used to add accent to the remaining beverage in the bottle.

As the triadic color scheme presents high-energy and contrast, the fourth sequence (Figure 5-37) presents the perfect quench. It is not necessary to show the woman in the design because she has fallen into a state of coolness. Two triadic color schemes are used to express the feeling of movement in terms of the extreme contrast.

The finished work (Figure 5-38) shows a series of four designs as a narrative. Colors enrich the layout, add emotion, and alter the viewer's perception of the design.

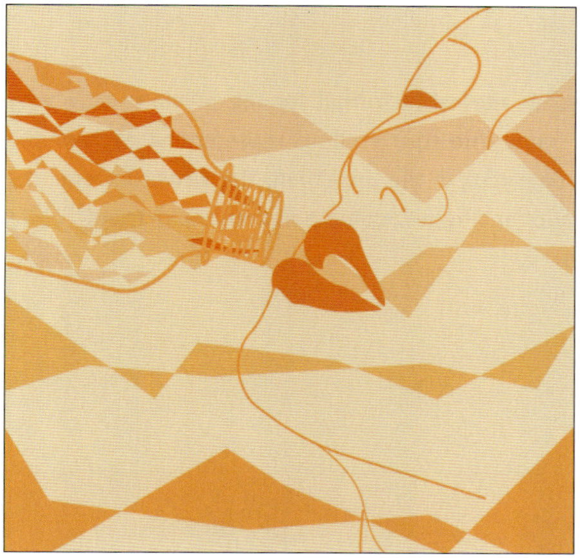

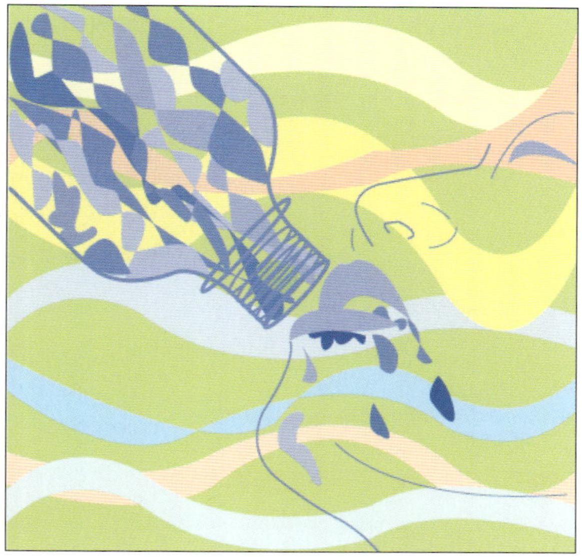

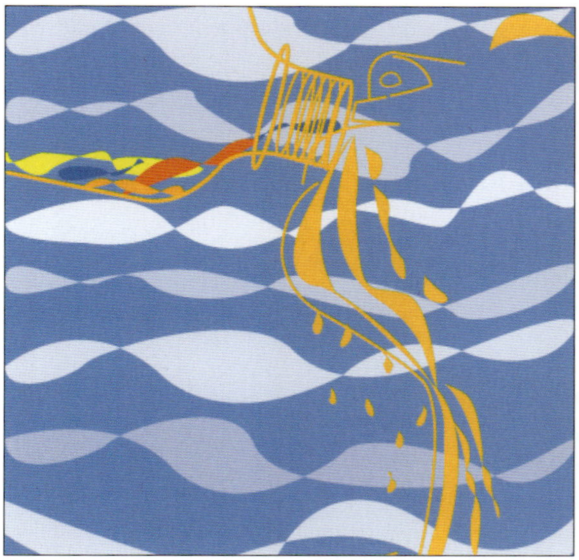

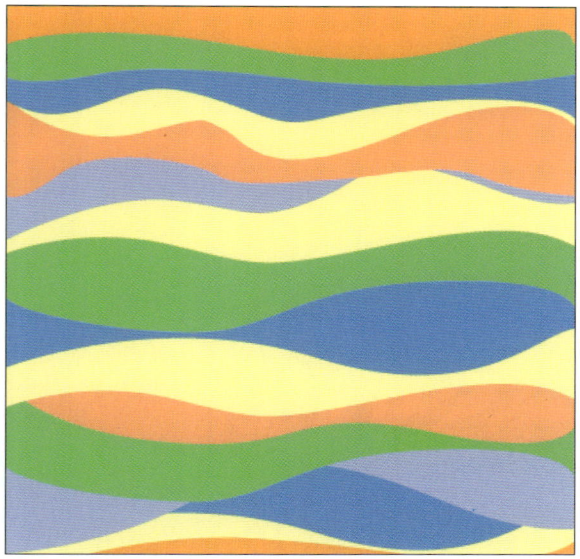

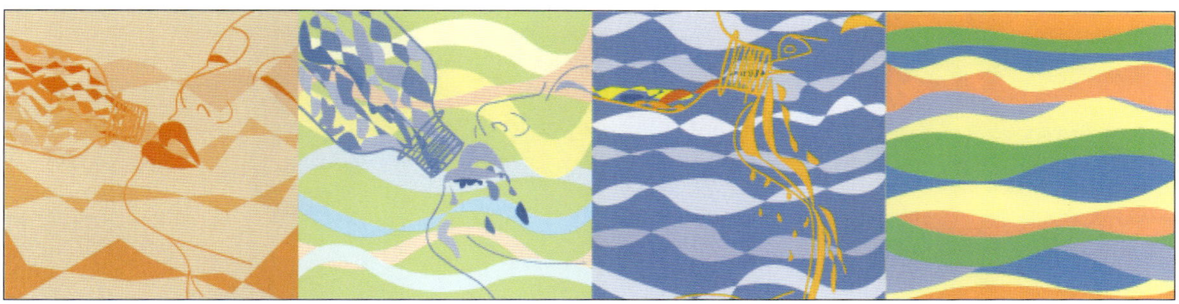

1 2
3 4
5

1 Figure 5-34. Monochromatic warm colors and sharp corners suggest thirst

2 Figure 5-35. Analogous colors and some curves promise relief

3 Figure 5-36. Complementary colors and many curves quench thirst

4 Figure 5-37. Triadic colors applied to a wavy pattern symbolize coolness

5 Figure 5-38. The entire sequence tells a story

## Flowers

Figure 5-39 shows an alternative format for the previous activity by dividing a single frame into four sections representing each of the color harmonies. Beginning in the upper left, the viewer experiences the monochromatic, analogous, complementary, and triadic color harmony schemes.

**1** Figure 5-39. The four color schemes applied to a single image

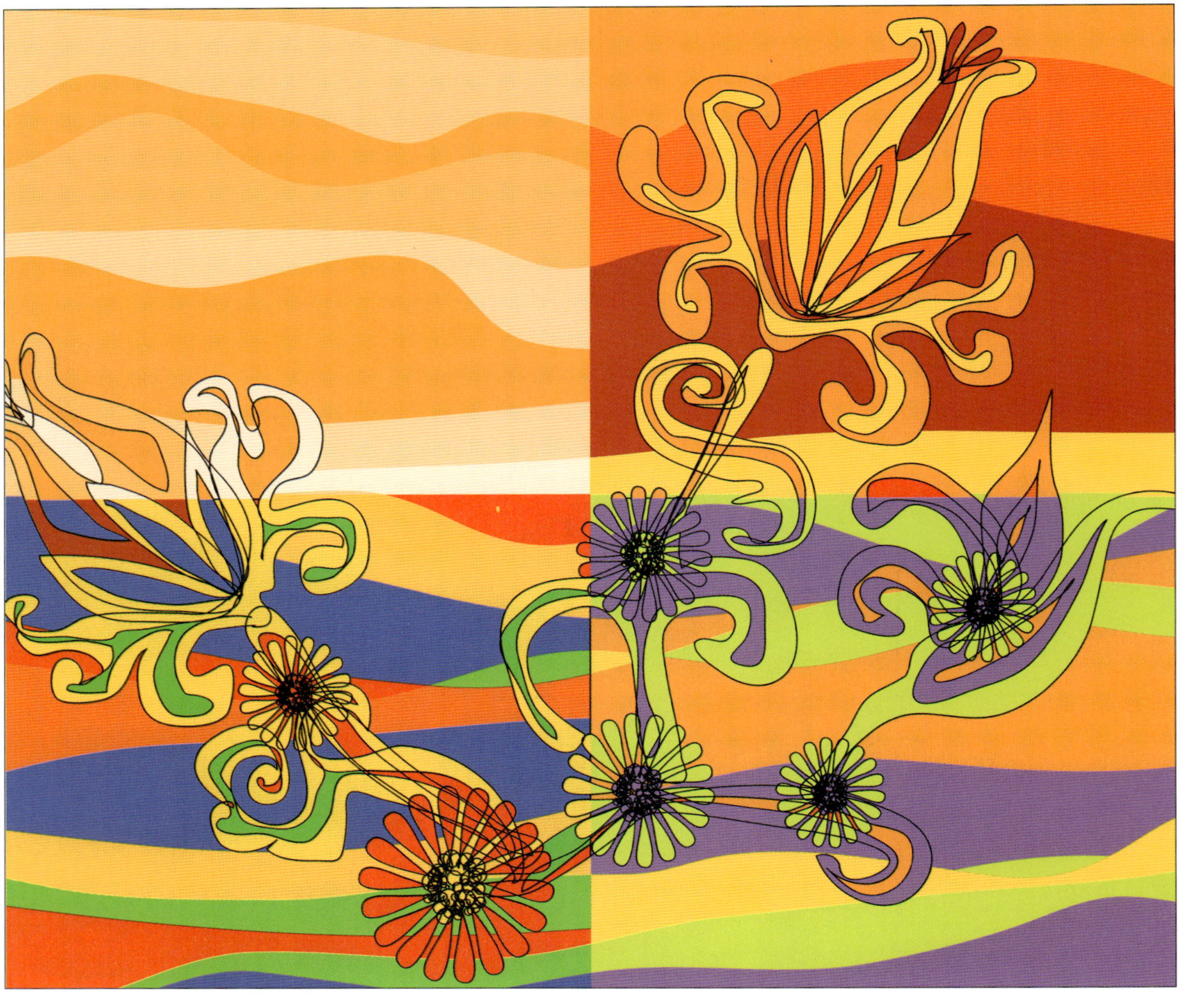

# Student Gallery
## A Sequence with Colors

This activity is to create the sequence of an event or a story with a specific color scheme.

- Activity theme: a story or event
- Software: Adobe Illustrator CS2
- Dimension: 320 x 320 pixels x 4
- Color scheme for each sequence: Monochrome, Analogous, Complementarys, and Triadic
- Format: publish a jpeg format from your work

### Marking Criteria (possible marks: 10)

Student will receive one of the marks in the following:

- 9 – 10: Successful design with creative solutions and professional finish
- 7 – 8: Successful design, but insufficient creativity and finish
- 5 – 6: Adequate, but lack of experiment or creativity
- 3 – 4: Inadequate, partly misunderstanding
- 2 – 0: Wrong theme or no submission

### Student Works - Dynamic Layout

- Joy Reynolds 2006

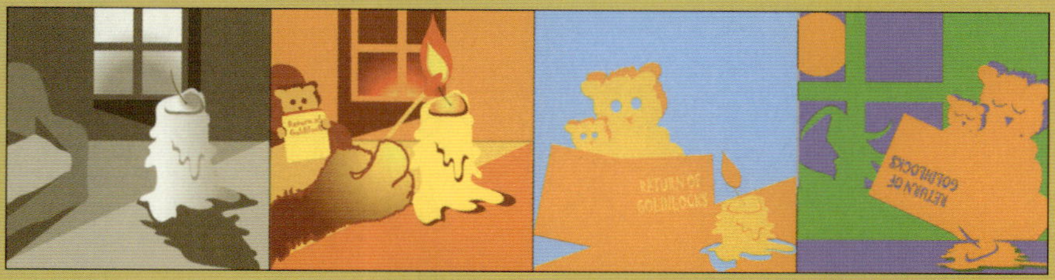

Four color schemes, monochrome, analogous, complementary, and triadic, were applied into four frames compromising a story. The above student's work is clearly telling a story within four sequences and the color schemes are appropriately applied into each sequence. The monochrome on the first sequence is very subtle and elegant due to a lack of color contrast. The analogous on the second sequence creates a warm mood and the complementary on the third sequence arouses a visual tension by adding a strong contrast between blue and orange color. The triadic scheme on the fourth reduces the tension and creates harmony.

Kaylene Court 2006

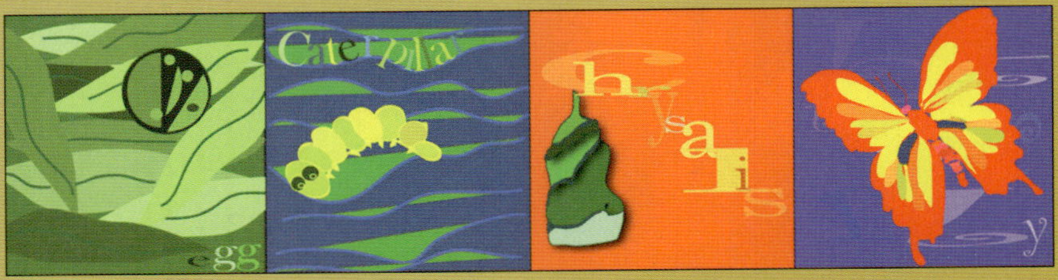


Krista Avila 2007

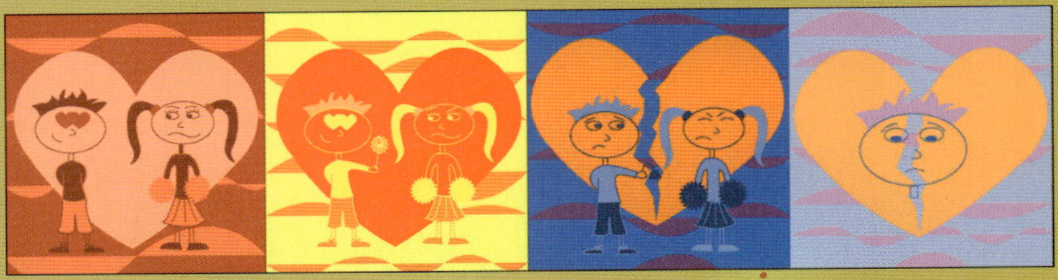

Elise Sondergeld 2007

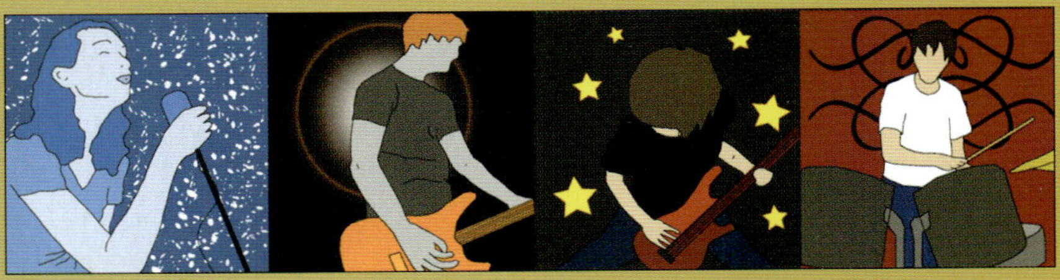

Karina Voss 2007

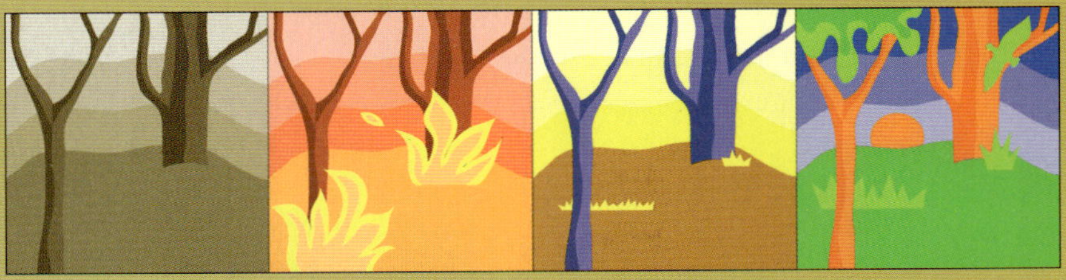

Natalie Gaye Clarke 2007

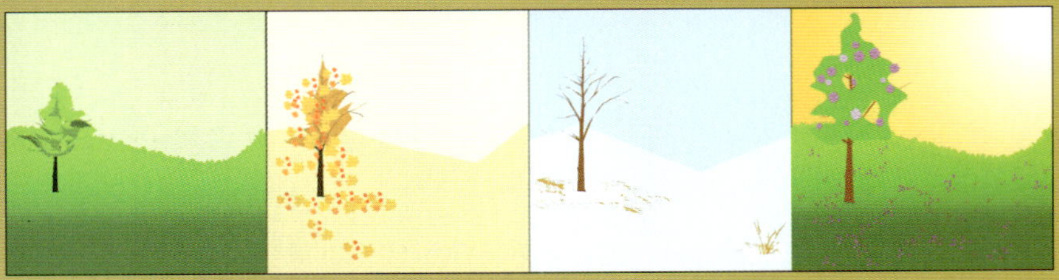

Chapter

[ 06 ]

# Shape

Shape in visual design refers to the outside edges of an object or its outline. Shapes are classified as geometrical, organic, stylized, and implied shapes. Visual design decomposes and composes shapes in order to create an intended visual structure.

# Defining Shape

A shape is a space enclosed by an outline, such as a circle, a square, or a triangle. Shapes are a fundamental element in design. Designs can exist without color, texture, or line, but rarely do they exist without shapes.

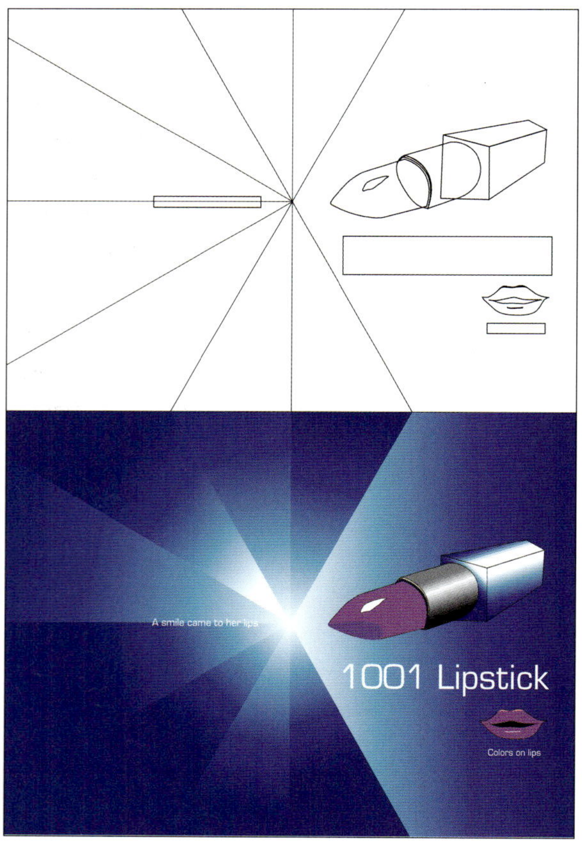


**1** Figure 6-1. Shapes are the basis for every layout or design

Shape refers to a two-dimensional object. Regardless of whether a shape is abstract or a representational form, designers arrange the elements and content within shapes. Figure 6-1 shows that a layout is nothing but a composition of shapes.

It is no exaggeration to say that shape is everything in visual design. All elements, such as text, lines, patterns, icons, or images, have different functions but are ultimately shapes. It can be said that a successful layout design is dependent on a successful composition of shapes.

# Types of Shapes

There are geometric shapes and organic shapes. An organic shape has irregular contours, much like shapes that appear in nature. Geometric shapes are made of regular contours. These are usually man-made shapes.

## Geometric Shape

The square, triangle, and circle are geometric shapes. These shapes are created artificially and do not appear in nature. Most designs use geometric shapes that have clear edges. The square (or rectangle) represents solidity and stability and symbolizes the ground and land. Squares are the most common geometric shapes found in modern environments. They bring with them a sense of comfort and familiarity. Sometimes, squares are uninteresting, but they can be easily manipulated to add excitement. Most of the time, however, manipulating a square risks losing its familiarity and comfort. When a square is skewed, it becomes a rhombus. The rhombus represents an energy more dynamic and progressive than a square, but its stability is reduced.

Figure 6-2 shows that there are many different ways to create a pattern using squares. Each design is unique and has its own beauty, but they all have the square as their common foundation. They all appear firm, solid, and constant.

The circle represents perfection and symbolizes energy. Circles suggest infinity and unity. They also denote rolling movement and energy. Like squares, circles are very common in modern environments. Some examples are holes, buttons, and balls (see Figure 6-3). Circle shapes are often used in logo design. Ovals, especially, suggest unity and imply innovation and progress. That is why many company logos use ovals.

Figure 6-3 shows some circular objects. They all suggest infinity and completeness. The circle shape of the no walking sign produces absolute power, perfection, and energy that stop you immediately. On the other hand, the basketball and soccer ball, because of their association with sports, produce infinite energy of movement.

1 2

1 Figure 6-2. Square-based geometric patterns
2 Figure 6-3. Common, everyday objects with circular forms

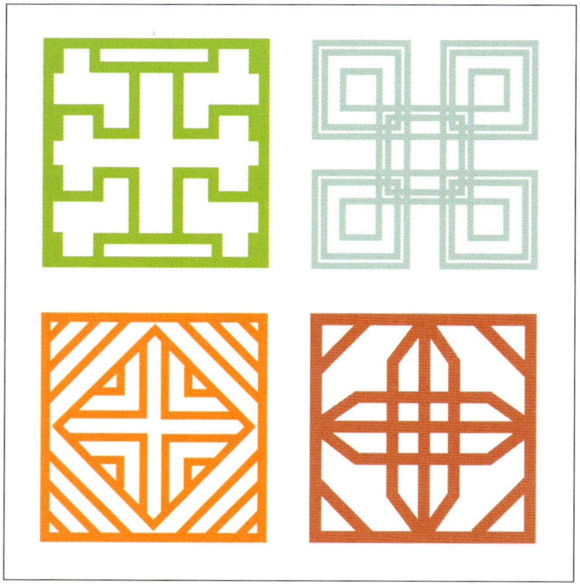

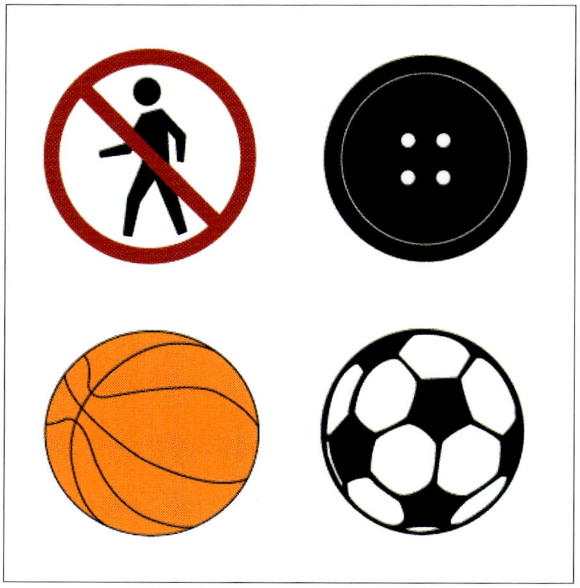

Triangles represent challenge, direction, dynamics, and action. A point-up triangle represents stability and positive growth; an inverted triangle has opposite meanings such as danger and aggression. Triangles are suggestive of various shapes by combination with other triangles. We are also familiar with the triangle such as pyramid, sign attention, and arrow. The shape of a star, as a result of the extension of triangle, implies transcendence and sacred power and is used in national flags.

As Figure 6-4 shows, triangles used in traffic signs symbolize direction and action. Triangles are also the backbone of well-structured architecture (see Figure 6-5).

1 2

1 **Figure 6-4.** Traffic signs use triangles to direct and attract attention
2 **Figure 6-5.** Triangles form a building's structure

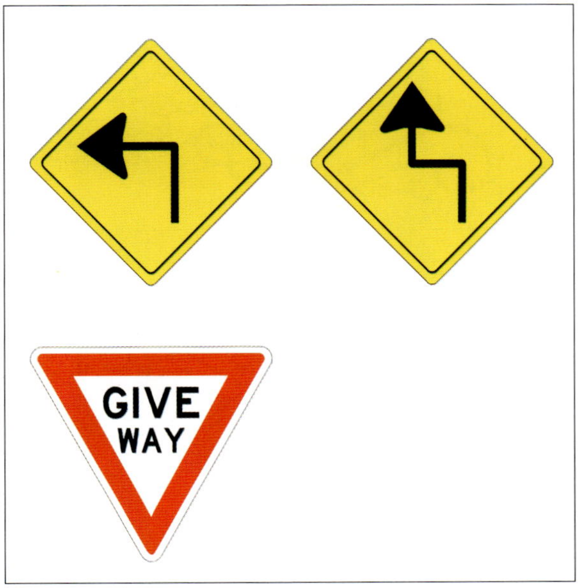


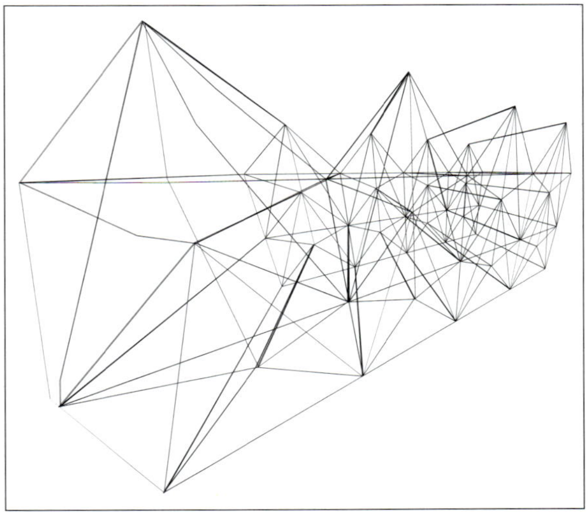

## Organic Shapes

Organic shapes have the irregular contours that appear in nature, such as the flowing, waving, and twisting banks of a river. Organic shapes are often playful, unpredictable, and whimsical, unlike the logical and systematic characteristics of geometric shapes. They are also freely formed and often abstract. Organic shapes, like clouds and amoebae, have natural, less well-defined edges.

Organic shapes in nature are full of inspiration that can be used to create beautiful, unique, and creative graphics. Figures 6-6, 6-7, 6-8, and 6-9 show stylized cloud images redesigned using traditional Korean cloud patterns. The outlines of clouds never remain exactly the same. They often change dramatically, even as they are being watched. The different organic outlines suggest different moods for each scene.

1 2
3 4

1 **Figure 6-6.** Warm, fast moving clouds
2 **Figure 6-7.** Cold, wintry clouds
3 **Figure 6-8.** Lazy, slow-moving clouds
4 **Figure 6-9.** Rainy, upper atmosphere clouds

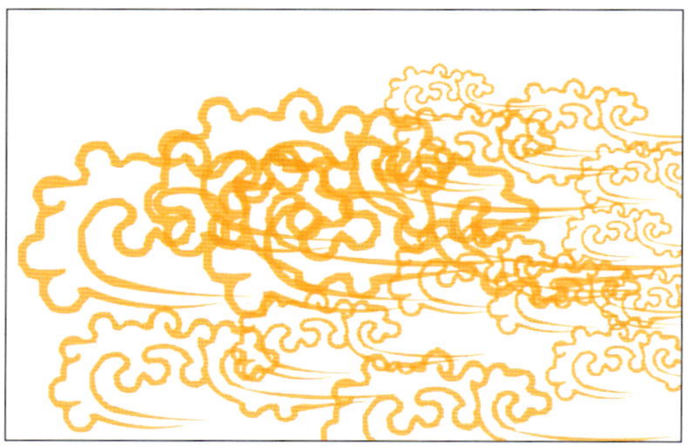

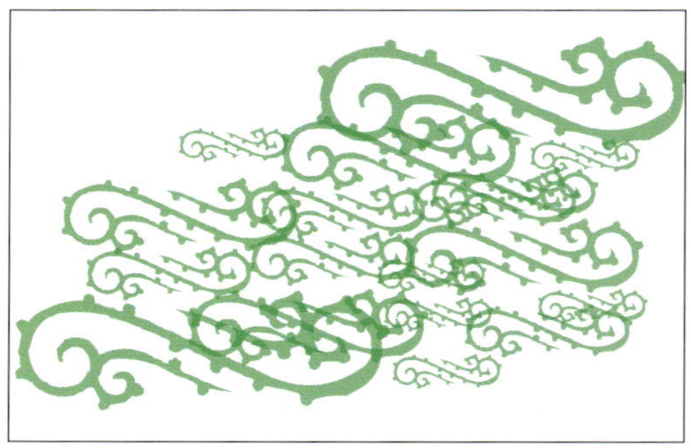

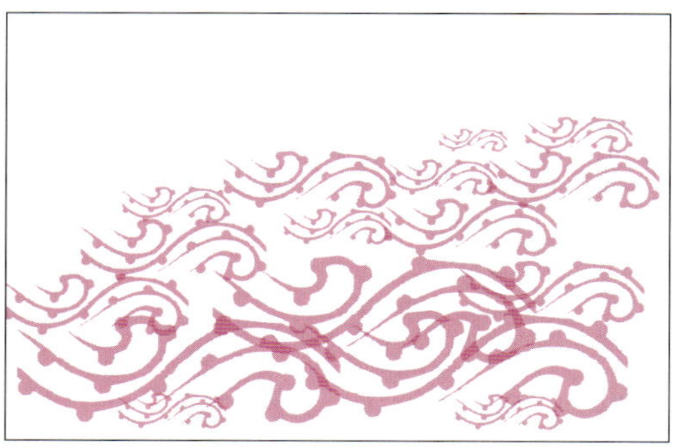

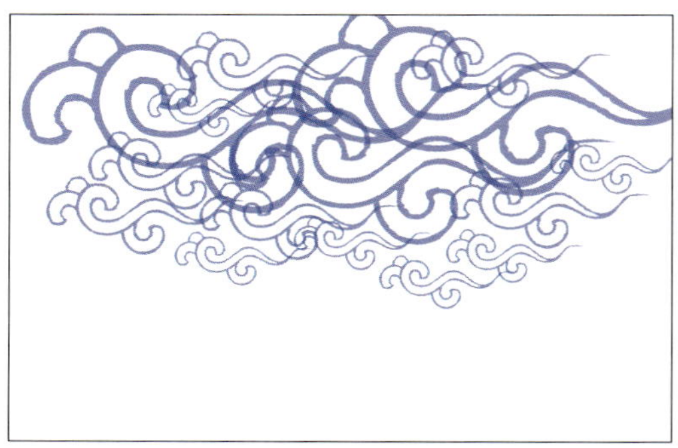

## Stylized Shapes

Organic shapes are non-representational, as opposed to stylized shapes which are representational. Stylized shapes symbolize, outline, and simplify an object or abstract idea for people to recognize.

Stylized shapes are often used as a visual language in public places, such as for restrooms in sports arenas and on fire signs in office buildings. Figure 6-10 clearly represents sports that most anyone would recognize. Figure 6-11 is a warning message with the flame shapes representing fire or a flammable substance.

An emoticon (emotion + icon) is a simple graphic symbol that visually represents a person, object, scene, or abstract idea. Emoticons can show various emotions with facial iconography and are frequently used in Internet communication. The left-hand image in Figure 6-12 represents anger or irritation, and the right-hand image represents happiness.

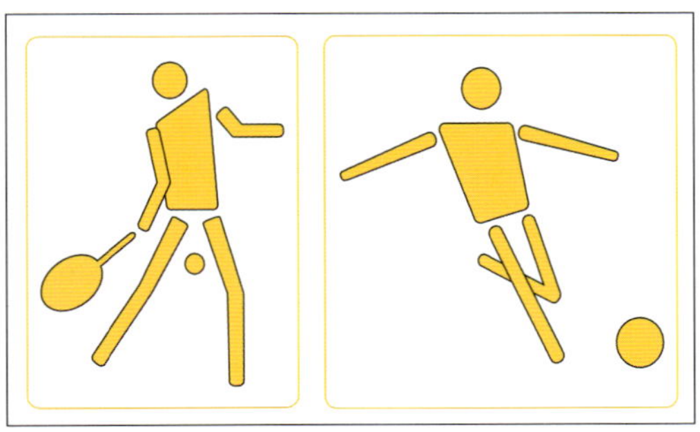

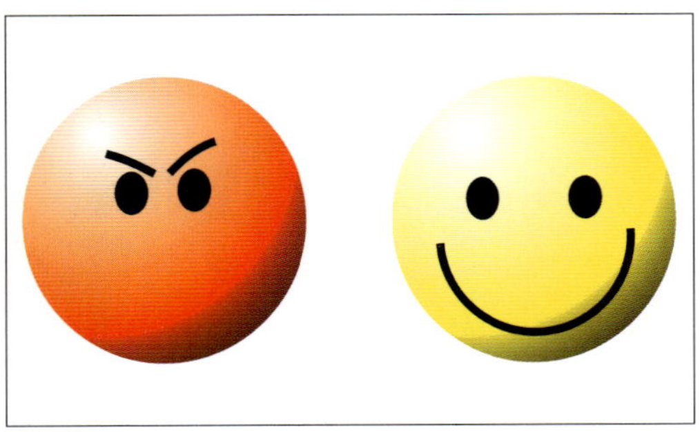

1 2
3

1 **Figure 6-10.** Sports: Simply stylized shapes create easily recognizable sports

2 **Figure 6-11.** Warning-Fire: Triangles and flame shapes indicate the potential for fire

3 **Figure 6-12.** Facial expressions: Emoticons express irritation and happiness

## Implied Shape

Implied shapes are incomplete shapes that rely on the viewer's mind to finish them based on recognizable features. The actual shapes shown in Figure 6-13 are a right angle and an arc, but the mind fills in the white areas to form a perfect square and a perfect circle.

Figure 6-14 looks like a labyrinth, and its right angles, repetitive rectangular patterning, and consistent spacing produce three-dimensional space and structure.

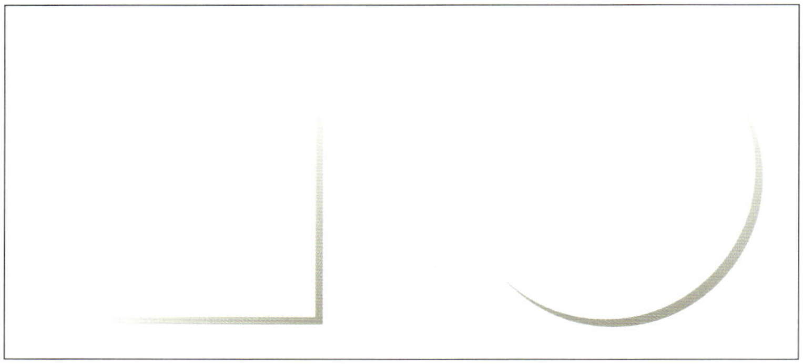

1
2

1 Figure 6-13. An implied square and circle
2 Figure 6-14. A maze pattern implies three-dimensional structure

## Positive and Negative Shape

—

A shape on a page is defined by the positive and negative areas present. The shape itself is the positive space and the rest of the area is the negative space. As Figure 6-15 shows, inverting positive and negative shape can create interesting contrast. Good composition requires that the negative area be considered as important a factor as the positive shape.

To make organic design active and lively, positive and negative areas must be considered carefully. All space in a page is active; there is no such thing as leftover space. This does not mean that you must fill up empty space. Instead, regardless of whether it is positive or negative, all space is meaningful. As Figure 6-16 shows, negative space can be used to complete a shape. Understanding the positive and negative qualities of shape in layout design is very important.

1 2

1 Figure 6-15. Inverted positive and negative shapes create balance

2 Figure 6-16. Negative shape mirrors and completes a positive one

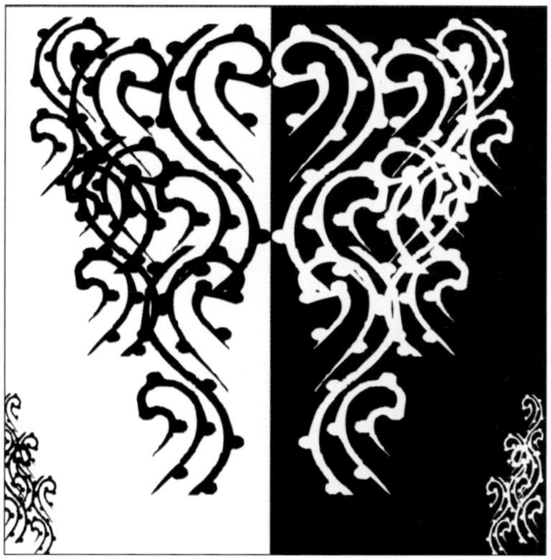

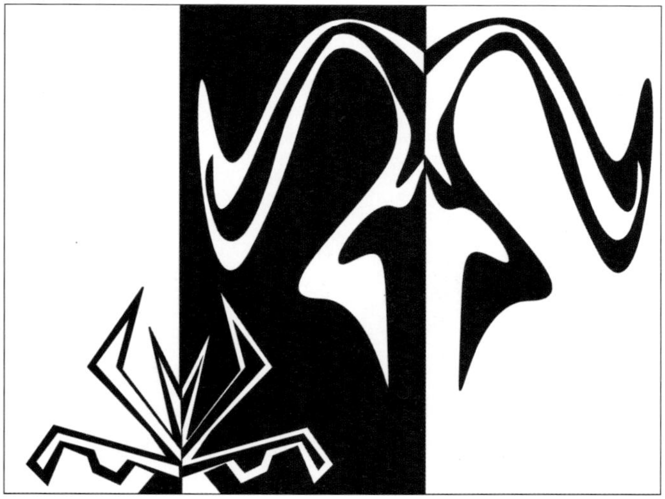

# Pattern

A pattern is created by repeating a visual element. Adding a pattern to a design gives it a particular rhythm. Patterns have a balancing and uniting effect in a design. Pattern design always considers positive and negative areas at the same time and manages the shape and the space as an organic whole. The pattern tile itself is an independent composition.

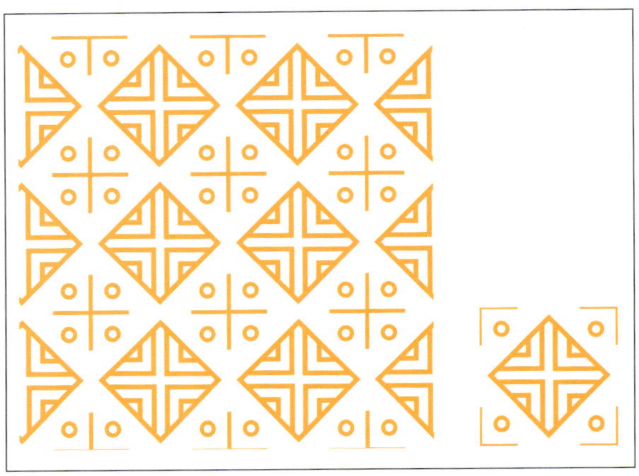

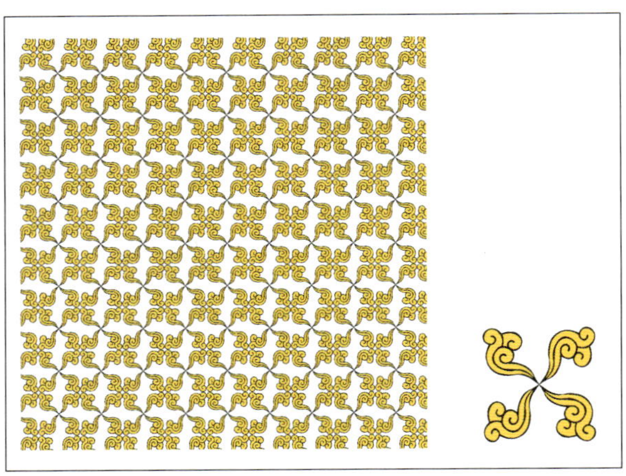

A pattern is created by repeating a visual element. Adding a pattern to a design gives it a particular rhythm. Figures 6-17 and 6-18 are examples of pattern designs with their base tiles on the right-hand side of each.

Patterns have a balancing and uniting effect in a design. Pattern design always considers positive and negative areas at the same time and manages the shape and the space as an organic whole. The pattern tile itself is an independent composition. Because it is the source of the pattern's rhythm, balance, and unity, it must be considered very carefully.

1 Figure 6-17. A pattern and its foundational square tile
2 Figure 6-18. A pattern and its foundational swirl tile

# **Design Studio:** Pattern Design

This activity involves creating a pattern tile, generating a pattern from the tile, and incorporating the pattern into a poster.

The steps are described below:

- Create a fictional organization, such as a sports club, design firm, or non-profit.
- Create a logo for the organization using its name and an appropriate image.
- Create a pattern tile from the logo image.
- Create a couple of different pattern designs with the tile using a canvas size of 500 × 500 pixels, then choose the best one.
- Merge the logo and the chosen pattern design and produce it as a poster.
- Artwork size: 500 × 500 pixels

Try to create a logo from scratch, or base your pattern on a pre-existing logo. The pattern tile can be based on the logo exactly as it is or by manipulating it somewhat. The final design can be in full color, if desired.

Shapes often make good motifs for pattern design. Logo design represents its subject's visual identity and suggests a direction of design. A successful logo design communicates the essential features of the subject without extraneous detail. The following examples demonstrate the process of converting a logo to a pattern and layout design.

## Zoo Poster

In Figure 6-19, the logo represents a zoo. A monkey hanging from a tree is used as the key shape in the logo design. It provides activity and dynamic energy, but also suggests a friendly zoo environment. This monkey shape provides a basis for the pattern design.

In Figure 6-20, the logo monkey has been flipped horizontally and then vertically. The left-hand figure shows the legs of four monkeys arranged to meet each other, and a square shape has been created in the middle of them. This arrangement has been repeated several times in the right-hand figure in a tiled layout. However, the pattern looks cramped.

In Figure 6-21, another monkey shape is added at the end of each monkey's hand. The square in the middle of the pattern tile is proportionally smaller than in the previous design. When tiles are added, as in the right-hand figure, a large rhombus is created inside each set. The rhombus adds good contrast and "breathing room" to the pattern design.

1 Figure 6-19. Basic logo design for the Royal Melbourne Zoo

2 Figure 6-20. A tile and cramped pattern based on the zoo's logo

3 Figure 6-21. A more open tile and pattern based on the zoo's logo

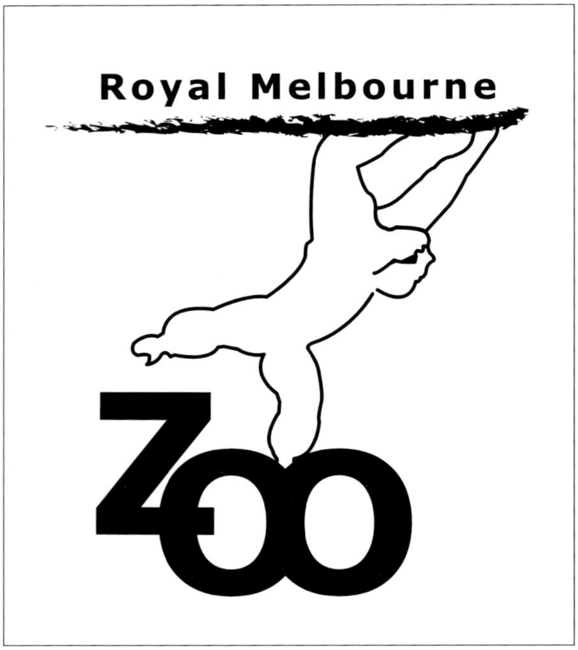


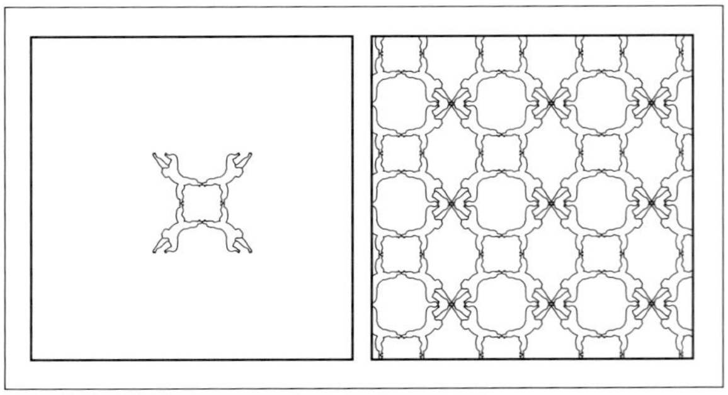

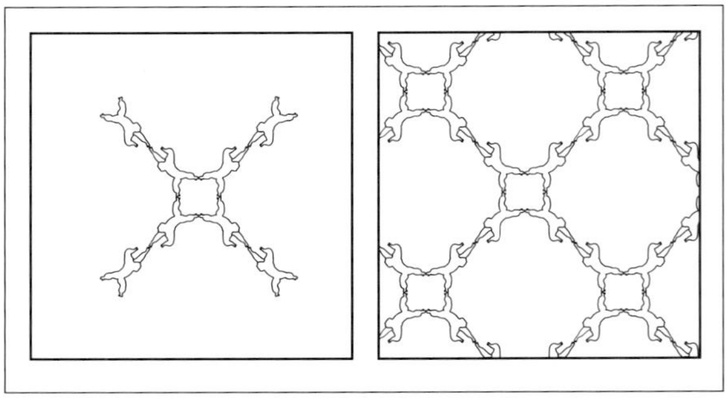

In Figure 6-22, the logo has been created in full color. It will be combined with the pattern design below.

Figure 6-23 shows the pattern design reproduced in color, which will be used for the background of the poster design.

The logo and pattern have been combined as an attractive poster design in Figure 6-24. This layout achieves consistency and unity between the elements.

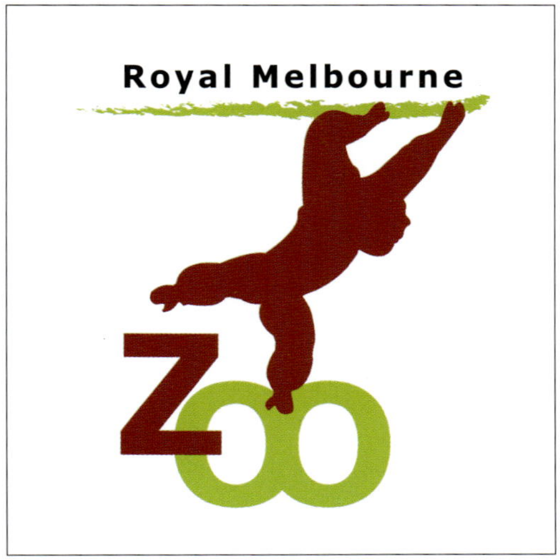


1 **Figure 6-22.** Zoo logo in full color
2 **Figure 6-23.** Monkey background pattern in color
3 **Figure 6-24.** Poster for the zoo combining the logo and monkey pattern

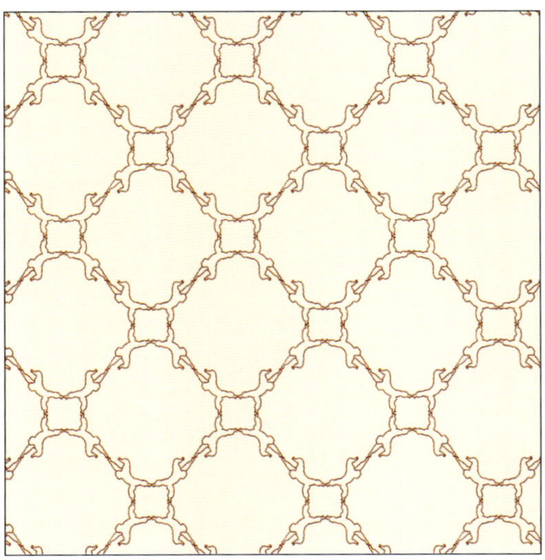

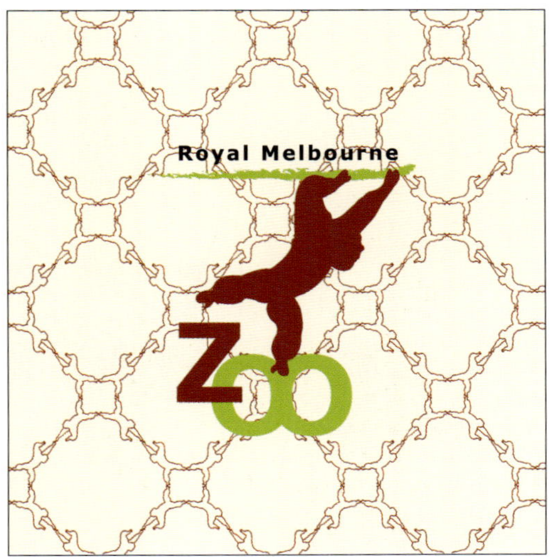

## Company Poster

Figure 6-25 is a logo design for a design company. The word kastor is from the Greek word for beaver. The logo image characterizes a beaver.

As shown in Figure 6-26, a pattern tile for Kastor Fakto is created by repeating and rotating the beaver logo image every 90 degrees using the beaver's eye (dot) as the pivot point.

As Figure 6-27 shows, you can apply different spacing and color to create a different pattern tile.

In Figure 6-28, the logo and pattern have been combined with the addition of an organic white shape overlaying the pattern design.

1 Figure 6-25. Color logo design for Kastor Fakto

2 Figure 6-26. A tile and pattern based on the company's logo

3 Figure 6-27. A tile and pattern design with tighter spacing

4 Figure 6-28. Poster for the Kastor Fakto firm

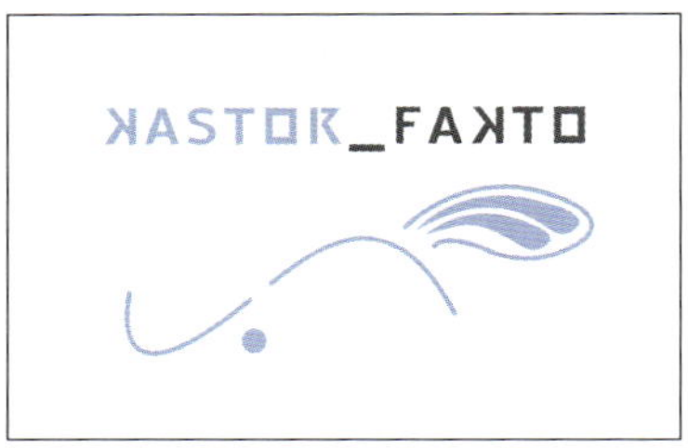

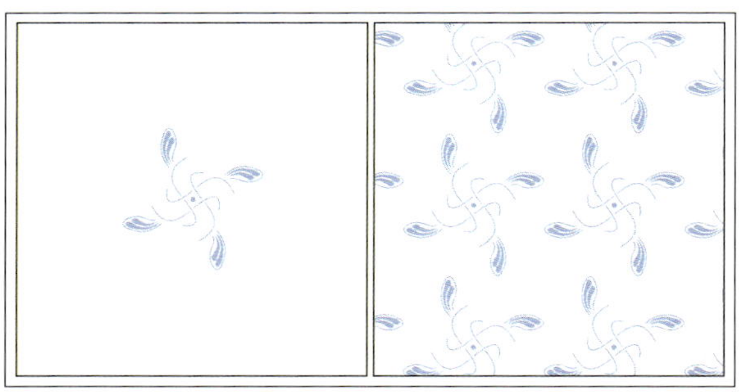

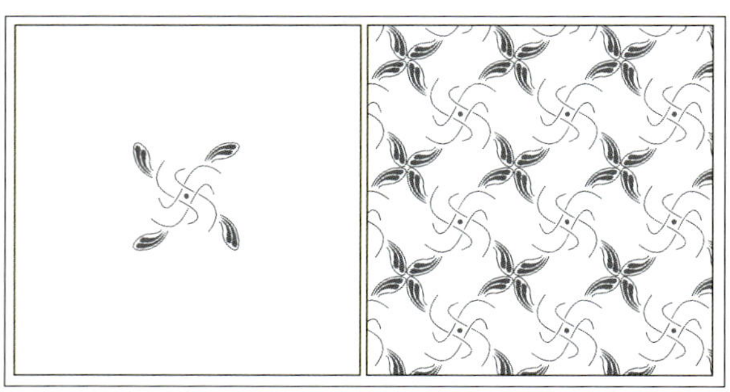

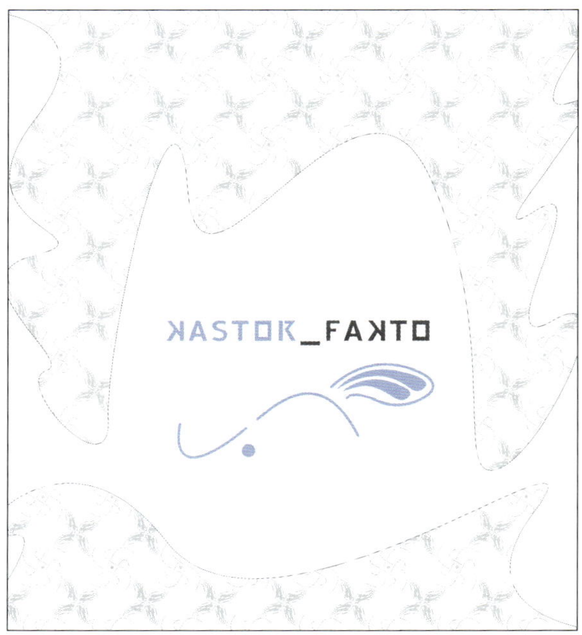

# Student Gallery
## Pattern Design

- You need to design your own logo and pattern design and apply it into a poster format.
  - Create a logo (a shape and a name)
  - Create a basic pattern tile and patterns
  - Merge the logo and the pattern as a poster format
- Software: Adobe Illustrator CS2 and Photoshop CS2
- Dimension:  500 x 500 pixels
- Format: publish a gif or a jpg format (depending on the image quality and file size) from your work

### Marking Criteria (possible marks: 10)

Student will receive one of the marks in the following:

- 9 – 10: Successful design with creative solutions and professional finish
- 7 – 8: Successful design, but insufficient creativity and finish
- 5 – 6: Adequate, but lack of experiment or creativity
- 3 – 4: Inadequate, partly misunderstanding
- 2 – 0: Wrong theme or no submission

### Student Works - Dynamic Layout

- Elise Sondergeld 2007

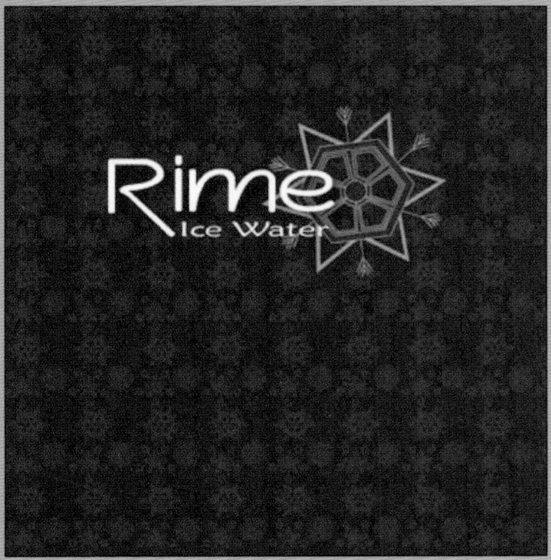


The work to the left done by Elise Sondergeld was chosen as the outstanding in this activity, logo design based pattern design. The work adopted a snow crystal for the logo symbol and pattern tile. The pattern design is beautifully balanced and contrasted and well supports the logo design.

Bradley John Acutt 2006

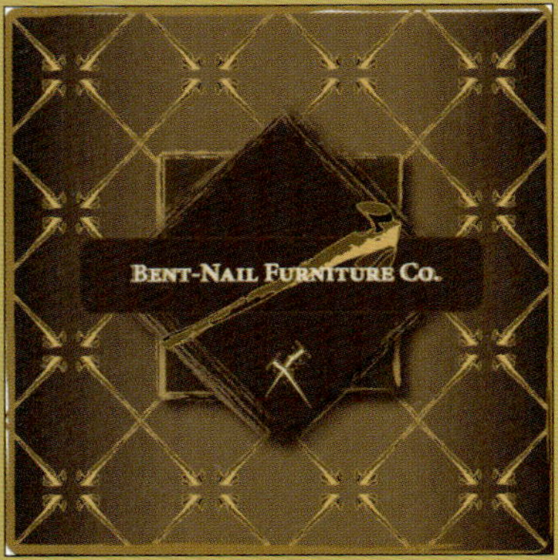


Joy Reynolds 2006

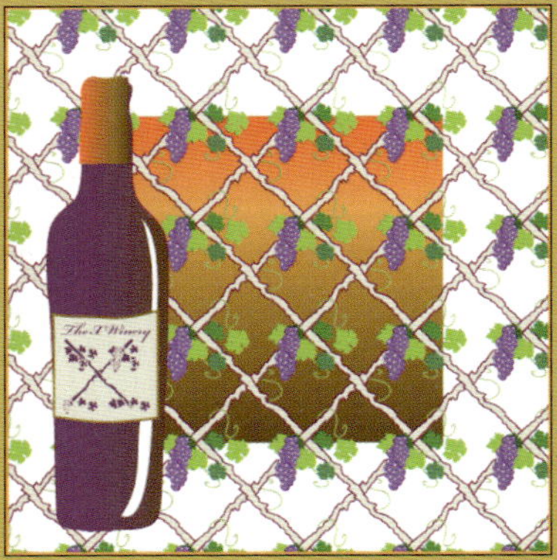

Sandra Mary Weedon 2006

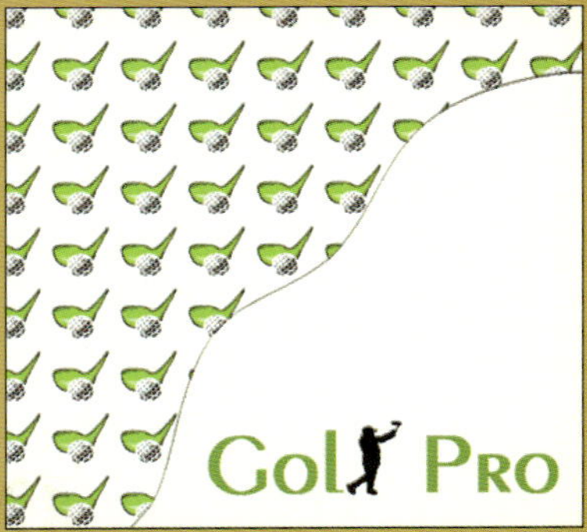


Krista Avila 2007

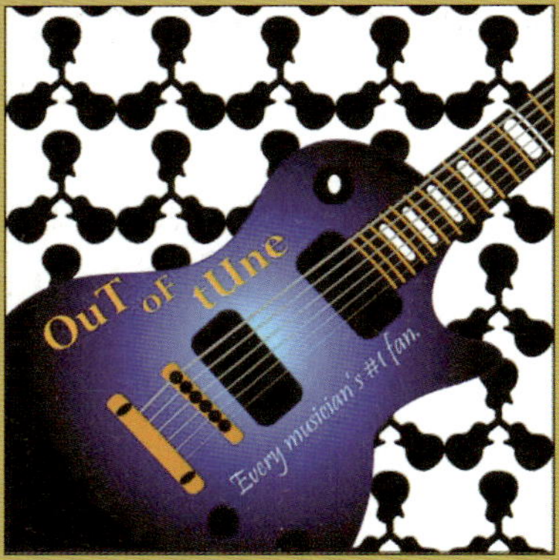


Natalie Gaye Clarke 2007

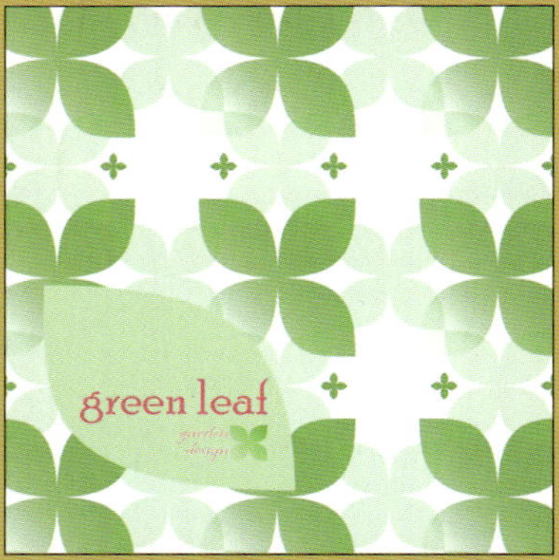


Justin Andrew Hawley 2007

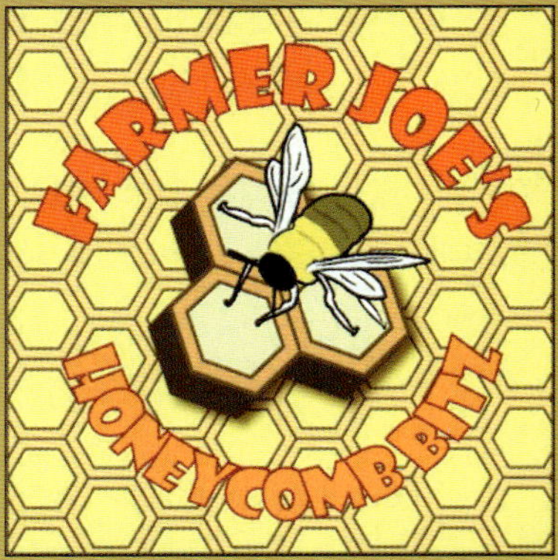


Chelsea Sutherland 2007

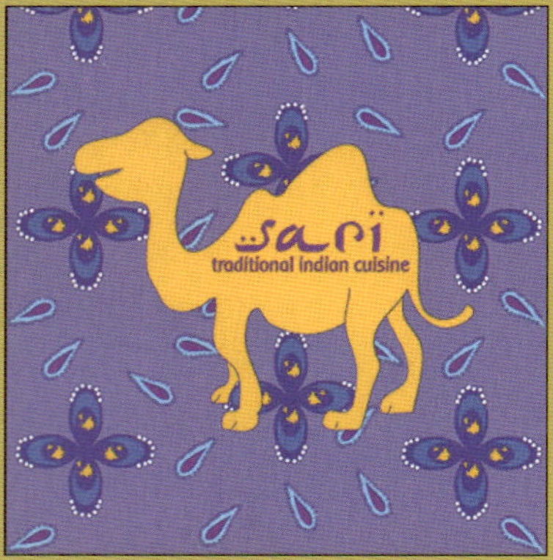


Karina Maree Voss 2007

Chapter

# [ 07 ]

# Lines

A line is not only a limitless form but an entity in itself. Lines can capture and depict the motion of an object, express emotion, or provide information. In addition, various types of lines, such as broken, thick, and thin, can produce an emotional experience.

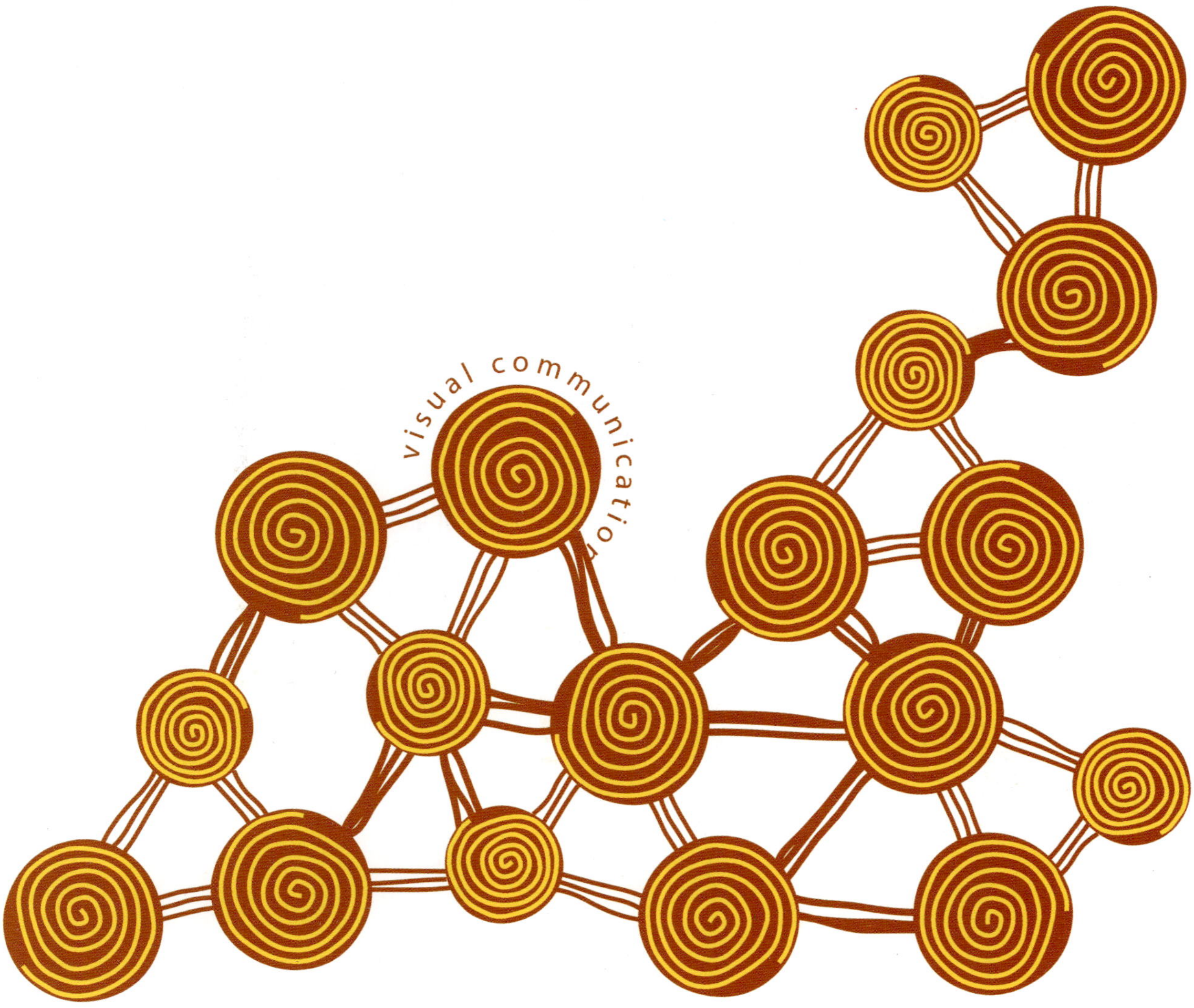

# Defining Lines

A line is a form with width and length, but no depth. We use lines to create forms and the outlines of objects.

Geometry defines a line as "an infinite number of points," but, typically, we see a line as the connection of points. Here are some of the characteristics that can define a line:

- Lines can be long or short, straight or curved.
- Lines can be horizontal, vertical, or diagonal.
- Lines can be solid, dashed, thick, thin, or of variable width.
- The endings of lines can be ragged, blunt, or curved.

The next two figures illustrate some of the properties a line can have. Figure 7-1 shows lines that vary in width, length, and direction.

Figure 7-2 demonstrates lines whose textures are derived from pens, pencils, and brushes.

There are two basic types of lines: straight and curved. Straight lines represent order, direction, and movement, while curved lines represent smoothness, freedom, and rhythm. These features can affect the composition of a design.

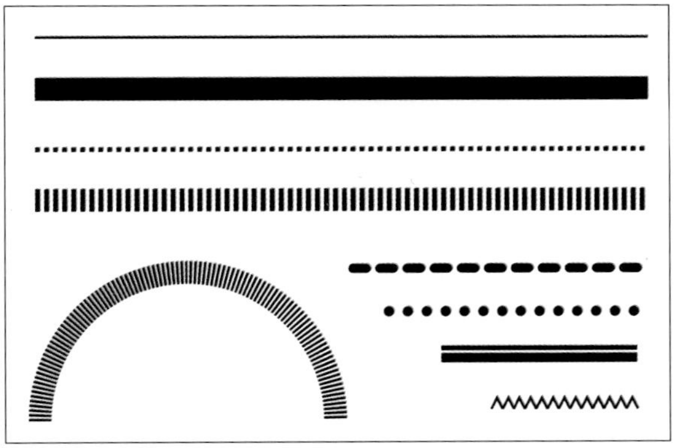

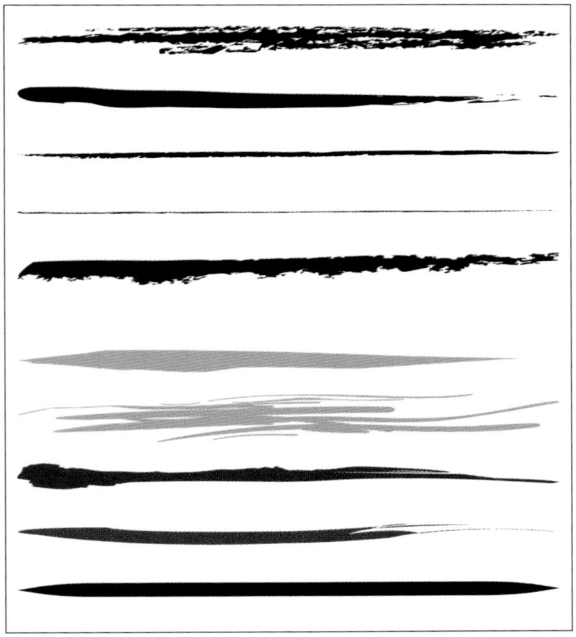

1 2

1 Figure 7-1. Various types of lines from Adobe® Flash® 8
2 Figure 7-2. Various brushes from Adobe® Illustrator® CS2

## Expressive Lines

—

Lines are placed between points and shapes. Lines are more concrete than points and less formative than shapes. However, a line is infinitely variable and can suggest very different emotional and visual expressions.

### 1 | Lines and Mood

The direction of a line can convey mood. Horizontal lines are calm and quiet, while vertical lines are more energetic and carry a sense of movement. Diagonal lines suggest dynamic force and a feeling of vitality.

## ■ Horizontal lines

Horizontal lines represent placidity and composure. Figure 7-3 illustrates gentle waves from the sea's horizon.

The angular horizontal lines in Figure 7-4 imply a desolate wilderness and a feeling of dreariness. However, the colorful plants enrich it with an exotic and tropical mood and reduce the jaggedness of the lines. The horizontal lines representing the ground support the plants with a sense of stability and balance.

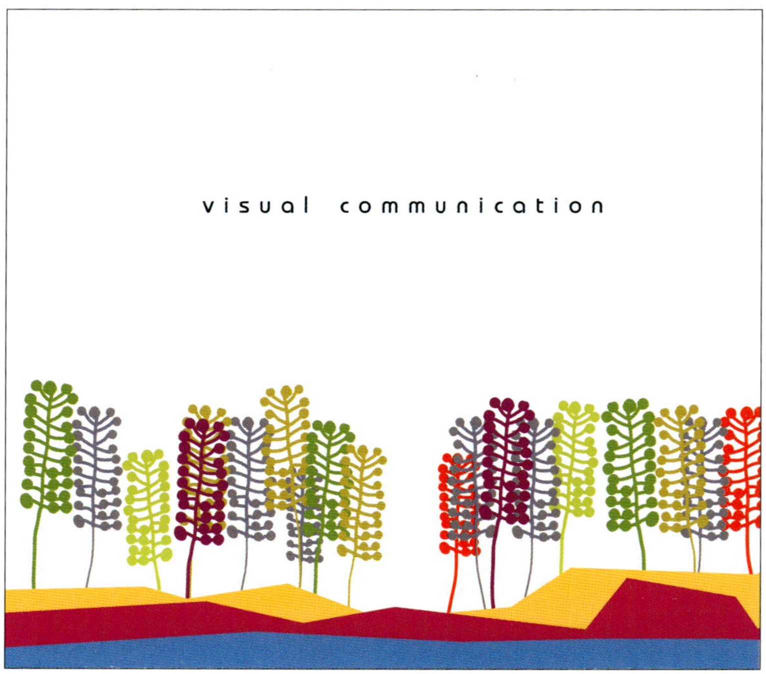


1 2

1 Figure 7-3. Horizontal lines represent gentle waves

2 Figure 7-4. Jagged horizontal lines are smoothed by the colorful plants

■ Vertical lines

Vertical lines represent a sense of movement and suggest eminence and nobility. Figure 7-5 illustrates the idea of an object moving quickly up or down.

Bamboo is a tall plant that is characterized by hard and hollow stems. The erect lines stand elegantly tall and seem to extend from the ground to the sky. As bamboo is associated with moral loftiness and uprightness, the vertical lines communicate a feeling of nobility and great height (see Figure 7-6).

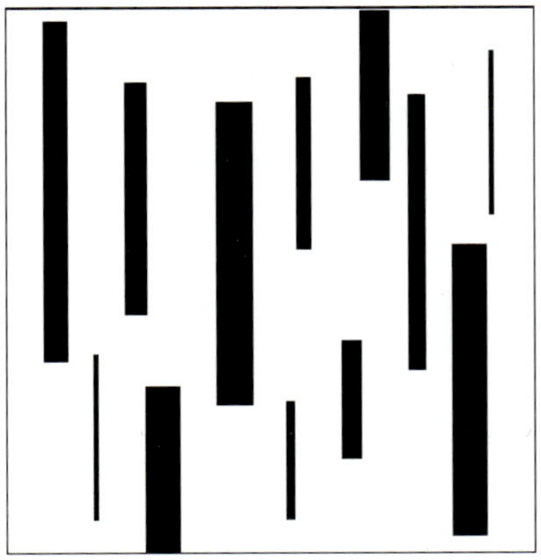

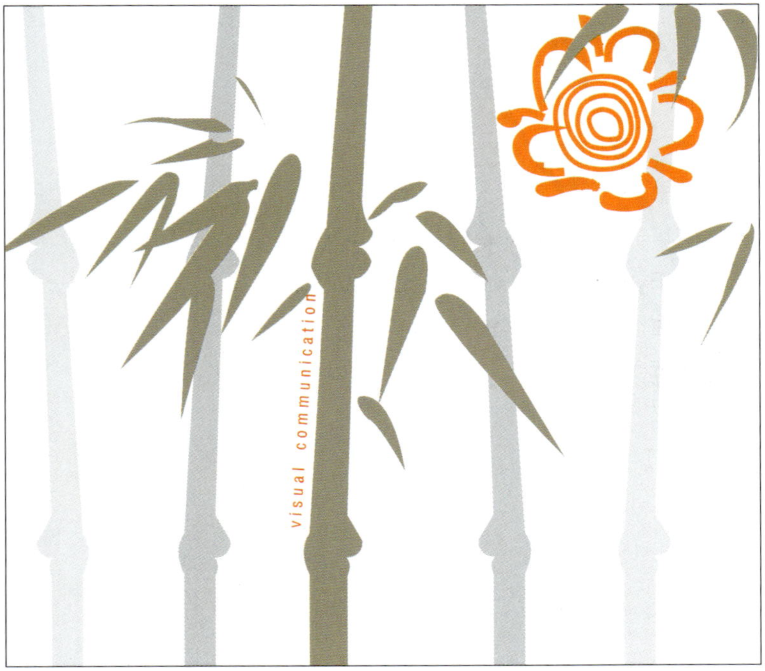


1 2

1 Figure 7-5. Vertical lines imply a quick fall or rise

2 Figure 7-6. Tall bamboo plants embody nobility and elegance

## ■ Diagonal lines

Diagonal lines have a sense of movement because of their angle. They suggest energy, excitement, and cheer. When formed as a zigzag, a line produces a strong sense of energetic movement and even a feeling of madness (see Figure 7-7).

The diagonal lines in Figure 7-8 not only form a structure by connecting the circular shapes but also suggest a feeling of direction and activity. The diagonal lines create support against gravity and impose a sense of solidarity and stability on the composition.

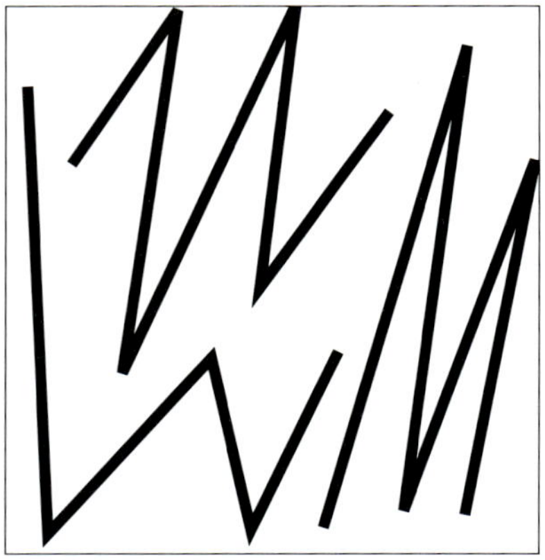

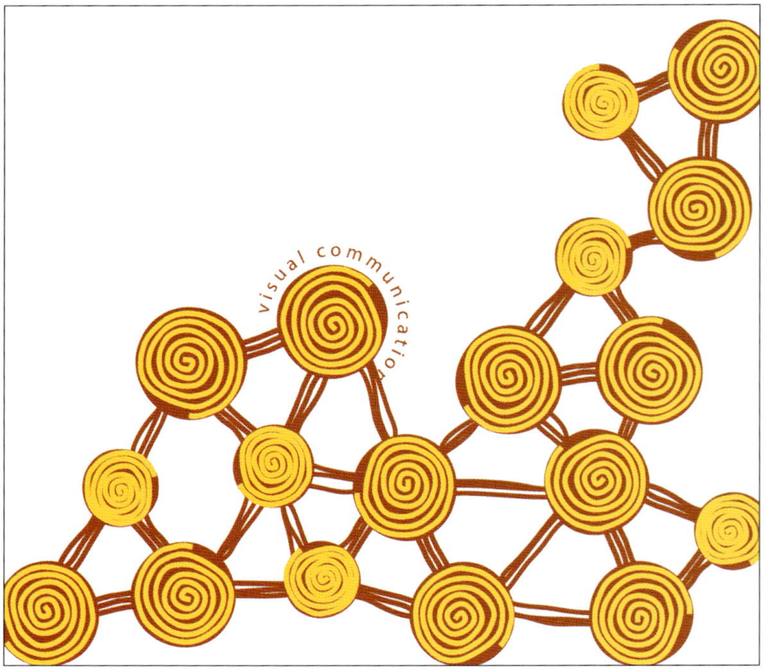


1 2

1 Figure 7-7. Diagonal lines suggest chaotic energy

2 Figure 7-8. Diagonal lines provide connection and activity

## Contour and Gesture

—

Simply drawing the outline of an object creates a shape that can be easily recognized. The outline of the object does not need to be colored or textured to express what it is. Lines used to follow the edges of forms are called contour drawings. There are two types of contour drawings: exterior and interior. Exterior outlines suggest a clean and connected line that has no shading. However, textured lines can add shading values to interior outlines giving the image a more three-dimensional feeling.

Figure 7-9 shows an exterior outline that depicts a woman posing with her right hand on her head and her left hand on her waist. With the exterior outline only, the viewer sees what the image is and what is happening. On the other hand, as Figure 7-10 shows, interior lines emit more detailed information. This creates texture or shading values that add depth to the scene.

1 2

1 **Figure 7-9.** Exterior outline of a woman

2 **Figure 7-10.** Interior outlines provide shading and depth

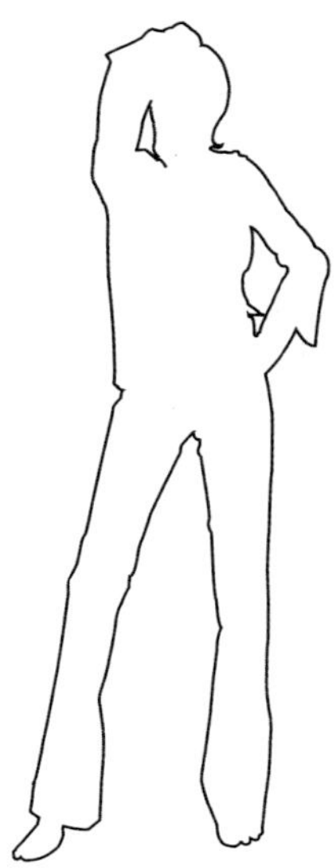

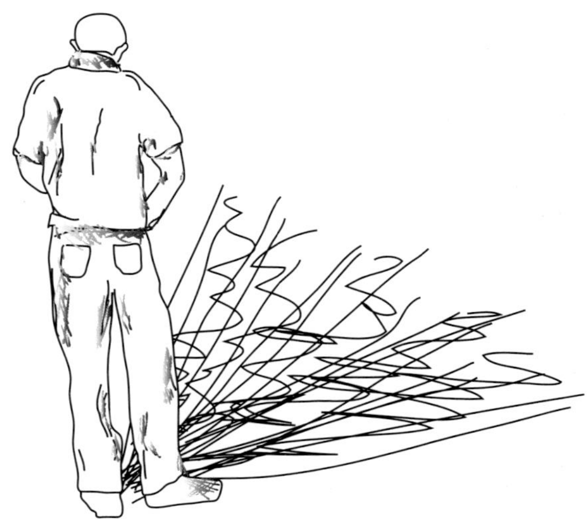

Drawings that incorporate motion lines around the primary outline are called gesture drawings. Drawing gestures requires careful observation and the ability to perceive areas of tension, direction, and movement in order to place motion lines effectively.

Figure 7-11 depicts a man who is running, and there are extra lines added to illustrate his running motion. His joints, such as elbows and knees, are bent repetitively, and his movement appears to displace the air.

The woman in Figure 7-12 seems to be trembling with fear. The extra lines around her outline add emotion and a story. She may fear that she is being followed by something and turns around to check and see.

1 2

1 Figure 7-11. Motion is exaggerated in a gesture drawing
2 Figure 7-12. Mood is represented in a gesture drawing

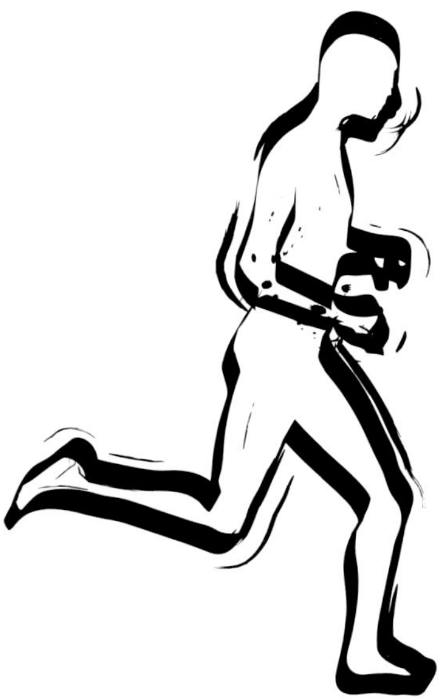

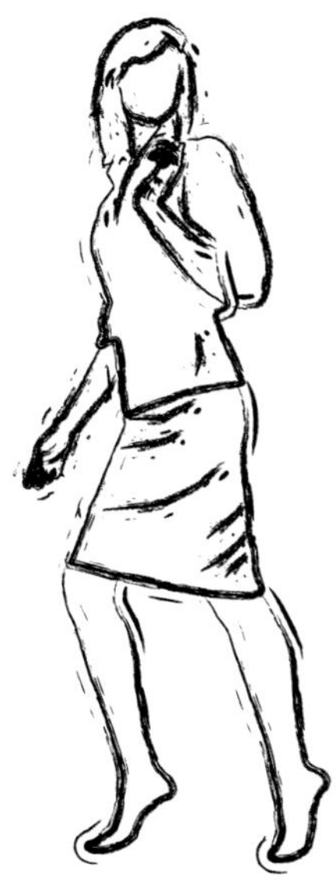

## Lines and Emotions

Lines are the most fundamental structural design elements. They can convey emotion as well as form. Lines can also produce textures that convey a sense of touch. The following hand images are some examples of the diverse qualities and infinite variations that can be achieved with lines.

In Figure 7-13a, the clear outline of the hand expresses elegant curves and detailed features. The detail lines convey the texture of the hand with fine wrinkles and provide a three-dimensional view. A line can express subtlety and roughness at the same time, as in Figure 7-13b. However, the lines used to draw Figure 7-13c are thick and sloped and suggest a laborer's rough and calloused hand.

**1 Figure 7-13.** Elegant, rough, and toughened hands

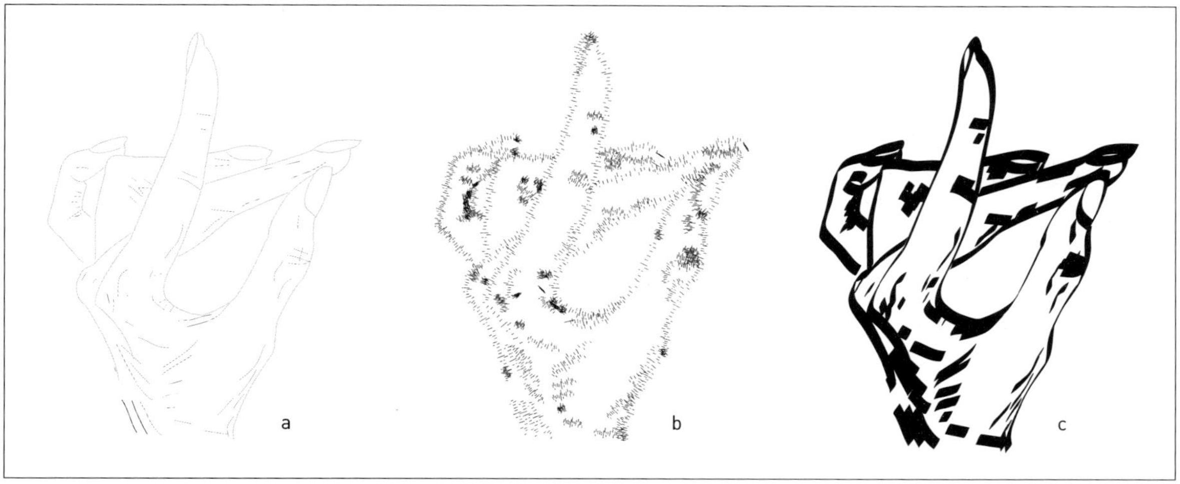

In Figure 7-14d, many short curved lines create roughness in the hand shape, but also weakness from undergoing many hardships. Striped lines may produce a patchy effect (Figure 7-14e). Overlapping thin lines and thick lines in a coursing style present movement and track the figure's previous locations (Figure 7-14f).

In Figure 7-15g, the contours of the hand are expressed with uneven lines. The irregular and repetitive lines in Figure 7-15h imply blurring and a lack of focus that projects a delicate motion. Figure 7-15i's mixed line types make it look like an acrobat's hand, which implies fun and playfulness.

1 Figure 7-14. Fragile, patchy, and active hands
2 Figure 7-15. Imperfect, unfocused, and playful hands

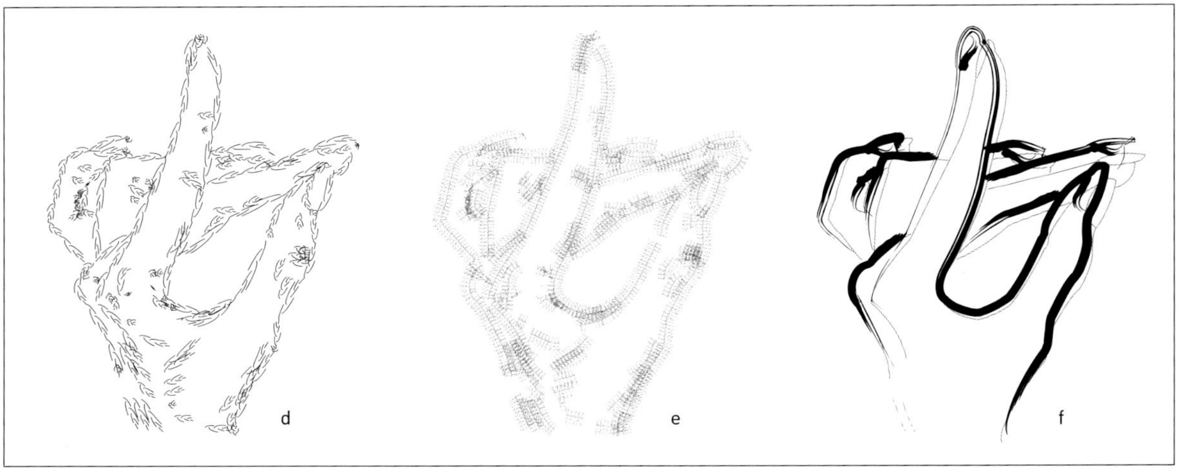


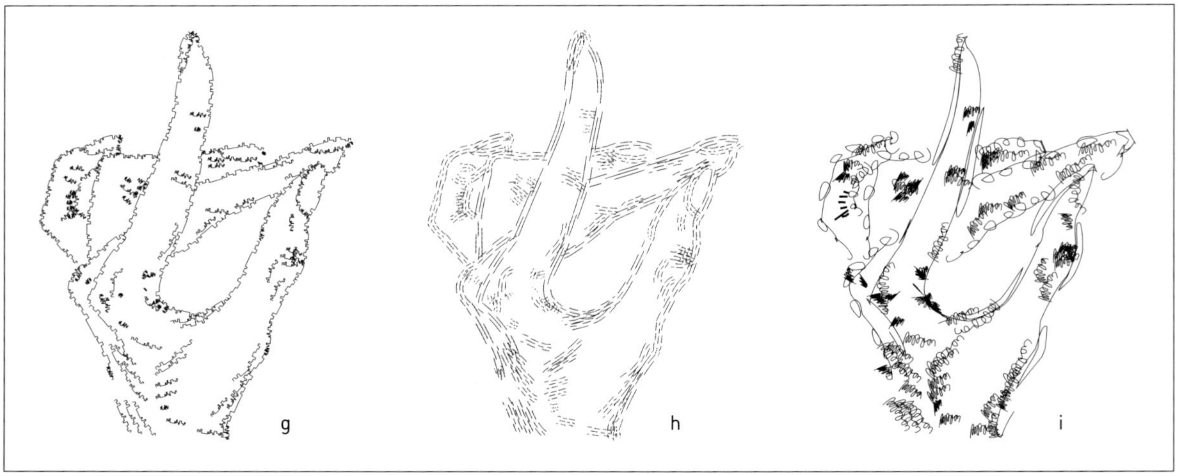

# **Design Studio:** Visual Journey

The aim of this visual journey is to practice using various types of lines in a design.

The recommended process follows:

- Choose a topic that can be visualized in a map format. It can be a trip, such as visiting a tourist spot, or it can be an abstract or ideal, such as love, history, or life.
- Visualize the topic primarily with various types of lines, but symbols and icons may be added, if necessary. However, the work must be done with black and white only.
- The finished work may be reproduced in full color, if necessary.
- Artwork size: 760 by 420 pixels or 420 by 760 pixels or 500 by 500 pixels

The map may be a drawing of a particular area or event such as a city or a festival. The map format can be used to conceptualize a journey from one place to another physically, spiritually, mentally, or emotionally. A map format works well for chronological journaling of a process or an event.

In Figure 7-16, the blue and orange lines represent different paths to reach destinations B and C, respectively, from point A. The map is a critical visual communication tool capable of presenting the process of a visual experience.

In Figure 7-17, the human digestive process is illustrated starting at the mouth, progressing through the stomach and bowels, and ending with excretion. The arrows show the entrance and exit clearly, and the eye will naturally travel from the green arrow to the orange arrow.

Figure 7-18 represents a chronology of the movements and schools in graphic design.

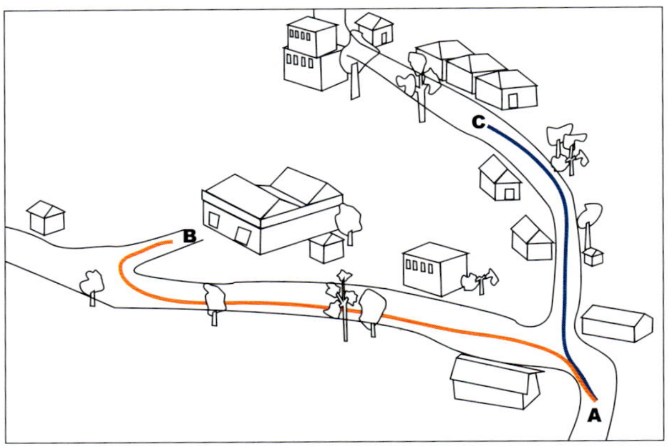


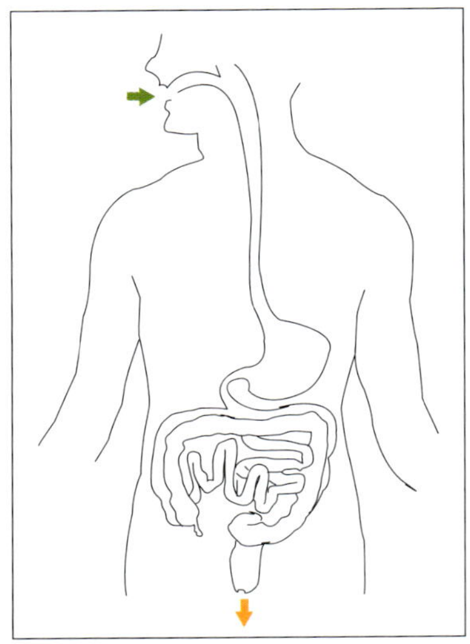

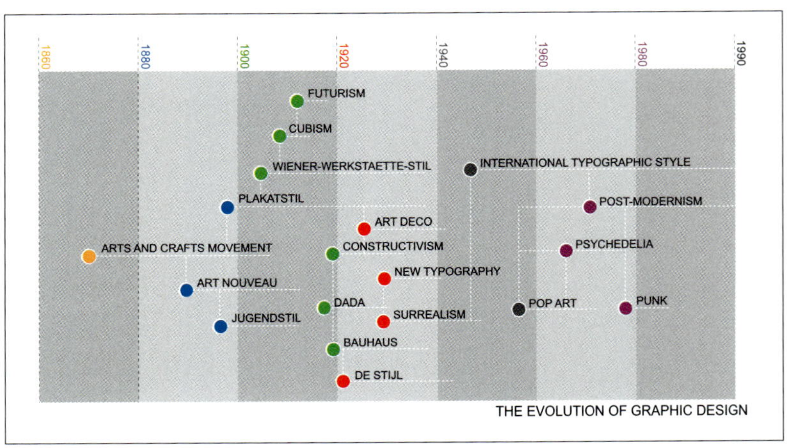


1 2
3

1 **Figure 7-16.** A map with different routes for different destinations

2 **Figure 7-17.** The human digestive process

3 **Figure 7-18.** A clean, linear history of graphic design

Figure 7-19 is essentially the same history but using spiral lines vertically to symbolize the evolution of graphic design.

Figure 7-20 is a good model for illustrating the active process of multimedia production. The complex procedure of developing a multimedia product is illustrated by icons that represent essential multimedia tools, such as images, video, sound, and text. The dotted arrowhead lines suggest the input (an idea) and the output (a finished multimedia product). The complex relationships between the elements and tools are embodied in the many circles and connected by the intersecting words "interaction" and "interface."

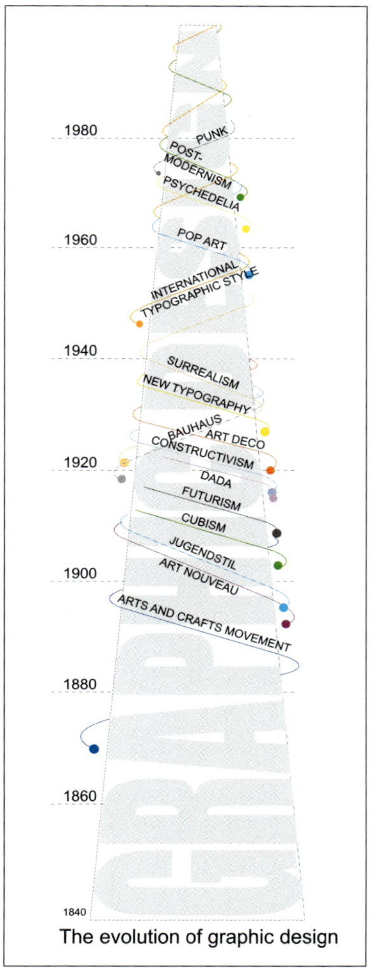


1 Figure 7-19. A creative, off-beat history of graphic design
2 Figure 7-20. The multimedia development process

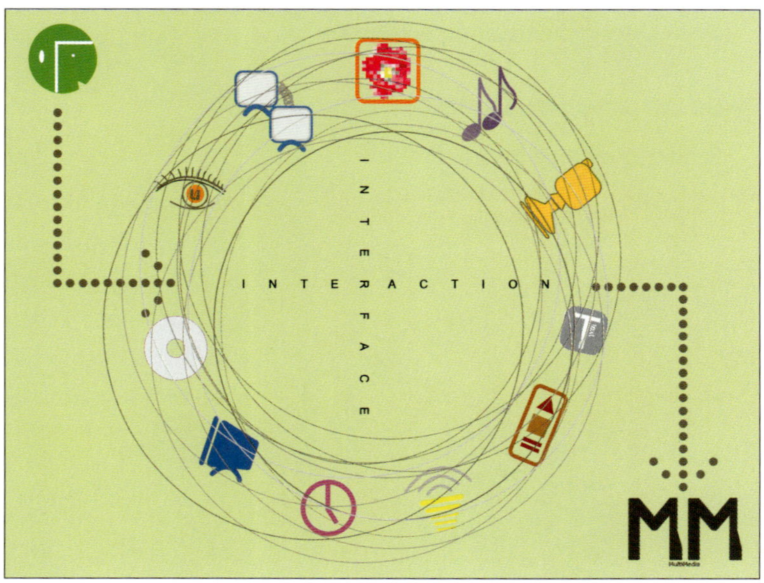

# Student Gallery
## Visual Journal with Lines

- The activity is to practice applying various types and styles of lines.
  - It could be a map format that represents a trip such as visiting a tourist spot.
  - It could be an abstract or ideal form such as love, history or life.
  - Various types of lines must be used.
  - The artwork may be in full color.
- Software: Adobe Illustrator CS2 and Photoshop CS2
- Dimension: 760 x 420 pixels or 420 x 760 pixels or 500 x 500 pixels
- Format: publish a gif or a jpg format (depending on the image quality and file size) from your work

### Marking Criteria (possible marks: 10)

Student will receive one of the marks in the following:

- 9 – 10: Successful design with creative solutions and professional finish
- 7 – 8: Successful design, but insufficient creativity and finish
- 5 – 6: Adequate, but lack of experiment or creativity
- 3 – 4: Inadequate, partly misunderstanding
- 2 – 0: Wrong theme or no submission

### Student Works - Dynamic Layout

- Sandra Mary Weedon 2006

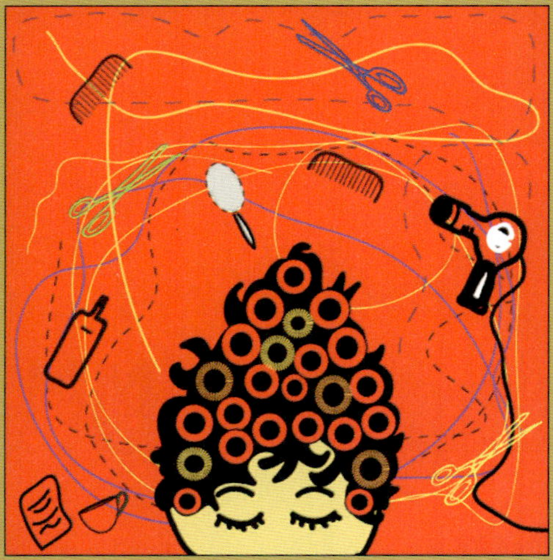

The key point in this activity is visualization of a process of an event by using various types and styles of lines. The work to the left done by Sandi Weedon 2006 presents a process at the hair salon according to use of hairdressing tools and equipment, such as comb, scissors, and hair dryer. The perm rollers with various types and colors of lines are terrific.

Bradley John Acutt 2006

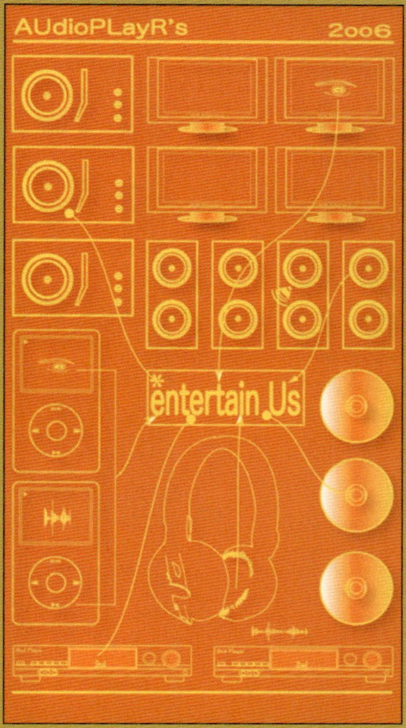


Kaylene Court 2006

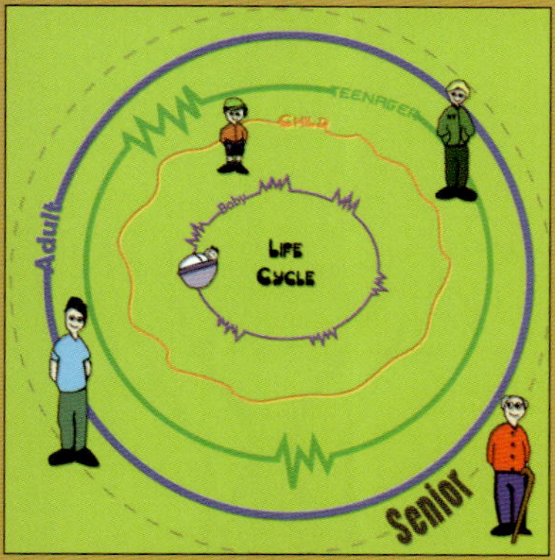


Joy Reynolds 2006

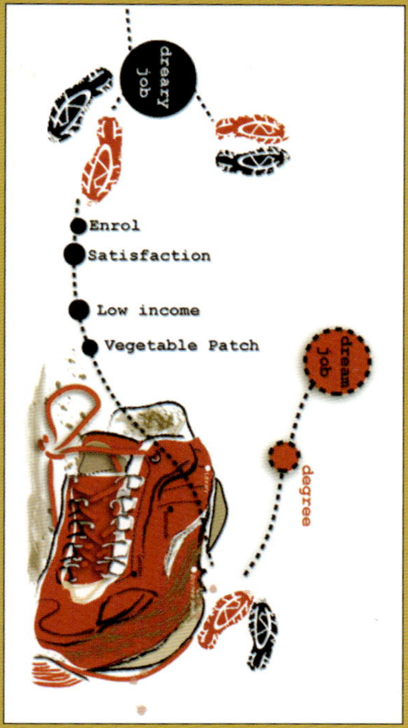


Douglas (Chak Cheung) Tsang 2006

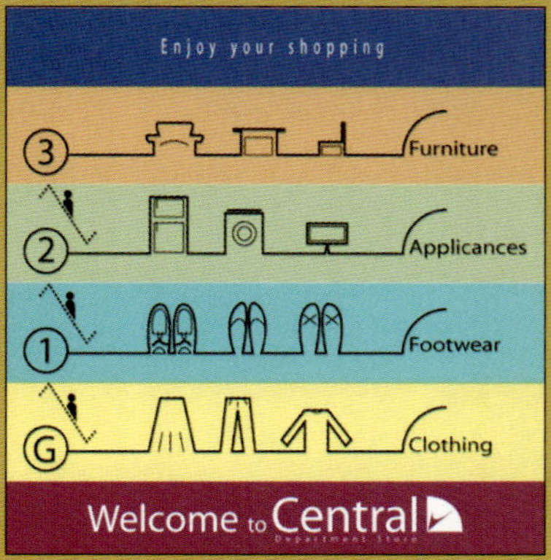


Natalie Gaye Clarke 2007

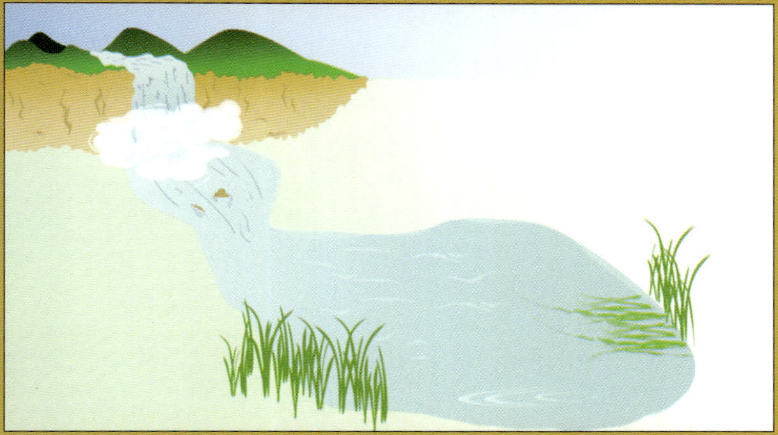

Justin Andrew Hawley 2007

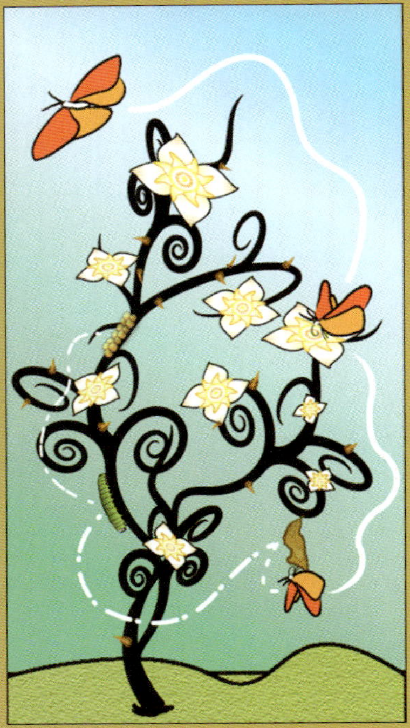

Karina Maree Voss 2007

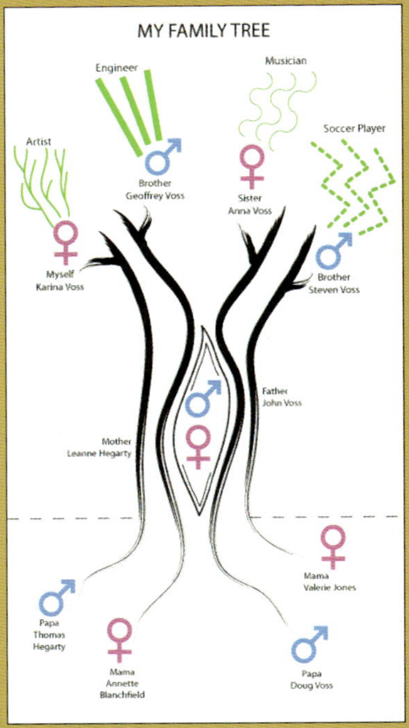


Elise Sondergeld 2007

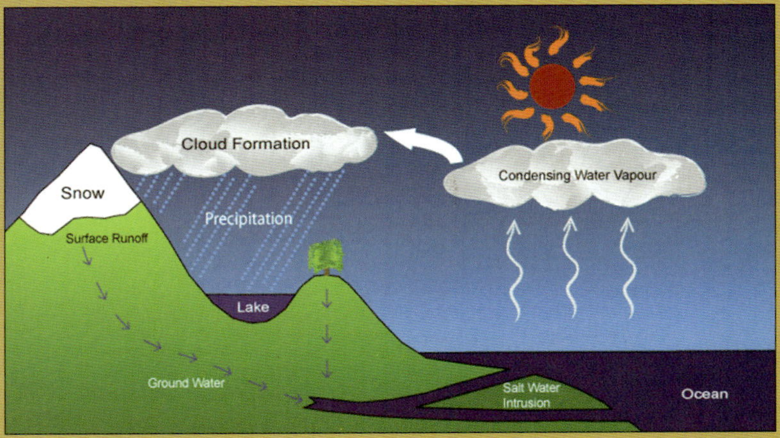

Chapter

# [ 08 ]

# Texture

Texture is a tactile experience of touching a specific object. Visual design is to create or arouse a particular visual experience in association with people's tactile experience. It refers to visual texture. Visual texture is able to deepen and enrich a layout design and produce various emotions and moods.

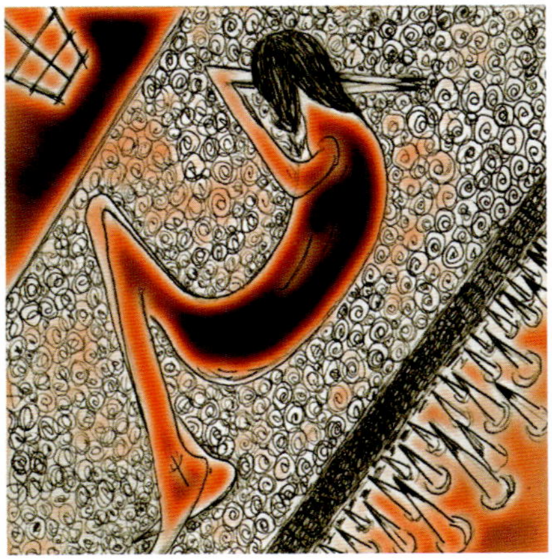

# Texture Defined

Texture is the surface quality of an object. Texture is experienced by touching objects. Every physical object has a texture. Some examples are smooth, rough, hard, and spiked. Texture, in terms of visual design, refers to creating tactile impressions. Texture design can add to the visual appeal and the impression of depth of an object. Visual texture links the experience of touching an object or a surface with an image.

Texture is the surface quality of an object. Texture is experienced by touching objects. Every physical object has a texture. Some examples are smooth, rough, hard, and spiked. Texture, in terms of visual design, refers to creating tactile impressions. Texture design can add to the visual appeal and the impression of depth of an object. Visual texture links the experience of touching an object or a surface with an image.

## Tactile Texture

Tactile texture is the actual feel of a surface through touch. It is the physical surface of an object that accompanies a three-dimensional experience. A tactile texture easily arouses the audience's emotions because it is associated with their tactile experience.

To get a good source for texture design, take photos of natural textures from the environment. Keen and minute observation reveals many beautiful textures. Creating a texture by hand is also a good idea in terms of achieving a unique and gorgeous texture. But, handmade textures may require much experimentation, time, and effort through combining natural textures with the designer's ideas. Impasto in painting, for example, takes advantage of tactile texture (see Figure 8-1). It adds a lively look to the painting's surface where the marks made by the brush or painting knife are visible.

Collage is a powerful medium for image texture made by gluing elements, such as colored paper, printed text and illustrations, photographs, and cloth, to a flat surface. A collage puts a three-dimensional and touchable experience into a design layout. It strengthens the design's reality and authenticity. A piece of paper can contribute greatly to the texture quality.

Figure 8-2 presents an image of a person who is sitting on a toilet. The toilet wall and floor tiles are composed of small pieces of torn and tightly-rolled paper. Collage enriches the realistic quality of the wall and floor, adding a sense of three-dimensionality to the image.

The pieces of broken glass in Figure 8-3 bring a sense of danger and tension to the atmosphere of the design.

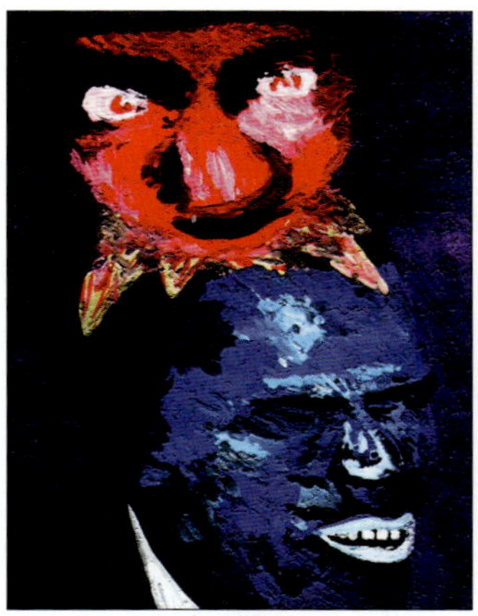

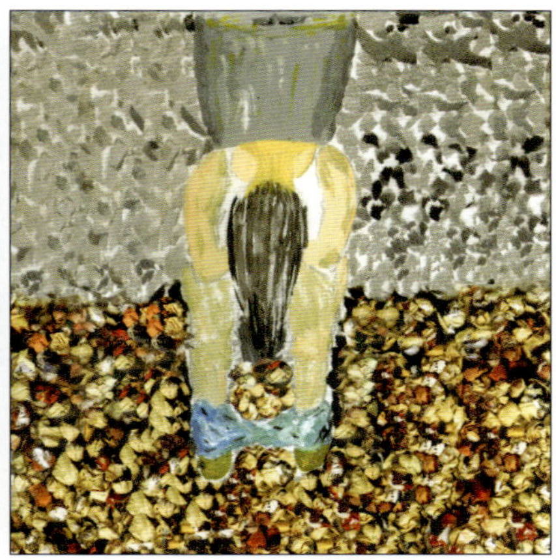

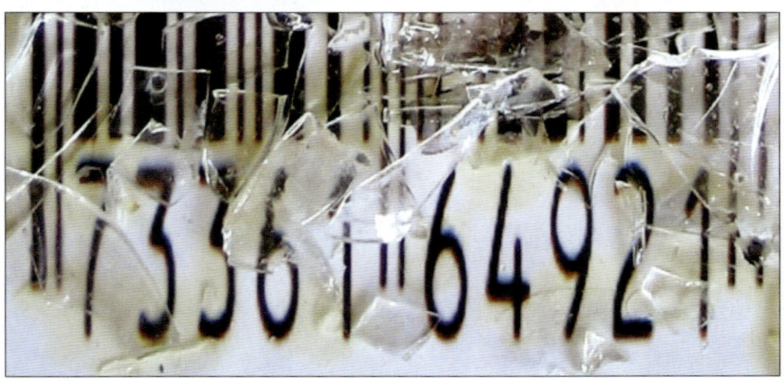

1 Figure 8-1. Impasto texture is achieved with strong paintbrush or knife marks

2 Figure 8-2. Collage uses different media to create a very three-dimensional texture

3 Figure 8-3. Jagged glass edges cause the viewer to feel vulnerable and fragile

## Computer-Aided Tactile Texture

The crab image in Figure 8-4a will be reproduced in Figures 8-4b through 8-4f with different textures to exemplify various tactile experiences. These texture transformations are produced from the Effect Gallery in Adobe Illustrator CS2.

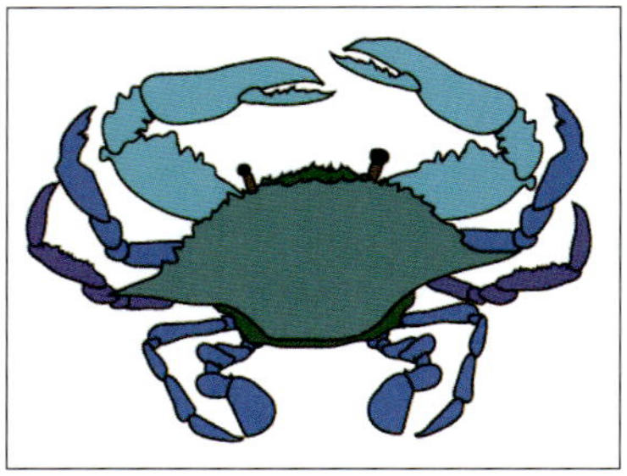

Figure 8-4a. A basic crab graphic

Craquelure in fine art refers to hairline surface cracking formed on old paintings. It is caused by age, climate conditions, and the materials used in the painting. The crab in Figure 8-4b seems to be painted on a rocky surface that produces not only a feeling of roughness, but also aboriginality and primitiveness.

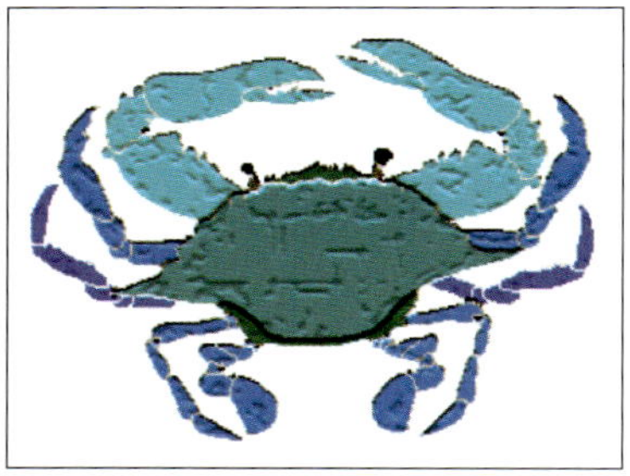

Figure 8-4b. Craquelure texture gives a sense of age

Patchwork is made by combining small pieces of material of different colors or patterns. The patchwork effect has been applied in Figure 8-4c. The small size of the patchwork squares in the crab image gives the impression of porcelain floor tiles, producing a mood of regularity and order.

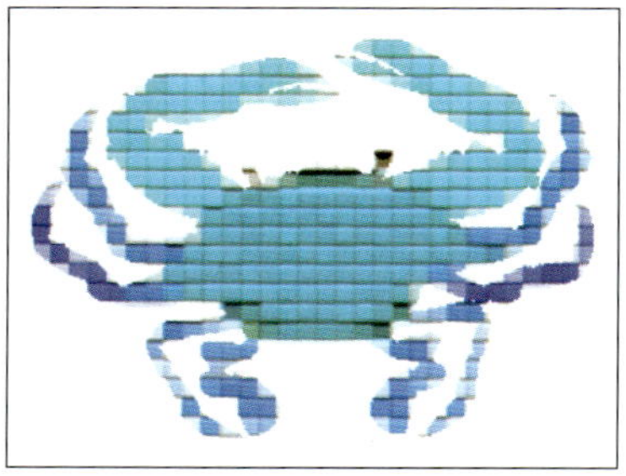

Figure 8-4c. Regularity and order are provided by a patchwork texture

A mosaic is a design that consists of small pieces of inlaid stone, glass, or similar materials. The mosaic effect has been applied in Figure 8-4d and produces a similar tactile experience to Figures 8-4b and 8-4c. However, it appears to be a more artistic form visually, as well as rougher and lumpier than patchwork because of its irregularity.

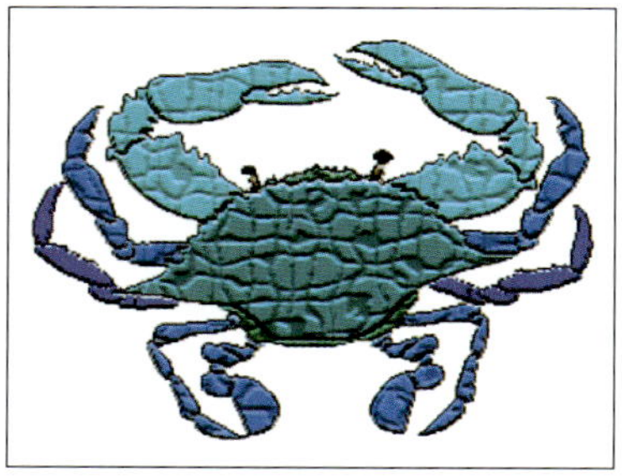

Figure 8-4d. A mosaic tile texture is artistic but rough-looking

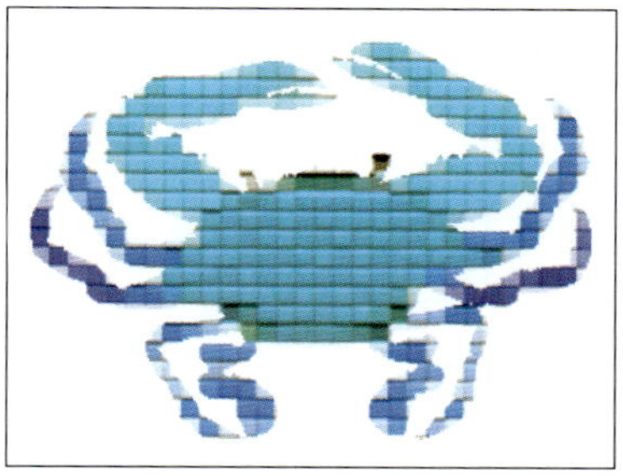

■ Figure 8-4e. A rough look is also achieved with a brick pattern

As Figure 8-4e shows, a brick texture produces a sense of roughness and grain.

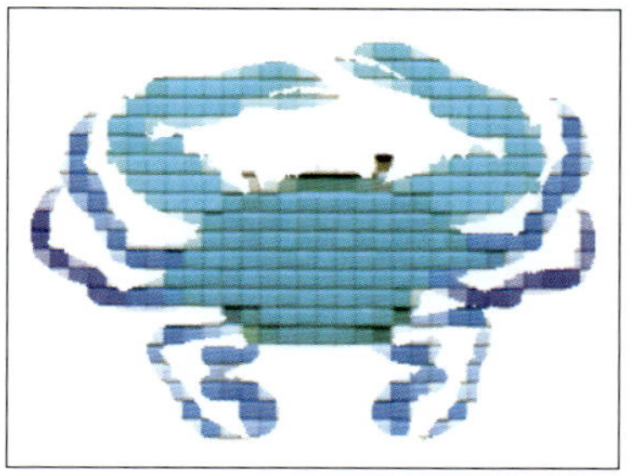

■ Figure 8-4f. A canvas texture makes the crab look painted

In Figure 8-4f, the crab's texture is reminiscent of a work produced on canvas.

# Visual Texture

Texture is the surface quality of an object. Texture is experienced by touching objects. Every physical object has a texture. Some examples are smooth, rough, hard, and spiked. Texture, in terms of visual design, refers to creating tactile impressions. Texture design can add to the visual appeal and the impression of depth of an object. Visual texture links the experience of touching an object or a surface with an image.

Good visual texture design is determined by representing a physical surface through imagery and creating the illusion of a surface texture that could be felt by a viewer if it were actually touched. Accomplishing a successful visual texture is done by accessing the viewer's tactile associations.

Figure 8-5 shows a strong sense of visual texture in an illustration of a person lying in a very uncomfortable bed. It symbolizes the person suffering from insomnia.

Simple lines or shapes can create symbolic textures to produce illusion and interest. Symbolic texture is a repetitive motif or pattern found in nature. The image in Figure 8-6 is patterned on a honeycomb. The overlapping circles in Figure 8-7 look like fish scales.

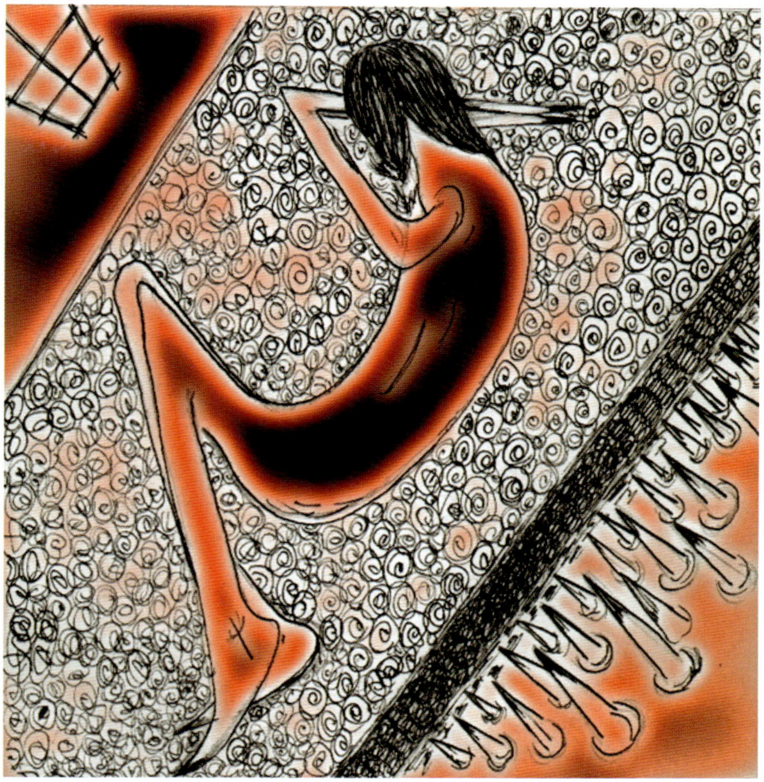

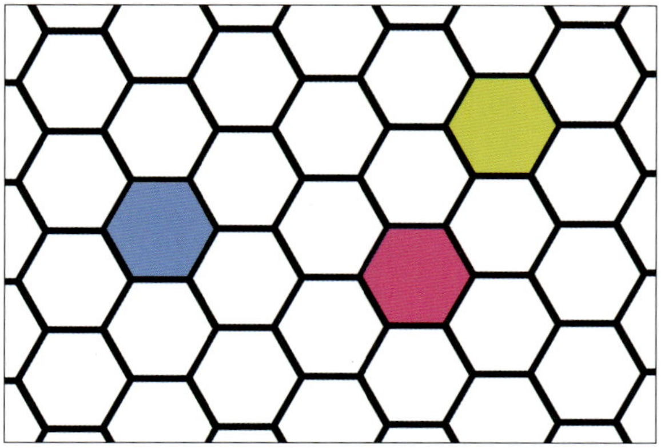

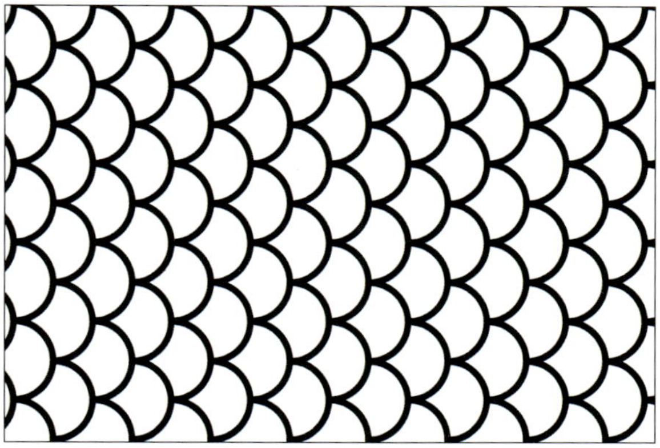

1 Figure 8-5. Insomnia torments its victim

2 Figure 8-6. A simple hexagon pattern creates a honeycomb texture

3 Figure 8-7. Overlapping circles suggest fish scales

## Computer-Aided Visual Texture

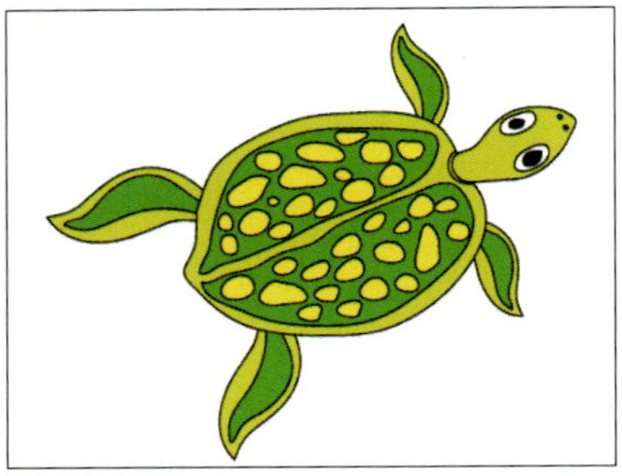

Figure 8-8a. A basic turtle image

The turtle graphic in Figure 8-8a will be reproduced in Figures 8-8b through 8-8f with different textures to provide a variety of visual experiences. These visual manipulations were created with the Effect commands in Adobe Illustrator CS2.

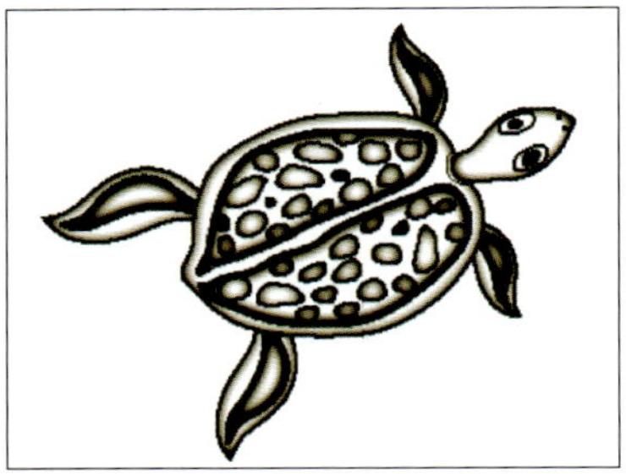

Figure 8-2b. The photocopy effect mixes softness with hard areas

A photocopied image is characterized by black and white colored areas highlighted with black around the edges. Figure 8-8b is a monochrome version of the original image. The midtone areas produce a visual softness and balance between the solid white and black areas, which produce more of a visual hardness.

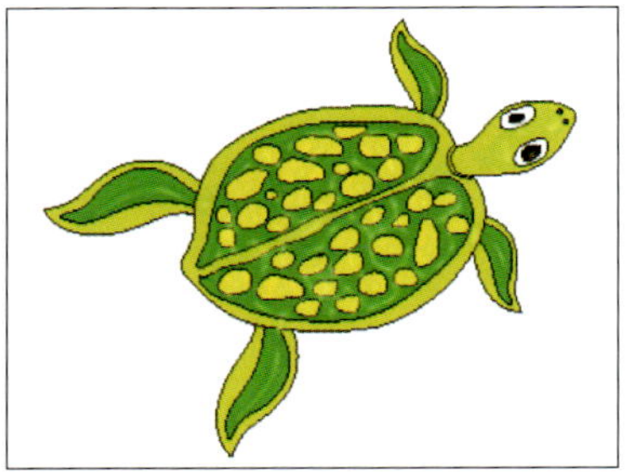

Figure 8-8c. A plastic wrap effect gives the turtle volume

The plastic wrap effect simulates covering an object with a thin, transparent, stretchy plastic. The surface of Figure 8-8c is accentuated with the shiny and glossy effect. The texture also produces visual volume and a three-dimensional effect.

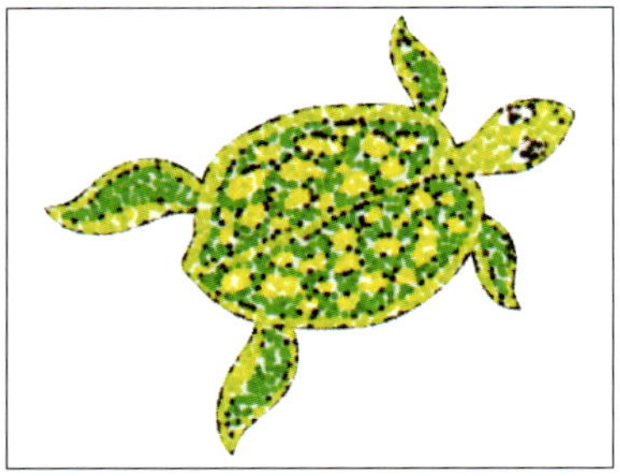

Figure 8-8d. Stylization is achieved with a pointillism approach

Pointillism is a style of painting in which many tiny dots are combined to form an image. The dot-based image in Figure 8-8d produces a feeling of smoothness and softness and looks artistic and stylized.

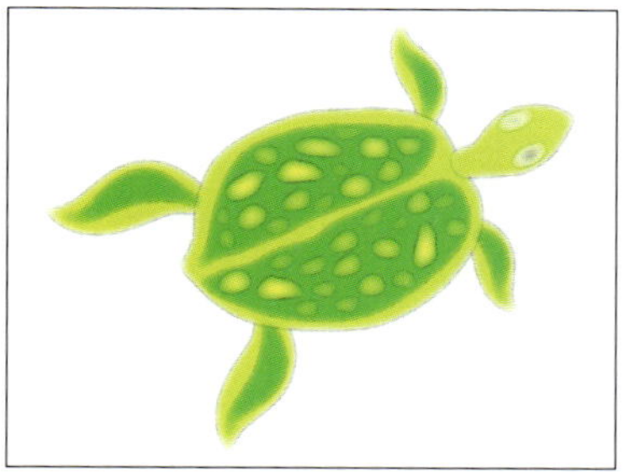

■ Figure 8-8e. Soft edges suggest a dreamlike state

Figure 8-8e is an example of feathered (or softened) edges that produce a warm and dreamlike feeling.

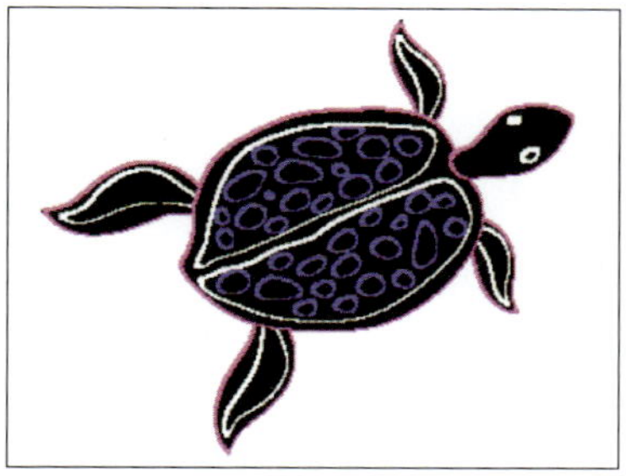

■ Figure 8-8f. A "glowing edges" effect gives the turtle an electric tinge

Figure 8-8f produces an impressionistic style of the turtle with highlights that outline areas of the image with different colors. This effect is called "glowing edges."

As Figure groups 8-4 and 8-8 demonstrate, visual and tactile textures create various surface qualities that produce different looks and feels. Textural design is critical in visual design for visual richness and depth.

# Texture and Emotions

Visual perception is associated to the tactile experience. A tactile experience can have much greater impact on the viewer's visual attention and emotional response than a visual experience.

The viewer's experience of a visual texture is subjective. When deciding on a texture, the designer should consider the average person's tactile knowledge of a particular object. Textures can arouse emotional responses from memories and associations.

As Figure 8-9 shows, broken and shattered pottery can evoke a sense of danger or violence. These experiences can be characterized with sharp and pointed shapes.

**Figure 8-9.** Sharp, pointed shapes invoke danger

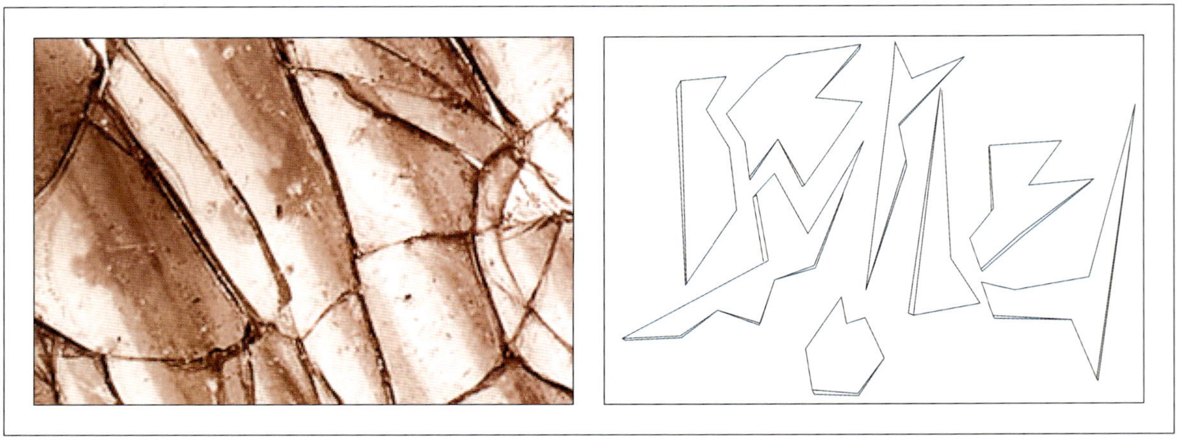

In Figure 8-10, the feathers and fluff in the left-hand image are soft and cushiony. This arouses a feeling of warmth and comfort. These emotions can be reproduced with many thin, fine lines, as shown in the right-hand graphic.

The spiky skin of a pineapple (see Figure 8-11, left-side) can be illustrated with repetitive spikes on overlapping semicircles (right-side).

The soapy water on the floor in Figure 8-12's left-hand image appears slippery and wet. As the right-hand image shows, various sizes of circles can represent bubbles of soapy water. They also produce a feeling of lightness.

1
2

1 Figure 8-10. Fine lines imitate the softness of down
2 Figure 8-11. Overlapping circles with spikes simulate pineapple skin

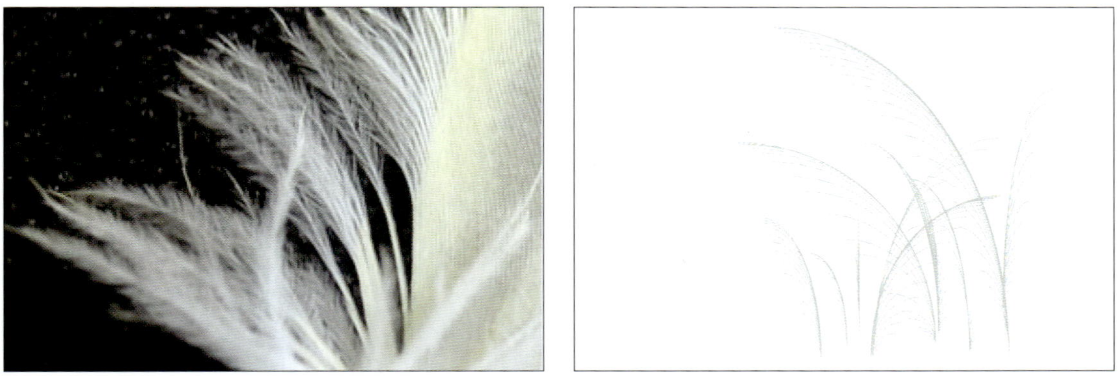

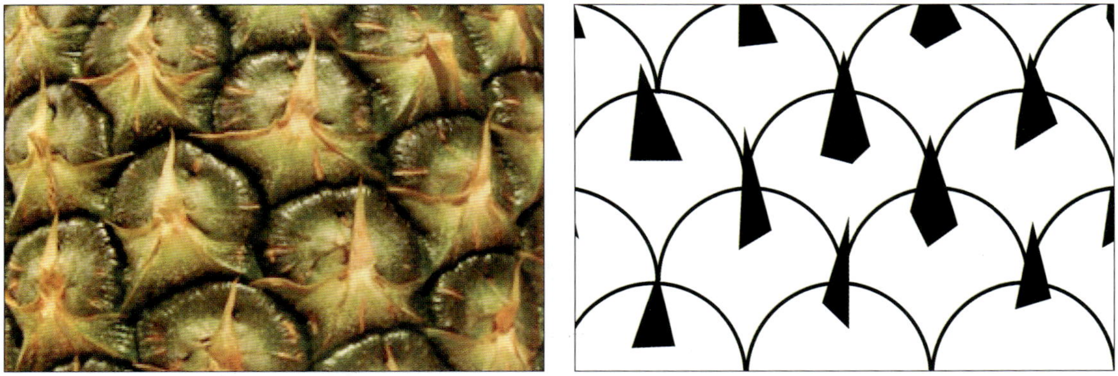

The metallic surface in Figure 8-13's left-hand image gives a cold feeling and the reflecting light produces a shiny white to gray gradient. The linear gradient in the right-hand image reproduces this cold, metallic sensation.

The surface of the bricks in Figure 8-14's left-hand image is coarse and uneven, but the right-hand design shows how the pattern can be standardized to suggest unity, balance, and uniformity.

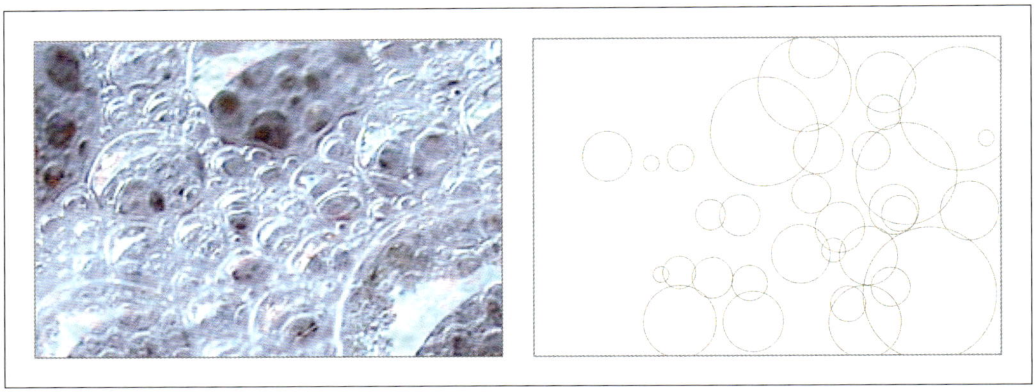

1 Figure 8-12. Differently-sized circles look like soft, airy soap bubbles

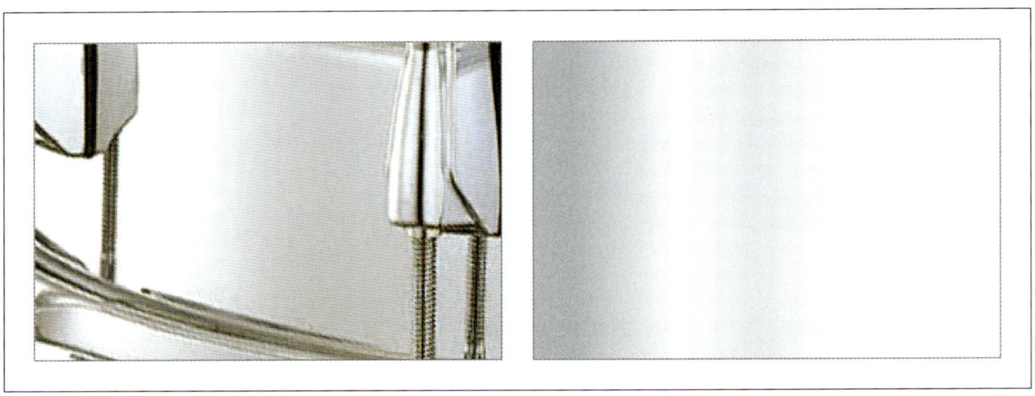

2 Figure 8-13. Metallic gradients appear cool and sterile

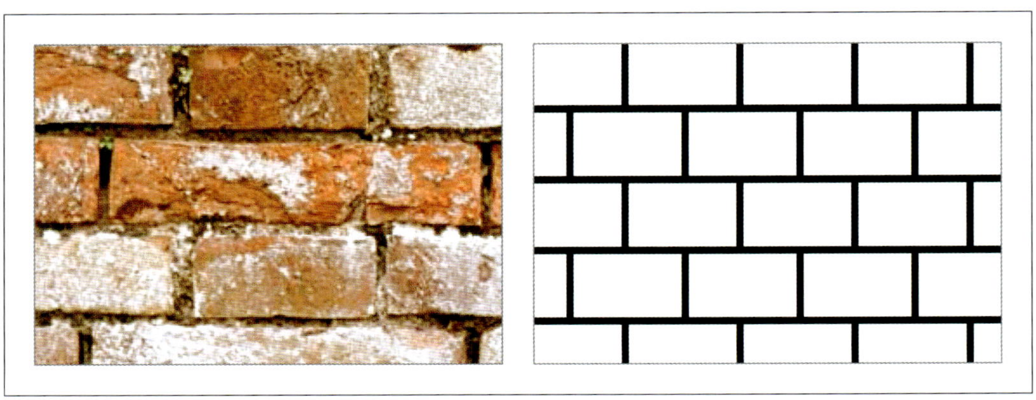

3 Figure 8-14. A uniform design can be derived from a rough brick wall

# Design Studio: Texture Design

The objective of this activity is to create a visual texture representing a compound noun such as a dragonfly.

The process follows:

- Choose one of the words from the list below or another compound noun
- Compose images or graphics to represent the chosen noun
- Create a texture that represents or connects with the noun and use it as the background
- Artwork size: 500 pixels by 500 pixels

**A list of compound nouns:**

- Bird dog
- Butterfly
- Dragonfly
- Firefly
- Flowerpot
- Frog fish
- Ladybird (or ladybug)
- Rose diamond
- Sea lion
- Tiger beetle

Figure 8-15 represents a ladybird (also known as a ladybug) that combines an image of a lady and a bird to depict the literal meaning of "ladybird." The background image is adopted from the insect's design, which enhances the audience's visual experience in relation to the ladybird.

Figure 8-16 is another example of this activity that represents the word dragonfly by combining a cartoon dragon and a fly's wings. The background texture is the stylized surface of a dragonfly's wing composed of a network of tubular veins coated with a transparent film.

1 2

1 Figure 8-15. A literal interpretation of a "ladybird"
2 Figure 8-16. A cartoonish rendering of a "dragonfly"

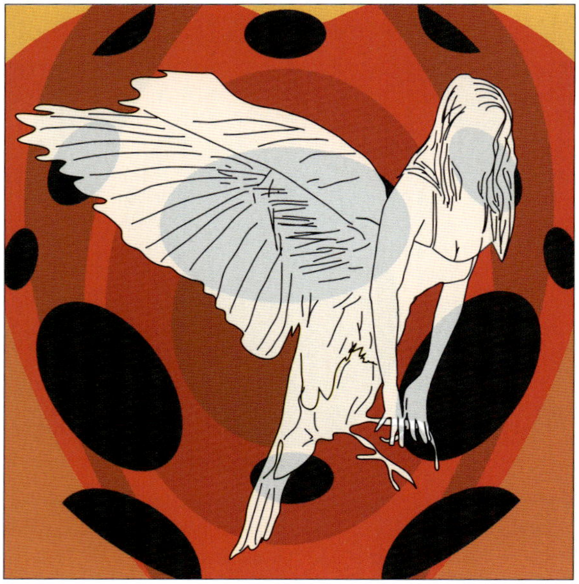

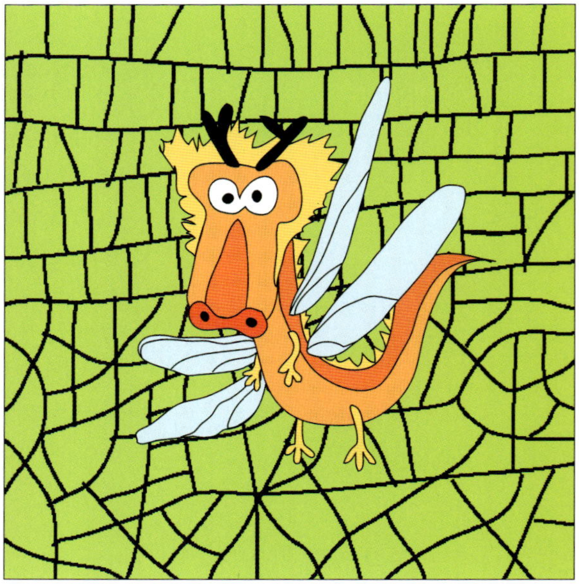

# Student Gallery
## Texture Design

The objective of this activity is to create a visual texture representing a compound noun chosen.

- Choose one of the words from the list
- Composite images or graphics to represent the chosen word
- Create a texture background which represents or associates with the real meaning of the word

- Software: Adobe Illustrator CS2 and Photoshop CS2
- Dimension:  500 x 500 pixels
- Format: publish a gif or a jpg format (depending on the image quality and file size) from your work
- Search a chosen word at Google Images (http://images.google.com) and it may gives you some ideas.

**Words list: compound nouns**

- Finger fish
- Monkey bread
- Flower bed
- Sea lion
- Frog fish
- Hair grass
- Tiger beetle
- Egg apple
- Bird dog
- Rose diamond

### Marking Criteria (possible marks: 10)

Student will receive one of the marks in the following:

- 9 – 10: Successful design with creative solutions and professional finish
- 7 – 8: Successful design, but insufficient creativity and finish
- 5 – 6: Adequate, but lack of experiment or creativity
- 3 – 4: Inadequate, partly misunderstanding
- 2 – 0: Wrong theme or no submission

## Student Works

- Douglas (Chak Cheung) Tsang 2006

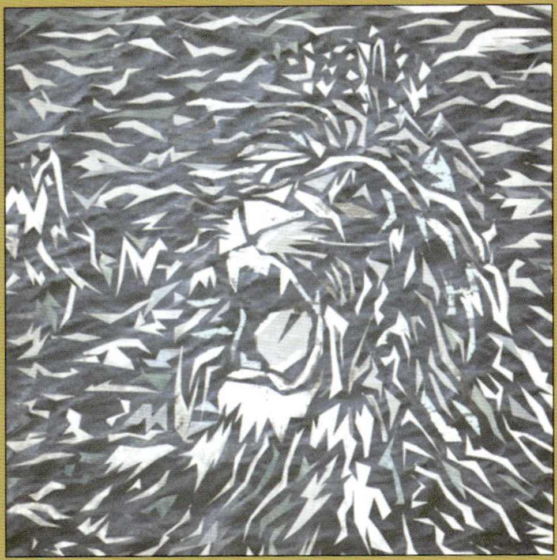

The activity required creating a texture design through visualizing a chosen compound noun. The most impressive work between 2006 and 2007 in my classes is the one to the left that defines a sea lion and its texture with a form of raging waves at the same time.

- Joy Reynolds 2006

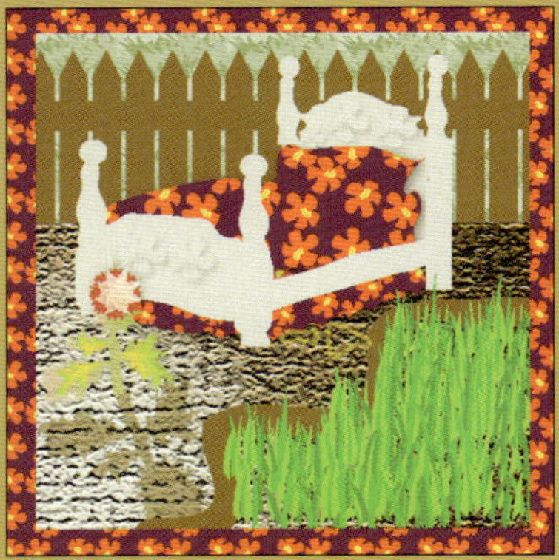

- Krista Avila 2007

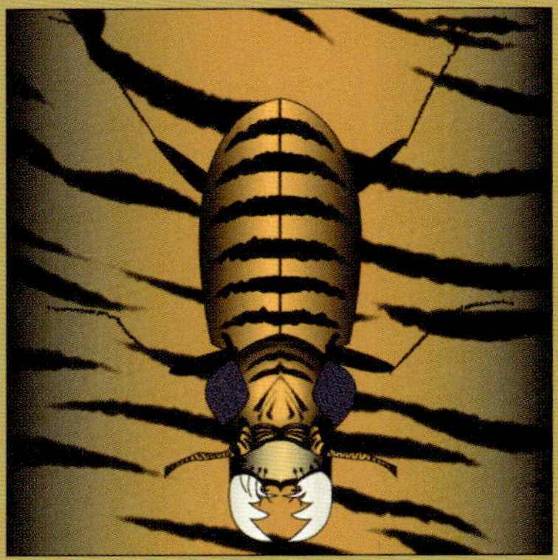

- Natalie Gaye Clarke 2007

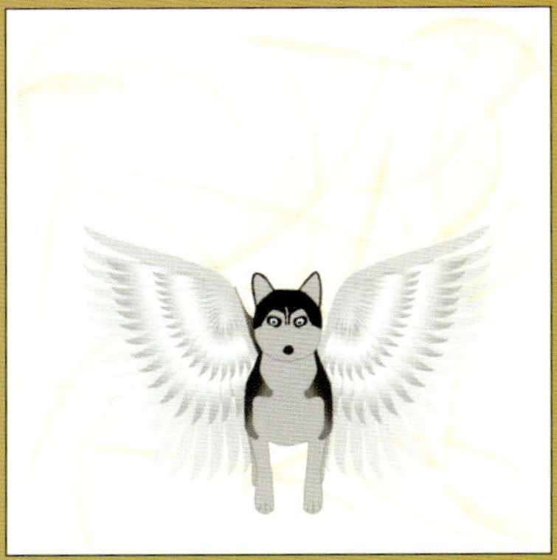

- Justin Andrew Hawley 2007

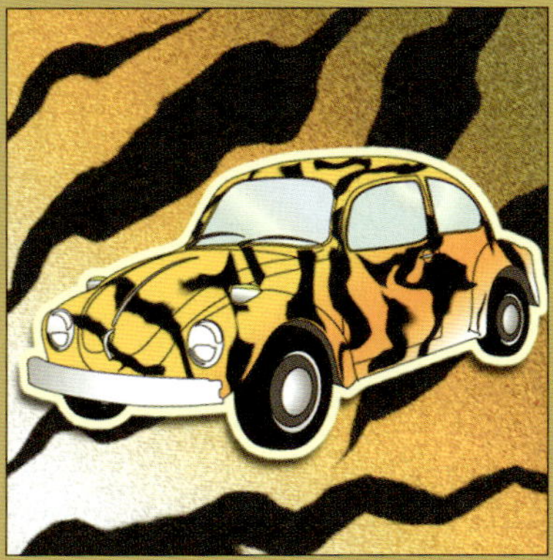

- Elise Sondergeld 2007

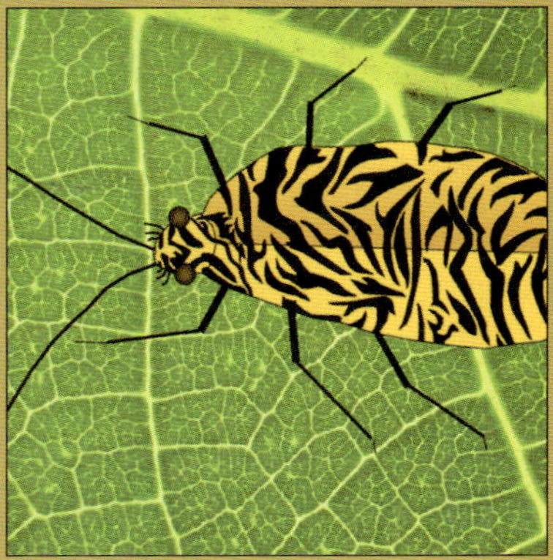

- Chelsea Sutherland 2007

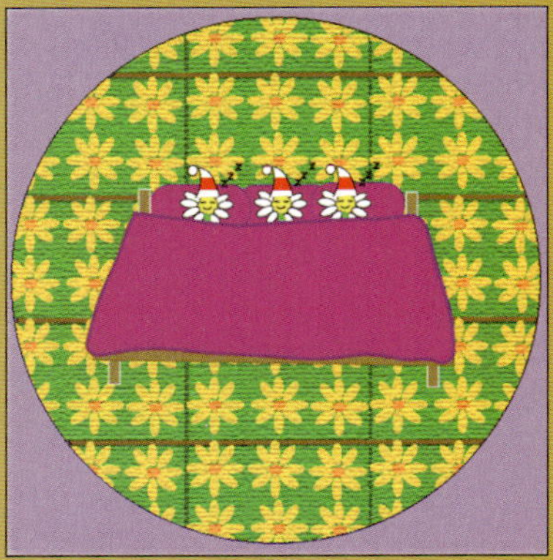

Chapter

# [ 09 ]

# Form & Perspective

Form refers to three-dimensional quality of an object which has its depth.
Light and dark areas of an object including its shadow determine its visual volume.

Perspective refers to the relationship between sizes and distances of objects in space. Perspectives in terms of visual design is to create a context of visual perception by arranging the objects in terms of their spatial relatives and traits.

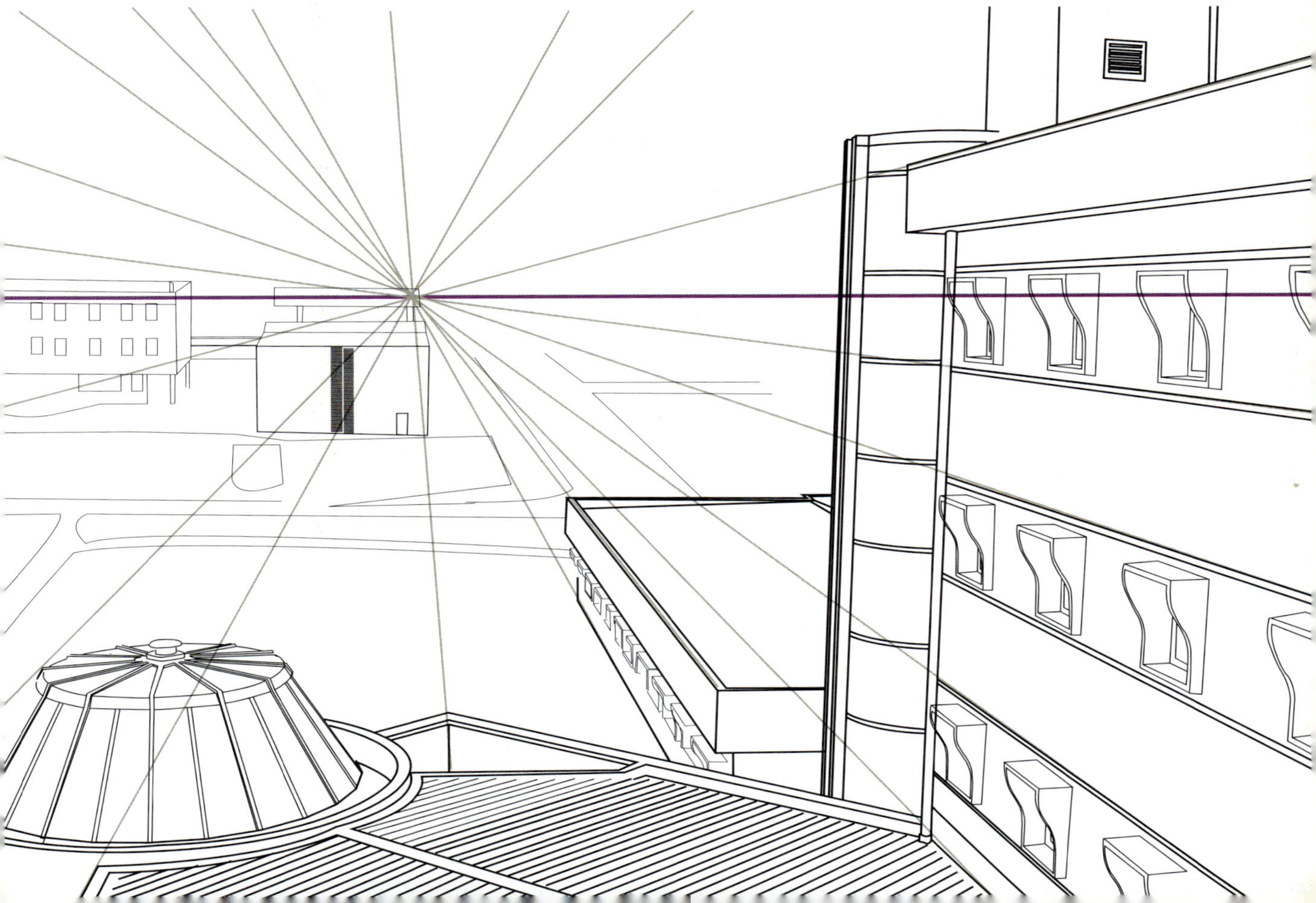

# Defining Form

Form and shape have similar characteristics. Shapes are 2-dimensional objects that have width and height, whereas forms are 3-dimensional and have depth as well as width and height. When you add depth to a shape, it becomes a form. Depth refers to the volume or thickness of an object. Technically, there are 2-dimensional and 3-dimensional forms. Strictly speaking, the former is a 2-dimensional image that creates the illusion of a 3-dimensional form, whereas 3-dimensional forms are tangible.

## Illusion of 3-Dimensional Form

A 2-dimensional form is a shape with depth. You can create a 2-dimensional form with lines that simply trace the dimensions of an object. Defining the structure of an object with lines can suggest its 3-dimensional form. As shown in Figure 9-1, a form may be drawn as if transparent, to show all the lines that define its edges.

Figure 9-2 shows an opaque version of the previous figures, again giving the illusion of depth. Both Figures 9-1 and 9-2 communicate form simply and efficiently using lines.

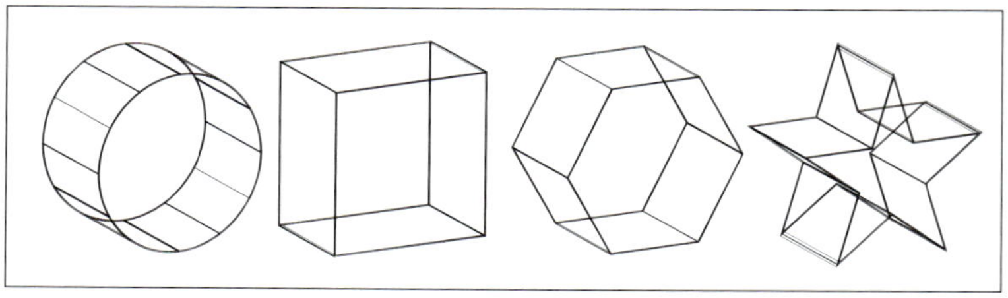

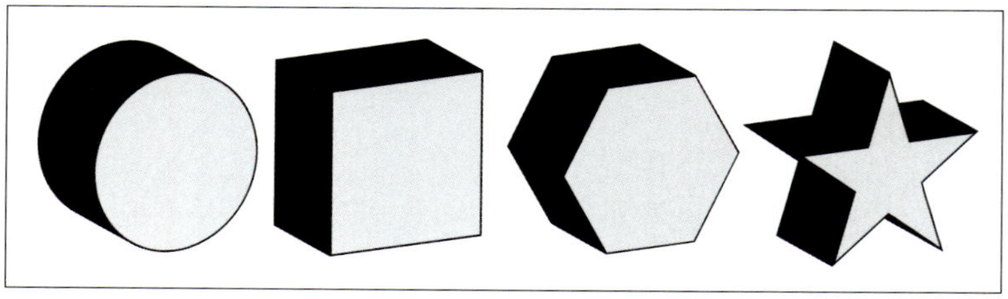

1
2

1 Figure 9-1. Outlines of transparent objects create the illusion of three dimensions

2 Figure 9-2. Solid forms of 3-dimensional figures

# Light and Shade

Light and shadow determines a 3-dimensional form in visual design. The light direction produces the shadow volume faces and light and dark areas within an image also suggest its visual volume.

Light and shade are fundamental aspects of 3-dimensional forms, and they must be taken into consideration when creating these forms for graphic design. More light on a surface of an object lightens its color, and less light suggests depth and shadow.

In Figure 9-3, the light is illuminating the person from behind. The person's body is blocking the light. Thus, the figure's front side is darkened, and the whole form is casting a shadow. Light and shade are fundamental to render form. They are intangible, but they create a spatial environment and increase realism. In Figure 9-4, shadows enable us to identify the source and direction of the light.

1 2

1 Figure 9-3. Shadow and shading create depth
2 Figure 9-4. Direction of light

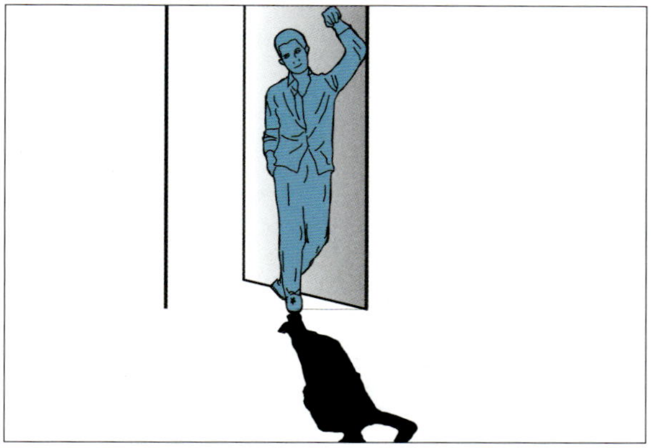

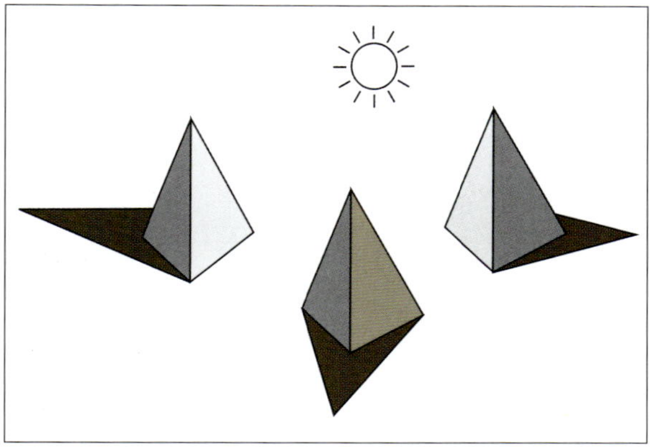

To create shadow, you need to consider three elements: light source, ground (angle of light), and direction of light. The vertical reference line and the horizontal vanishing point assist in creating a 3-dimensional object. First, the light source could be the sun or an artificial light. The ground is the spot where the light hits directly on the ground, determining the angle at which the light falls on object. In Figure 9-5 the light source is behind the box and beaming from 11 o'clock, or 120 degrees.

This image has been revised from Hagan's shadow basic (Learning How to Draw, http://www.geocities.com/%7Ejlhagan/K9-14/introduction.htm).

As Figure 9-6 shows, if the light source is located behind the object, it is necessary to consider the vanishing point of the shadow, determined by the direction of light. The shadow is cast at the intersection between the lines from the ground (the light angle) and the vanishing point of the shadow on the ground.

This image has been revised from Loomis' Perspective Shadow, Figure 4 (A. Loomis 1951, Successful Drawing, p. 84).

1 2

1 Figure 9-5. Principles of light, shadow, and perspective
2 Figure 9-6. Using perspective lines to place shading

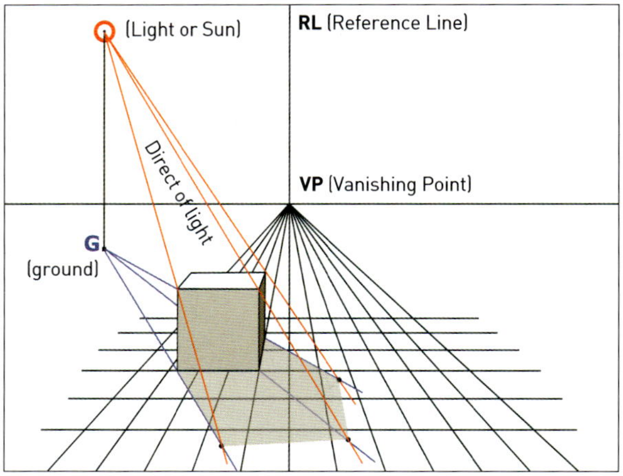


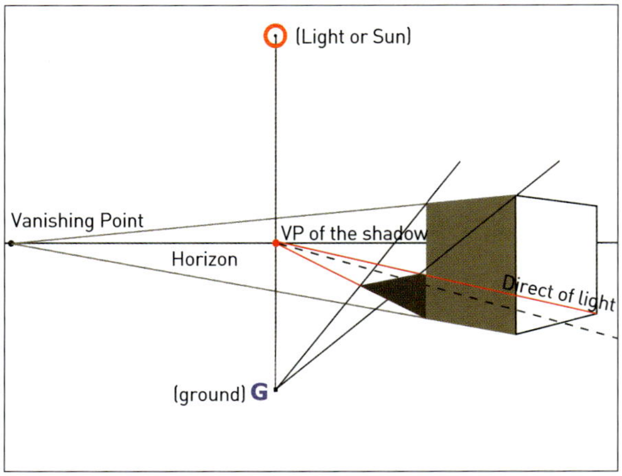


• This image is my outcome and its manipulation from LESSON - PERSPECTIVE EIGHT - BASIC SHADOWS, Learning How to Draw, (http://www.geocities.com/~jlhagan/K9-14/draw_eight.htm)

There are three elements to be considered when applying shading on an object: highlights, halftones, and shadows. Highlights collect more light rays than any other area so it will be the lightest area. Halftones collect fewer rays. Shadow begins where the light rays are at a tangent to the surface.

It is useful to note that the band of darker shadow in Figures 9-7 and 9-8 appears between the halftone and the reflected light within the shadow. As shown in Figure 9-8, the shadow cast on the ground under diffused light starts from this band (Loomis 1951, p. 81).

A 3-dimensional form is essentially a structure of shading, balanced between highlight, halftone, and shadow.

1 2

1 **Figure 9-7.** Highlights, halftones, and shadow
2 **Figure 9-8.** Shadows under indirect or diffused light

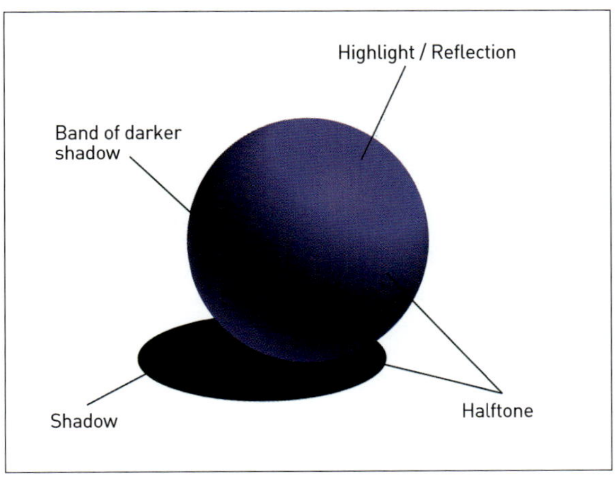


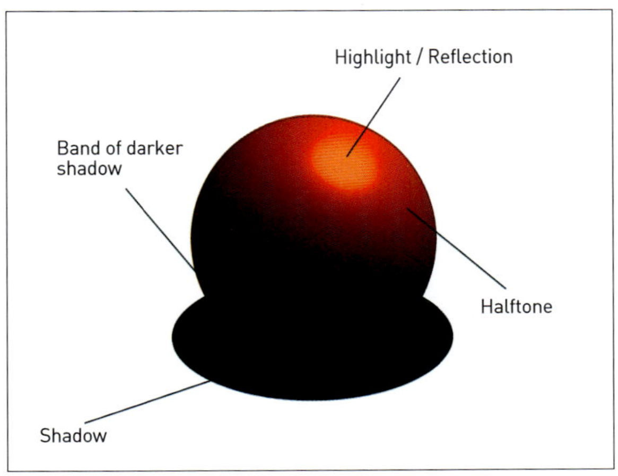


• Loomis, A. (1951). Successful Drawing, Viking Press, p. 81

# Perspective

Perspective is the art of adding an impression of depth in a 2-dimensional image. A good control of perspective creates a relative relationship between objects and their environment. For example, larger, detailed objects appear closer whereas smaller, blurred objects appear further away.

Perspective is the art of adding an impression of depth in a 2-dimensional image. A good control of perspective creates a relative relationship between objects and their environment. For example, larger, detailed objects appear closer whereas smaller, blurred objects appear further away.

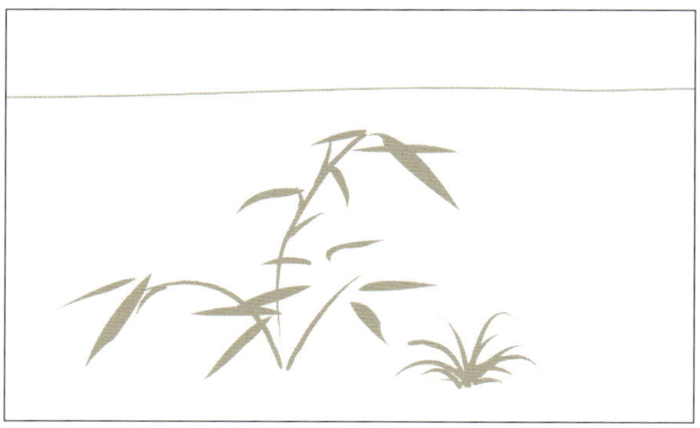

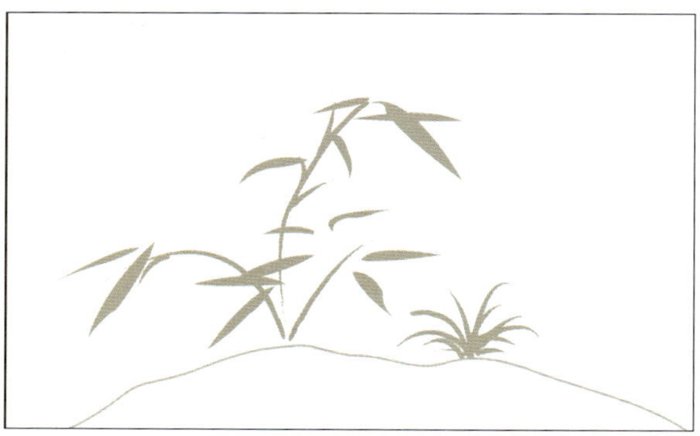

1 Figure 9-9. A high horizon line implies looking down
2 Figure 9-10. A low horizon line implies looking up

The horizon is a reference point that represents our eye level. It determines the position of an object in an image. It can be said that the horizon is a movable line that can change the view of perspective. In Figure 9-9 the viewer is looking down onto plants in a field. The viewer is in front of the plants and the horizon is above. In Figure 9-10, the viewer is looking up the plants on a hill. As demonstrated here, the horizontal line determines where your eye level will be.

Another important element of perspective are vanishing points, the points in the distance where parallel lines seem to meet. When viewing a road or a railway it seems to stretch until it narrows to a vanishing point where it meets the horizontal line. The horizon line and vanishing points determine the size and form of an object in 3-dimensional space.

## 1-Point Perspective

As Figure 9-11 shows, a 1-point perspective converges at one vanishing point. It is a parallel perspective because the object viewed runs parallel to the perspective lines.

To draw this 1-point perspective, one vanishing point is set on the horizon line. As Figure 9-12 shows, the vanishing point and the horizon line are at the same eye level, and the trees diminish parallel to that perspective. Figure 9-13 is another example of 1-point vanishing view, with the horizon and vanishing point at the same level. The buildings are drawn following the radial lines created in proportion to the perspective.

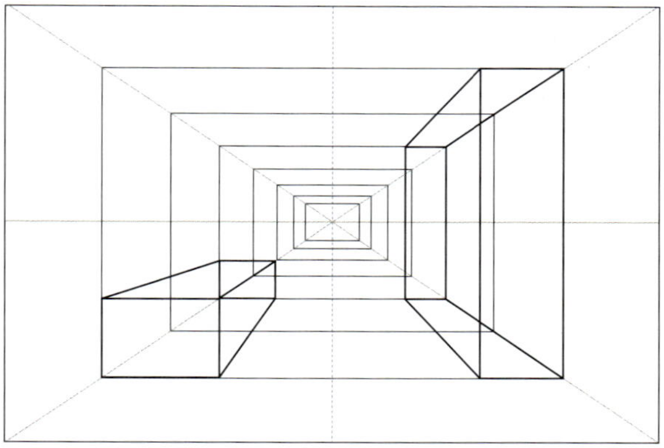

1 Figure 9-11. 1-point perspective
2 Figure 9-12. Images sized parallel to the 1-point perspective
3 Figure 9-13. The vanishing point is set on the horizon line

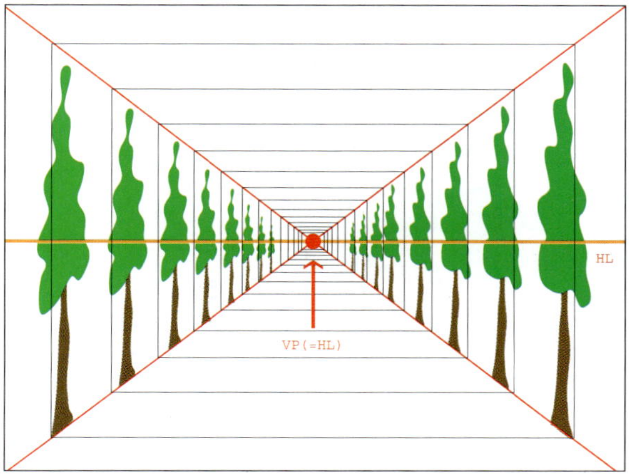


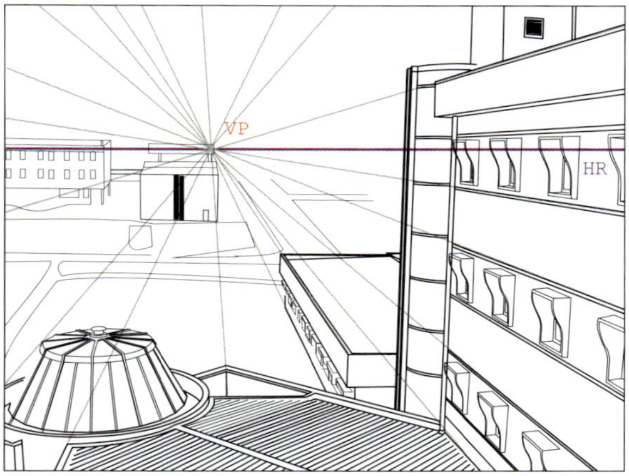

## 2-Point Perspective

As Figure 9-14 shows, 2-point perspective uses two vanishing points and is more realistic than the 1-point perspective. When you look at the corner of an object, there are two vanishing points that recede to the left and right.

To draw in 2-point perspective, both left and right vanishing points are placed on the horizon line. As shown in Figure 9-15, when you draw multiple objects in this perspective, multiple reference lines (RL, RL-1 and RL-2) may be necessary. Figure 9-16 is an example of a 2-point view with vanishing points outside the image frame.

1 2
3

1 Figure 9-14. 2-point perspective uses two vanishing points

2 Figure 9-15. Multiple reference lines are used with 2-point perspective

3 Figure 9-16. Vanishing points fall beyond the frame

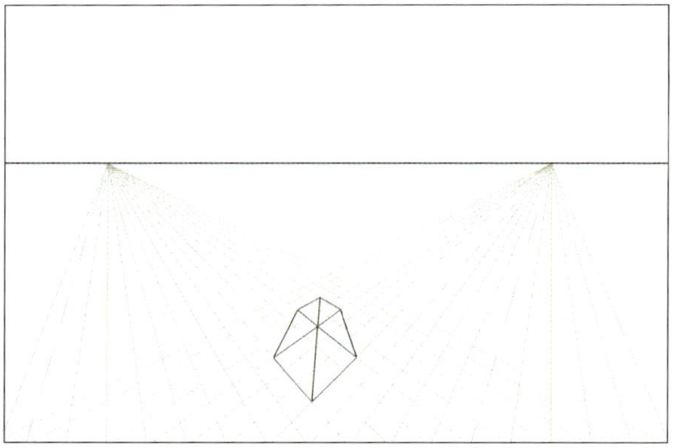

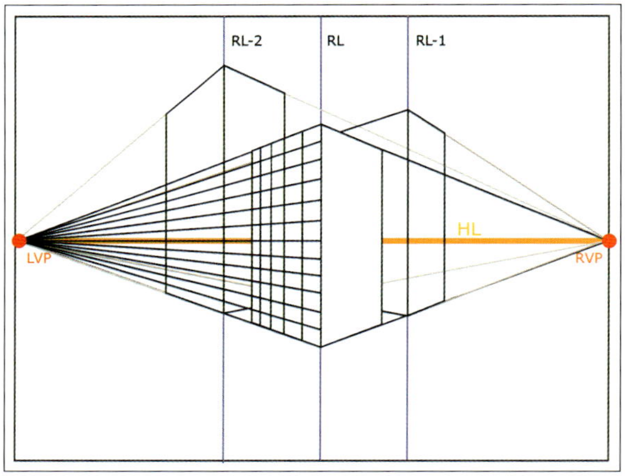


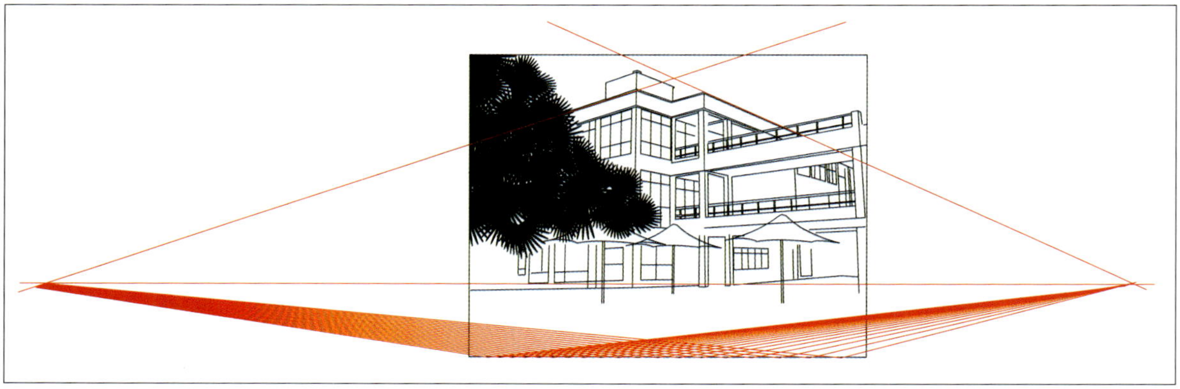

## 3-Point Perspective

The 3-point perspective uses three vanishing points, including the right and left vanishing points on the horizon line and one vertical vanishing point above or below the horizon (see Figure 9-17).

To draw three vanishing points, the left and right vanishing points are placed on the horizon line (LVP and RVP, Figure 9-18). Then a central vanishing point (CVP, Figure 9-18) is placed above or below the horizon. Figure 9-18 sets the central vanishing point on the same level as the horizon line. Figure 9-19 uses a central vanishing point above the horizontal line and left and the right vanishing points outside the image frame.

1 2
3

1 Figure 9-17. The 3-point perspective has horizontal and vertical points

2 Figure 9-18. 3 points vanishing: 2 points horizontal and vanishing and vertical vanishing point

3 Figure 9-19. A central vanishing point above the horizon

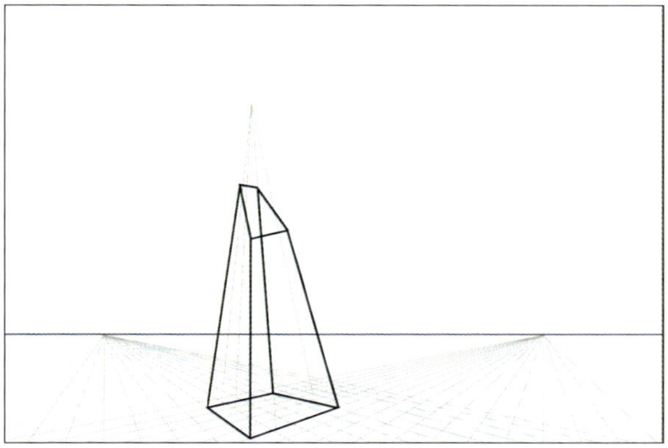

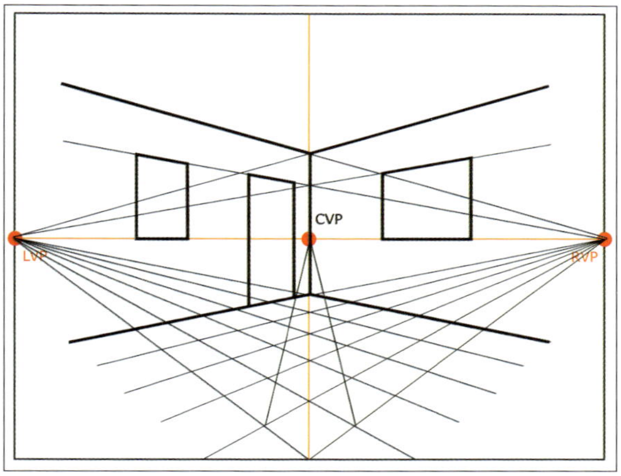


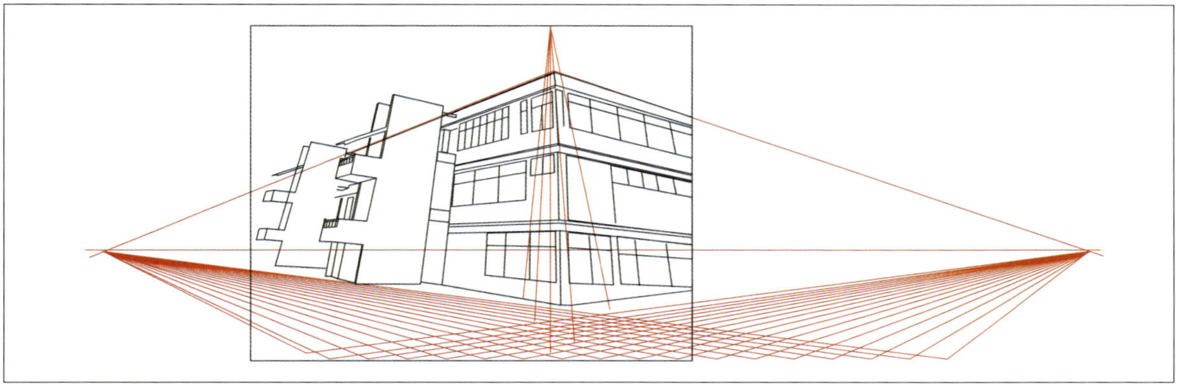

## Perspective and Layout

A 3-dimensional form and perspective are often used for a layout design to bring about visual interest and reality. A 3-dimensional spatial format may be a more effective and persuasive presentation because people live in 3-dimensional space. Figure 9-20 is an example of an interface design using a metaphor of a reception desk. There are hot spots indicating where the user is able to access to and the red arrows guiding direction in which the user moves.

A 3-dimensional space used for an interface design encourages familiarity and assimilation in terms of the user's experience. Figure 9-21 is an interface design using a landscape as a background. The hill landscape arouses a sense of tranquility and peacefulness. Three-dimensional perspectives in layout design can grab the user's attention and encourage their participation, thereby enhancing the interactive experience.

1 2

1 Figure 9-20. Interface design using a reception desk
2 Figure 9-21. A hilly landscape enhances the interactive experience

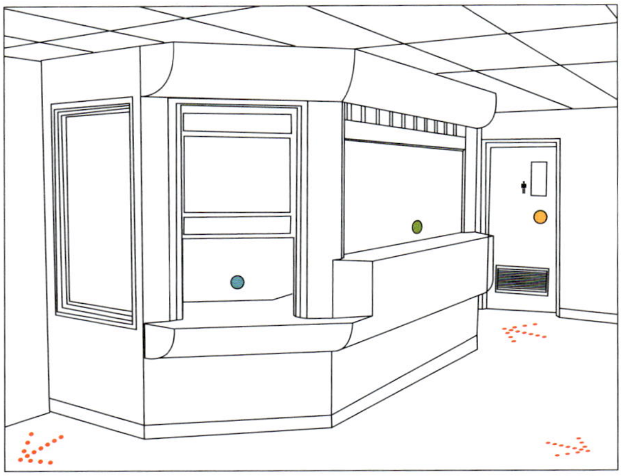

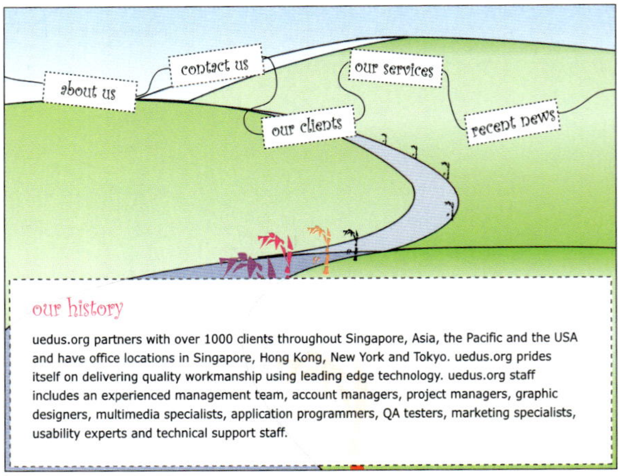

# Origami

Origami is the Japanese name for the art of paper folding. The folding technique is good practice for developing a sense of three-dimensional design.

Origami is applied to create a concept of the layout design that, when used as material for an interface design, can stimulate the user's interest. Figure 9-22 shows three origami ducks and one swan associated with Hans Christian Anderson's "Ugly Duckling" story.

In Figure 9-23, the previous image has been reproduced in a poster format with added graphics: an image of the "ugly duckling," the story title, and additional graphics.

1 2

1 **Figure 9-22.** Origami depicts characters from the "Ugly Duckling" story

2 **Figure 9-23.** Ugly duckling origami layout poster

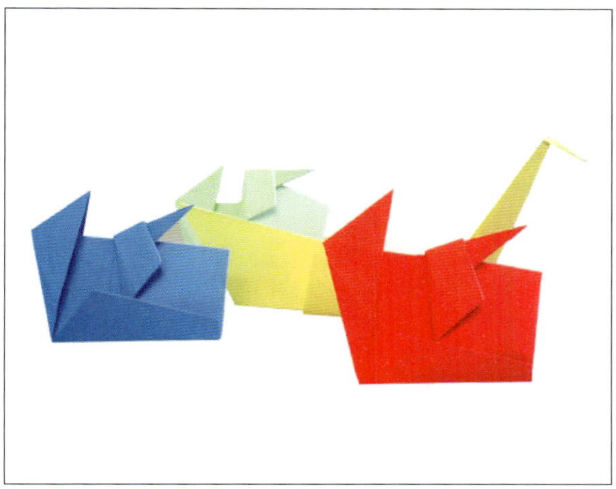

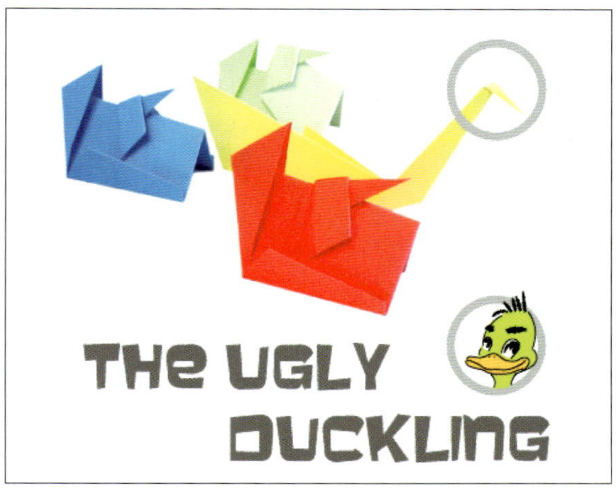

Figures 9-24 and 9-25 are additional examples of using folded paper for a visual work. Figure 9-24 shows paper folded at regular intervals and Figure 9-25 shows paper used as a background for a sign for a baby changing table.

1 2

1 **Figure 9-24.** Origami paper folded accordion-style

2 **Figure 9-25.** Folded paper used as background for a baby changing sign

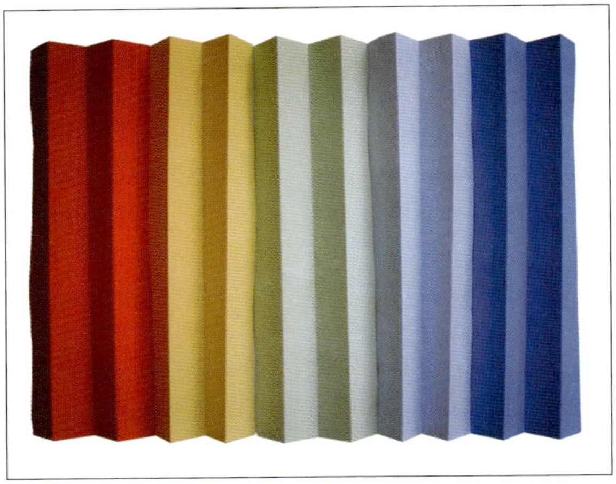

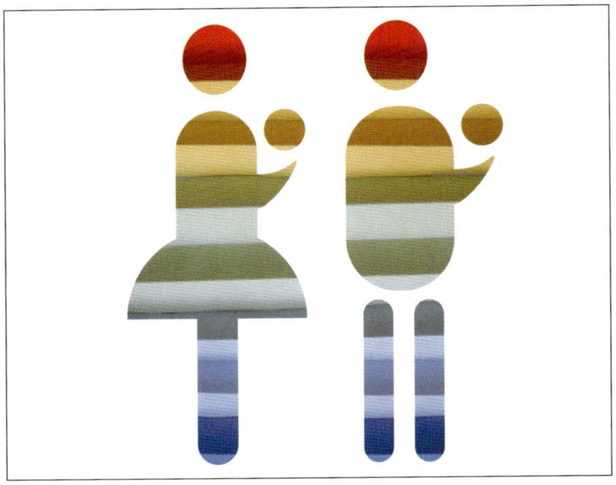

# Design Studio:
# Aluminum Foil Package Design

The objective of this activity is to cultivate your sense of 3-dimensional design.

Your task is to create an interface design for the aluminum foil package. You don't have to print it out and develop a real package, but you should keep the real form in mind while designing the interface. Consider using a metaphor for this package design with an emotional appeal. For example, an interface of a household pet produces a feeling of comfortable familiarity, while an interface design of animals such as frogs and monkeys suggests a more exotic, exciting feel.

- Choose an animal that can appeal to the customer emotionally
- Draw a drawing plan for the aluminum foil package, as in Figure 9-26
- Illustrate and stylize the animal to fit the format, as shown in Figure 9-27

Package design helps you to foster a sense of 3-dimensionality. Dealing with a package or brainstorming to create a unique package design requires the creator to understand the functions and use of the package and the procedure for usage. While developing a package design, consider every step of the process from the 3-dimensional aspect and from the customer's perspective.

As Figure 9-26 shows, the drawing plan has to be done correctly and accurately in terms of measurements and functions. The drawing plan helps the designer to imagine a finished form.

Once you complete the drawing plan, you are ready to design the interface. While designing the interface, it is still necessary to consider the finished form in order to apply graphics correctly. The metaphor of the interface design is inspired by a tree frog. The aim is to produce a stylized and friendly aluminum foil package. Figure 9-27 is a finished form of the interface design.

Figure 9-28 is the finished work seen from various perspectives. You don't have to do this final step, but if possible, you can create the final form of the package using a design program such as Adobe Illustrator or Photoshop. Like a real package design, the digital design also demands the same techniques, such as cutting, pasting, and 3-dimensional transformation.

1 3
2

1 Figure 9-26. Drawing plan for aluminum foil package design

2 Figure 9-27. Design for an interface package styled like a green frog

3 Figure 9-28. Finished interface package design

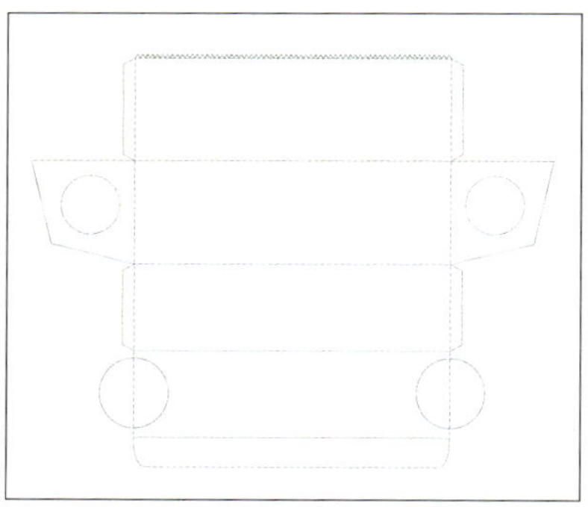

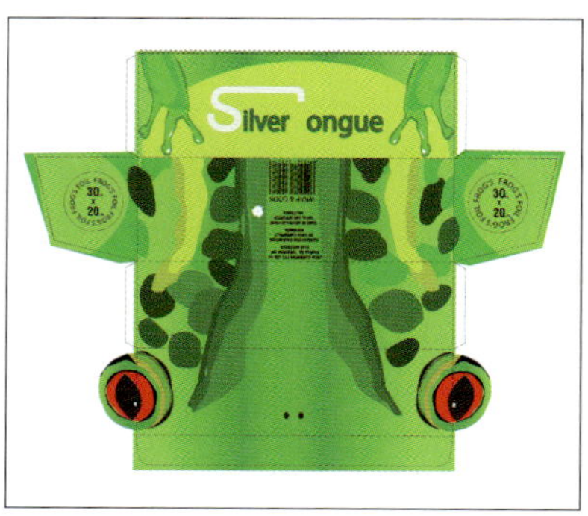


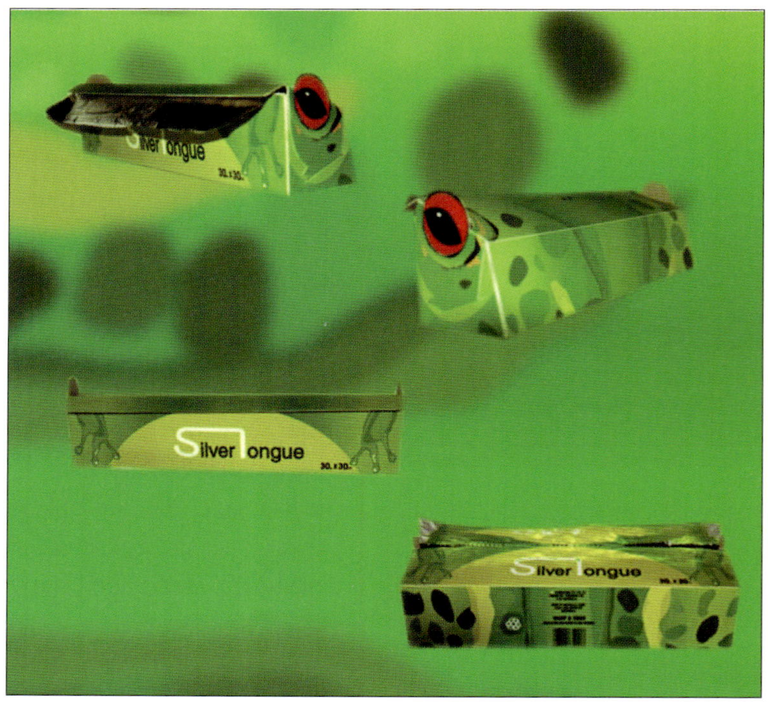

# Student Gallery
## Package Design - Digital Format

The objective of this activity is to create a package design using aluminum foil.

- Choose an animal which can appeal to the customer emotionally
- Illustrate the animal to fit the format provided

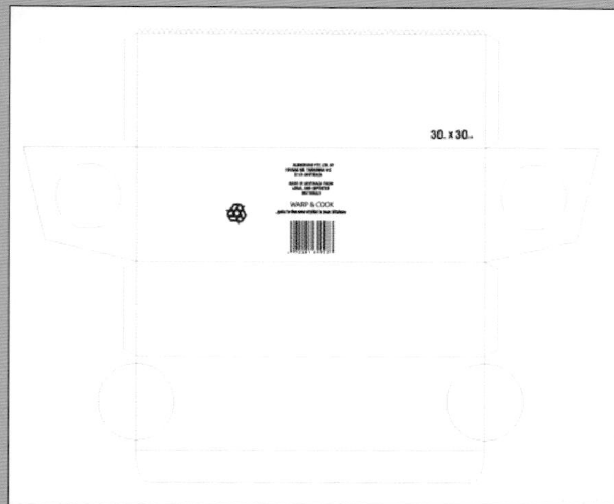


- Software: Adobe Illustrator CS2 and Photoshop CS2
- Dimension: the same size of the interface supplied
- Format: publish a gif or a jpg format (depending on the image quality and file size) from your work

### Marking Criteria (possible marks: 10)

Student will receive one of the marks in the following:

- 9 – 10: Successful design with creative solutions and professional finish
- 7 – 8: Successful design, but insufficient creativity and finish
- 5 – 6: Adequate, but lack of experiment or creativity
- 3 – 4: Inadequate, partly misunderstanding
- 2 – 0: Wrong theme or no submission

## Student Works - Dynamic Layout

- Natalie Gaye Clarke 2007

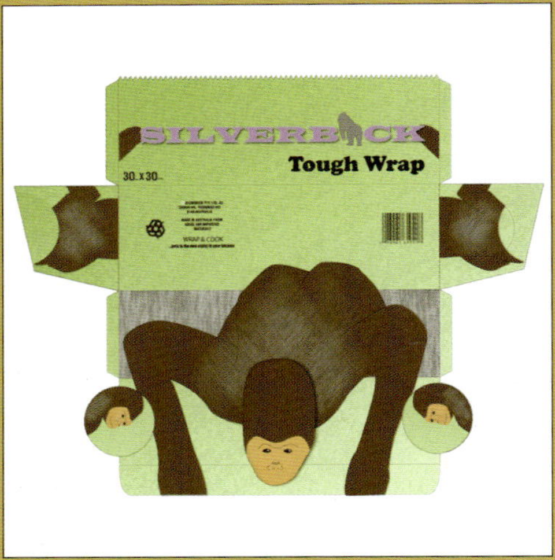


Natalie applied a monkey metaphor into a package for a plastic food wrap named 'Tough Wrap.' The drawing of the monkeys creates friendliness and intimacy and the elements are arranged well for being fitted into the 3–dimensional surface.

- Bradley John Acutt 2006

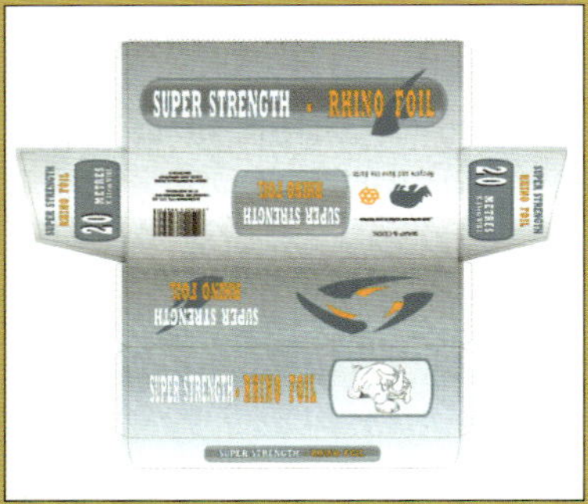


- Krista Avila 2007

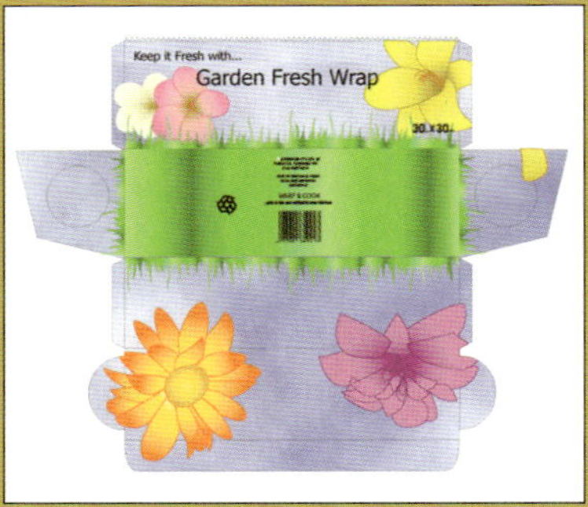


- Elise Sondergeld 2007

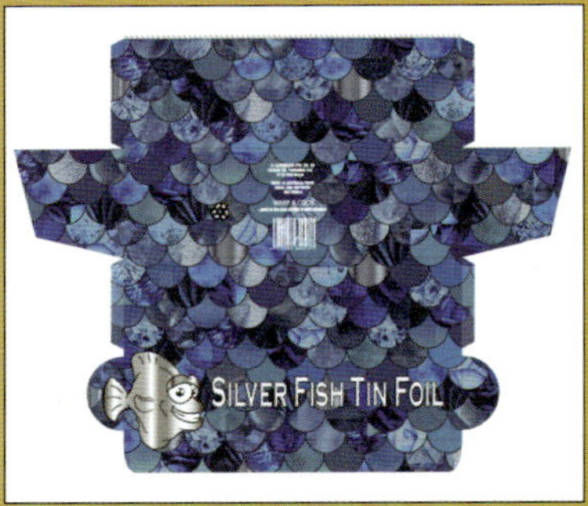


- Karina Maree Voss 2007

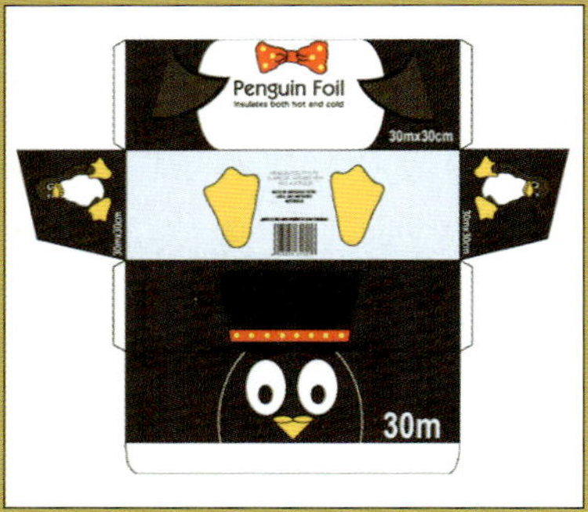

Chapter

# [ 10 ]

# Typography

Traditionally typography refers to the art and technique of designing letterforms, but in visual design it means the arrangement and appearance of text on a page or a screen. In addition, the art and technique of expression with animated text is called kinetic typography. Typography in visual design concerns the most effective way to control text and other design elements according to the design objectives.

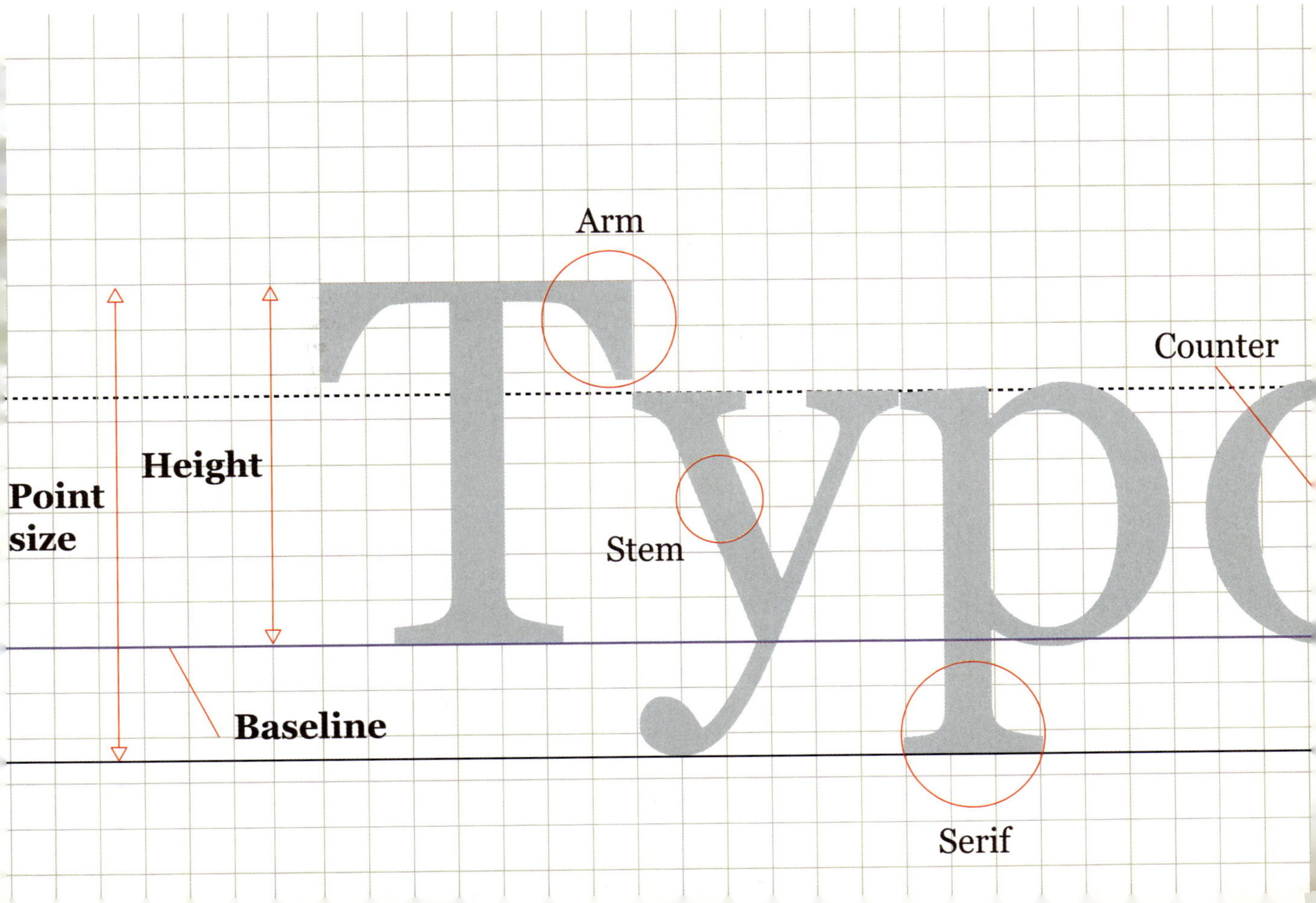

# Terminology

Typography provides the most important and fundamental understanding of graphic design. It covers layout, color, shape, form, and so on. However, this section will not be dealing with how to create a typeface, but will instead focus on how text information functions as a visual design element.

Figures 10-1 and 10-2 present terminology in typography with letters in Georgia typeface. There are many more characteristics in typography that would require a more in-depth review. Fur further study of typography, read technical books on the subject. The following two figures intend to give you a brief introduction to common terms that define the visual structure of letters. It is not necessary to memorize all of them, but the terms will help you to be familiar with the structural view of the letterform and understand the text's function and aesthetic form.

Some of the terms used in the figures are defined below:

- **Arm**: The horizontal stroke on some letters, such as the top of the capital T and the horizontal strokes of the F and E.
- **Ascender**: The upward vertical stem on some lowercase letters, such as b, h, and l that are above the x-height.
- **Apex**: The point at the top of a character, such as the uppercase A.
- **Bar (cross bar)**: The horizontal stroke across the middle of uppercase A and H.
- **Baseline**: Visible bottom line of letters that can align with the uppercase or some lowercase letters.
- **Bowl**: The curved or circular part of the uppercase C and D and the lowercase b, o, and p.
- **Counter**: The enclosed or partially enclosed circular and curved

space of some letters, such as d, o, and s.

- **Descender**: The downward vertical stem on some lowercase letters, such as g and p, that is below the x-height.
- **Ear**: A decorative flourish usually on the upper right side of the bowl, such as on a lowercase.
- **Hairline**: The thinnest stroke.
- **Kerning**: The adjustment of distance between specific pairs of characters.
- **Leading**: The space between lines of text.
- **Link**: A curved stroke that connects the bowl and loop of a double-story.
- **Loop**: The enclosed and partially enclosed counter below the baseline that is connected to the bowl by a link.
- **Serif**: The little extra stroke found at the end of main vertical and horizontal strokes of some letterforms.
- **Spline**: The main left to right curving stroke in S and s.
- **Stem**: The main vertical stroke of a letterform.
- **Tail**: The decorative curved stroke in the descender, such as on g, j, and y.
- **Terminal**: The end of a stroke in sans-serif letterform.
- **Tracking**: The adjustment of space for the whole body of text.
- **Height**: The height of a lowercase x in a particular font. The x-height is a factor in typeface identification and readability.

1
2

1 Figure 10-1. Typography terms
2 Figure 10-2. More typography terms

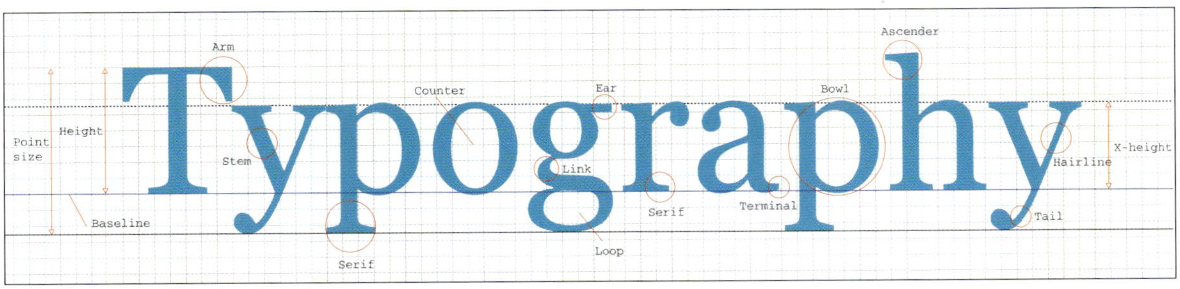


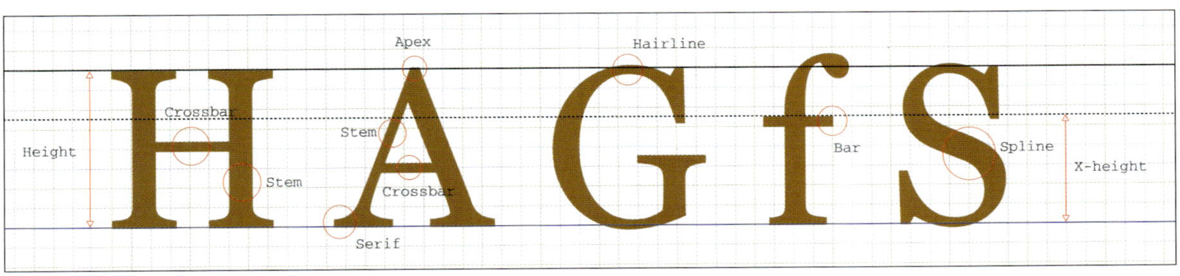

# Typeface Attributes

When selecting (or creating) a typeface, consider certain attributes: weight, width, posture, and whether it is serif or sans-serif. These four attributes determine the structural features of a typeface.

## Weight

Type weight refers to how thick a given character is. Typefaces can look heavy, light, or slender. There is a wide range of weights, including extra light, light, semi-light, regular, medium, semi-bold, bold, extra-bold, and ultra-bold. In general, however, these can be classified with three types: Regular, Bold, and Light. The range of weights available for a typeface will vary. Figure 10-3 is an example of various weights for the Arial typeface. Notice how the different weights "feel."

Regular is the standard weight class. Regular typefaces are almost always used for the main body of a text document because they are more readable than bold and light typefaces. Bold typefaces are heavier and slightly wider than regular ones. They are mainly used for emphasizing text such as a title or headline. Italic typefaces are mainly used to emphasize words, sentences, or paragraphs within the body of a text. Light typefaces are slender and lighter than regular. They are often used for creating a minimalist look.

| | |
|---|---|
| HOW DO I LOOK? | Arial Regular 14pt |
| *HOW DO I LOOK?* | *Arial Italic 14pt* |
| **HOW DO I LOOK?** | **Arial Bold 14pt** |
| ***HOW DO I LOOK?*** | ***Arial Bold Italic 14pt*** |
| **HOW DO I LOOK?** | **Arial Black Regular 14pt** |
| HOW DO I LOOK? | Arial Narrow Regular 14pt |
| *HOW DO I LOOK?* | *Arial Narrow Italic 14pt* |
| **HOW DO I LOOK?** | **Arial Narrow Bold 14pt** |
| ***HOW DO I LOOK?*** | ***Arial Narrow Bold Italic 14pt*** |

**Figure 10-3.** Arial typeface and weights in a comparative line-up

## Width

Typefaces have a variety of widths that are generally categorized into two types: condensed and extended. A condensed form is one where letters are closer together, creating a tighter letterform than the standard. Conversely, an extended form is wider than the standard. Figure 10-4 shows the condensed form of the Gill Sans typeface and the extended form of the Eurostile-Roman-DTC typeface.

When a typeface is created by a professional, it is designed with proportion and balance. It is unwise to change the width of a typeface without good reason; not using a given typeface's width is likely to break its structural aesthetic and destroy its beauty.

| | |
|---|---|
| HOW DO I LOOK? | Gill Sans MT 14pt |
| HOW DO I LOOK? | Gill Sans MT Condensed 14pt |
| **HOW DO I LOOK?** | **Gill Sans MT Ext Condensed 14pt** |
| HOW DO I LOOK? | Eurostile-Roman-DTC 14pt |
| HOW DO I LOOK? | EurostileExtended-Roman-DTC 14pt |

**Figure 10-4.** Standard, condensed, and extended width typefaces

## Posture

Type posture refers to the inclination of a typeface. It is a way of adding expression, such as activity, seriousness, or whimsy to the typeface. Italic and oblique are the normal categorizations of posture. Italic types slant to the right and are used for emphasis of text. The degree of slant for each letter in an italic typeface is different. The inclination of each letterform has been adjusted to maintain a good visual balance. Oblique types also slant, but the letters all slant at the same angle without exception.

Figure 10-5 shows the difference between italic and oblique forms in the same typeface, Bodoni MT. The second line is the italic and the third line is oblique with a slope of 10 degrees. To emphasize the difference, the fourth line shows both postures with the italic form in black overlaying the oblique form in orange. In the italic posture, some letters have different inclinations, such as the letter W, and the kerning has been adjusted.

| | |
|---|---|
| HOW DO I LOOK? | Bodoni MT Regular 14pt |
| *HOW DO I LOOK?* | *Bodoni MT Italic 14pt* |
| *HOW DO I LOOK?* | Bodoni MT Regular 14pt: a slope of 10 degrees |
| *HOW DO I LOOK?* | *Italic VS.* a slope of 10 degrees |

■ Figure 10-5. A comparison of italic and oblique typeface postures

## Serif and Sans-Serif

Typefaces can be divided in two visual classes: serif and sans-serif. Serif typefaces have curls and small appendixes on the extremities of the characters to aid in reading recognition. The serifs help the reader's eye connect a sequence of letters. Serif typefaces are commonly used for print media, such as newspapers and books. Serif typefaces are suitable for the bodies of printed texts. In titles and headlines, however, serif fonts reduce the visual sense of simplicity and clarity. Sans-serif typefaces (typefaces with no serif) are more appropriate for headlines and titles, as they are simple and unadorned. Figures 10-6 and 10-7 show examples of sans-serif and serif typefaces.

Be aware that mixing more than three typefaces in a page can severely reduce readability, especially if mixing multiple serif and sans-serif typefaces. However, whether the typefaces have serifs is not the prime factor in determining readability. Rather, font size, leading, and kerning (or tracking) are priorities in readability.

| sans-serif, 24pt | Arial Regular |
|---|---|
| | Century Gothic Regular |
| | GilSans Regular |
| | Tahoma Regular |
| | Verdana Regular |

| serif, 24 pt | Baskerville Old Face Regular |
|---|---|
| | Bookman Regular |
| | CenturyOldStyle Regular |
| | Georgia Regular |
| | times New Roman Regular |

1 Figure 10-6. Examples of sans-serif fonts
2 Figure 10-7. Examples of serif fonts

# Suggestions for Web Typography

Good typography can be produced through a combination of scientific approach and creative solutions. The scientific approach considers how various features of online situations affect typography. Creativity is required to effectively integrate typography with other design elements for a cohesive graphic design.

## Choosing a Font

Selection of typefaces is limited in online situations, and only some default fonts provided by the Internet browser may be available. If a chosen typeface might not be installed on the viewer's computer or device, the font must be embedded for the viewer's browser to display it. Embedding a font within a web page requires font embedding technology and the perpetual license to distribute it.

Even with limited fonts, there are still many decisions to be made. Font selection is usually determined by the content and structure of the text information. Texts are classified according to their function, such as headline and body text. The simplicity of a sans-serif typeface can emphasize the importance of a headline. Body text should be either serif or sans-serif but no smaller than 10 points in size. Fonts in diverse text formats, such as headlines, captions, and quotations, should be harmonized in terms of visual balance and readability so that they are neither too similar nor incompatible.

Font size, leading, kerning (tracking), and font color are considerable factors that determine degrees of readability. For example, the following are attributes of Times New Roman that give it an optimistic feel: 12-point font size, 13-point leading, and a color scheme for the font and its background that uses complimentary or adjacent complimentary colors.

Font size can seriously affect the readability of text on the web. For example, small font sizes, such as six or seven points, are readable in print media, but less than 10 points may be unreadable on the web.

## Leading and Legibility

The most influential factor in typographic legibility is leading. Leading refers to the space between lines of text. Figures 10-8 and 10-9 display the body text using different leading values. Figure 10-9 uses greater leading and is more comfortable to read and less visually tense.

15cm (425 pixels)

Most Internet browsers apply leading that is 10 percent larger in points than the font size. For example, when a 12-point font is used, the browser applies approximately 13.2 points for the leading. However, the leading may need to be adjusted according to the amount of text and length of rows. If you select a 12-point font and leave the default leading value, the length of each row should not be more than about six inches (425 pixels). At this font size, row lengths longer than six inches cause the reader to hunt for the next line or skip it entirely. That is to say, the longer the row length, the greater the leading needs to be. The importance of proper leading is due to the fact that the average reading speed on the web is 30% slower than for print.

Arial Regular 12 pt, **leading 14.4 pt**

15cm (425 pixels)

Most Internet browsers apply leading that is 10 percent larger in points than the font size. For example, when a 12-point font is used, the browser applies approximately 13.2 points for the leading. However, the leading may need to be adjusted according to the amount of text and length of rows. If you select a 12-point font and leave the default leading value, the length of each row should not be more than about six inches (425 pixels). At this font size, row lengths longer than six inches cause the reader to hunt for the next line or skip it entirely. That is to say, the longer the row length, the greater the leading needs to be. The importance of proper leading is due to the fact that the average reading speed on the web is 30% slower than for print.

Arial Regular 12 pt, **leading 18 pt**

1 Figure 10-8. Smaller leading is visually tense
2 Figure 10-9. Larger leading is easier to read

Most Internet browsers apply leading that is 10 percent larger in points than the font size. For example, when a 12-point font is used, the browser applies approximately 13.2 points for the leading. However, the leading may need to be adjusted according to the amount of text and length of rows. If you select a 12-point font and leave the default leading value, the length of each row should not be more than about six inches (425 pixels). At this font size, row lengths longer than six inches cause the reader to hunt for the next line or skip it entirely. That is to say, the longer the row length, the greater the leading needs to be. The importance of proper leading is due to the fact that the average reading speed on the web is 30% slower than for print. In general, designers try to put about 40 to 50 characters or about 9 to 10 words into each row of body text.

It is also important to consider that type displayed on a Windows web browser will look two to three points larger than the equivalent typeface on a Macintosh. Windows operating systems use a 96ppi (points per inch) display setting, while Macintosh uses 72ppi.

## Scrolling

In printed text, such as newspapers and books, the average reader grasps the visual structure of the whole text and then starts to read. On the other hand, as shown in Figure 10-10, a web browser window is limited as to the amount of text that is visible at a given time, and the user may have to click pages forward and backward, or scroll up and down repeatedly, to understand the whole structure. In the case of important and large amounts of text, most people prefer to print a hard copy to read.

Scrolling a web page up and down often causes a user to give up reading. Scrolling a page prevents the user from following the flow of text from top to bottom and breaks the visual structure of the text. Scrolling pages makes the user too busy. Page-based view is a better way to display large amounts of text information. Just as turning the page of a book refreshes the reader before moving to the next page, so clicking the next page link on a web page provides the user a short break. Alternatively, you can display a summary of the text information on a web page and provide a printable version as an option (see Figure 10-11).

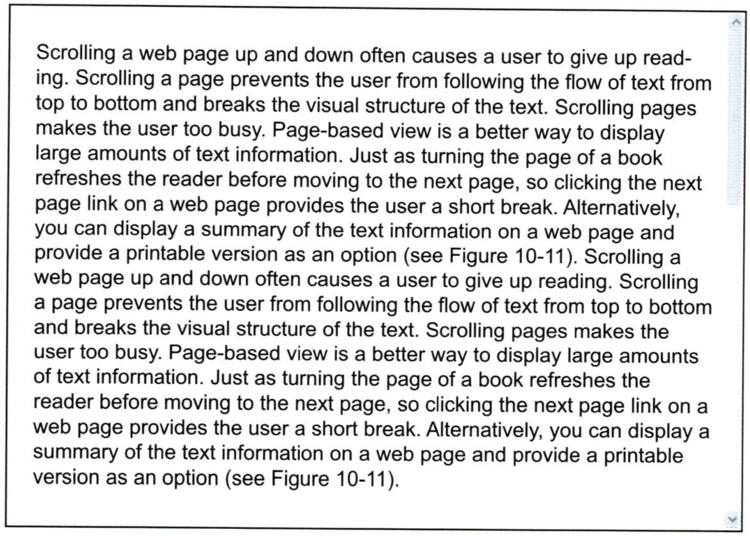

Scrolling a web page up and down often causes a user to give up reading. Scrolling a page prevents the user from following the flow of text from top to bottom and breaks the visual structure of the text. Scrolling pages makes the user too busy. Page-based view is a better way to display large amounts of text information. Just as turning the page of a book refreshes the reader before moving to the next page, so clicking the next page link on a web page provides the user a short break. Alternatively, you can display a summary of the text information on a web page and provide a printable version as an option (see Figure 10-11). Scrolling a web page up and down often causes a user to give up reading. Scrolling a page prevents the user from following the flow of text from top to bottom and breaks the visual structure of the text. Scrolling pages makes the user too busy. Page-based view is a better way to display large amounts of text information. Just as turning the page of a book refreshes the reader before moving to the next page, so clicking the next page link on a web page provides the user a short break. Alternatively, you can display a summary of the text information on a web page and provide a printable version as an option (see Figure 10-11).

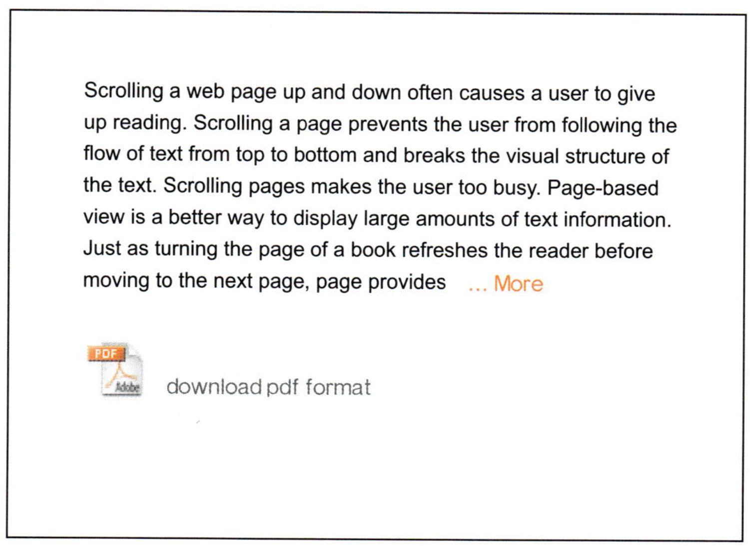

Scrolling a web page up and down often causes a user to give up reading. Scrolling a page prevents the user from following the flow of text from top to bottom and breaks the visual structure of the text. Scrolling pages makes the user too busy. Page-based view is a better way to display large amounts of text information. Just as turning the page of a book refreshes the reader before moving to the next page, page provides ... More



1 Figure 10-10. Grasping the structure of text is hindered by scrolling

2 Figure 10-11. Providing a printed version of a web page is often appreciated

## Word Spacing (Kerning and Tracking)

Both kerning and tracking in typography refer to the adjustment of space between characters. Both of these factors of adjustment affect the amount of positive and negative space on a graphic plane. Kerning is the process of adding or subtracting space between specific pairs of characters, whereas tracking is the adjustment of space for the whole body of text. Tracking can change the visual appearance and affect the readability of the text. It is important to know that appropriately controlling kerning and tracking contributes to a professional level of design and helps to foster a subtle sense of visuality.

In web site design, many designers prefer to use CSS (cascading style sheets), which allows adjustment of word spacing and leading, whereas regular HTML does not. Spacing that is too tight causes words to become indistinguishable; however, too wide of spacing reduces legibility. Word spacing looks tighter on the web than in print, but there is no standard for it. Ideally, the reader will read the text smoothly and rhythmically, and will not need to reread a row.

Word spacing affects how many words you can put in a row. As stated above, with a 12-point font size, the length of a row should be no more than about six inches. In other words, about 40 words should be placed in a row. Another method for examining word spacing is to put a lowercase i between a set of words and judge the visual balance of spacing on either side of the letter. Figures 10-12 and 10-13 show the same paragraph using different letter spacing, line height, and word spacing. Figure 10-13 is much more readable and pleasing to the eye.

Kerning is the process of adding or subtracting space between specific pairs of characters, whereas tracking is the adjustment of space for the whole body of text. Tracking can change the visual appearance and affect the readability of the text. It is important to know that appropriately controlling kerning and tracking contributes to a professional level of design and helps to foster a subtle sense of visuality.

**Times New Roman: 12 pt, letter-spacing: normal, line-height: normal, word-spacing: normal**

Kerning is the process of adding or subtracting space between specific pairs of characters, whereas tracking is the adjustment of space for the whole body of text. Tracking can change the visual appearance and affect the readability of the text. It is important to know that appropriately controlling kerning and tracking contributes to a professional level of design and helps to foster a subtle sense of visuality.

**Times New Roman: 12 pt, letter-spacing: 1 pt, line-height: 18pt, word-spacing: 1pt**

**1 2**

**1** Figure 10-12. Normal letter spacing can be harder to read

**2** Figure 10-13. One-point letter spacing is easier to read than normal spacing

## Indent and Outdent

Indenting the first line of a paragraph is common. Indentation helps the reader find the beginnings of and distinguish between separate paragraphs (see Figure 10-14). Indentation of a paragraph may not be necessary as long as a blank line is inserted between the paragraphs (see Figure 10-15).

**1 2**

**1** Figure 10-14. Indentation quickly identifies new paragraphs

**2** Figure 10-15. Blank lines also separate paragraphs

  Indenting the first line of a paragraph is common. Indentation helps the reader find the beginnings of and distinguish between separate paragraphs (see Figure 10-14). Indentation of a paragraph may not be necessary as long as a blank line is inserted between the paragraphs (see Figure 10-15).

  In general, indentation uses em, or the width of the letter m in that font, as a standard unit. An em for a 12-point font would equal to 12 points, so 2em equals 24 points (12 points×2). An indentation of 2em may too strongly emphasize the paragraph. Alternatively, you can apply an indentation with two spaces using the space bar.

  Another alternative for distinguishing between paragraphs is to use an outdent. Outdented paragraphs may express a fresh and unique mood because this style is not as common (see Figure 10-16).

Arial 12 pt, text-indent: 12 pt

Indenting the first line of a paragraph is common. Indentation helps the reader find the beginnings of and distinguish between separate paragraphs (see Figure 10-14). Indentation of a paragraph may not be necessary as long as a blank line is inserted between the paragraphs (see Figure 10-15).

In general, indentation uses em, or the width of the letter m in that font, as a standard unit. An em for a 12-point font would equal to 12 points, so 2em equals 24 points (12 points×2). An indentation of 2em may too strongly emphasize the paragraph. Alternatively, you can apply an indentation with two spaces using the space bar.

Another alternative for distinguishing between paragraphs is to use an outdent. Outdented paragraphs may express a fresh and unique mood because this style is not as common (see Figure 10-16).

Arial 12 pt, Non-indent

In general, indentation uses em, or the width of the letter m in that font, as a standard unit. An em for a 12-point font would equal 12 points, so 2em equals 24 points (12 points × 2). An indentation of 2em may too strongly emphasize the paragraph. Alternatively, you can apply an indentation with two spaces using the space bar.

Another alternative for distinguishing between paragraphs is to use an outdent. Outdented paragraphs may express a fresh and unique mood because this style is not as common (see Figure 10-16).

> Indenting the first line of a paragraph is common. Indentation helps the reader find the beginnings of and distinguish between separate paragraphs (see Figure 10-14). Indentation of a paragraph may not be necessary as long as a blank line is inserted between the paragraphs (see Figure 10-15).
>
> In general, indentation uses em, or the width of the letter m in that font, as a standard unit. An em for a 12-point font would equal to 12 points, so 2em equals 24 points (12 points×2). An indentation of 2em may too strongly emphasize the paragraph. Alternatively, you can apply an indentation with two spaces using the space bar.
>
> Another alternative for distinguishing between paragraphs is to use an outdent. Outdented paragraphs may express a fresh and unique mood because this style is not as common (see Figure 10-16).

Arial 12 pt, text-indent: -12 pt

**Figure 10-16.** Outdentation provides a unique approach

## Alignment

Text can be aligned in four ways: left-aligned, right-aligned, centered, and justified. The most common type is left-alignment, which is also the default alignment in Internet browsers. The main disadvantage of using left-aligned text is that the rows differ in length, which may make it difficult to locate the next line and increases eye strain. As an example, compare the left-aligned paragraphs against the justified ones in Figure 10-17. However, this disadvantage is less serious than the drawbacks of the other alignment options.

As shown in the right-hand image in Figure 10-17, justified text has the advantage of creating the same margins on the left and right. It appears well-structured and visually stable, unlike the other alignments. However, it often creates uneven word spacing that can look crowded or too spread out. It also applies hyphenation to automatically narrow word spacing. As a result, you may need to look at each word or row in detail and adjust as necessary.

■ Figure 10-17. Left-aligned and justified text compared

Text can be aligned in four ways: left-aligned, right-aligned, centered, and justified. The most common type is left-alignment, which is also the default alignment in Internet browsers. The main disadvantage of using left-aligned text is that the rows differ in length, which may make it difficult to locate the next line and increases eye strain. As an example, compare the leftt-aligned paragraphs against the justified ones in Figure 10-17. However, this disadvantage is less serious than the drawbacks of the other alignment options.

As shown in the right-hand image in Figure 10-17, justified text has the advantage of creating the same margins on the left and right. It appears well-structured and visually stable, unlike the other alignments.

left-aligned text

Text can be aligned in four ways: left-aligned, right-aligned, centered, and justified. The most common type is left-alignment, which is also the default alignment in Internet browsers. The main disadvantage of using left-aligned text is that the rows differ in length, which may make it difficult to locate the next line and increases eye strain. As an example, compare the left-aligned paragraphs against the justified ones in Figure 10-17. However, this disadvantage is less serious than the drawbacks of the other alignment options.

As shown in the right-hand image in Figure 10-17, justified text has the advantage of creating the same margins on the left and right. It appears well-structured and visually stable, unlike the other alignments.

justified text

Right-aligned text (see the left-hand figure in Figure 10-18) is not often used because the beginnings of the lines are uneven.

For the same reason, center-aligned text is rarely used. Centered text (see Figure 10-19) is appropriate for headlines and sub-headlines. Both right-alignment and center-alignment are often used to emphasize short, narrow paragraphs.

1
2

1 Figure 10-18. Right-aligned text has an uneven and jagged appearance

2 Figure 10-19. Center-aligned text appears doubly jagged and uneven

Text can be aligned in four ways: left-aligned, right-aligned, centered, and justified. The most common type is left-alignment, which is also the default alignment in Internet browsers. The main disadvantage of using left-aligned text is that the rows differ in length, which may make it difficult to locate the next line and increases eye strain. As an example, compare the leftt-aligned paragraphs against the justified ones in Figure 10-17. However, this disadvantage is less serious than the drawbacks of the other alignment options.

As shown in the right-hand image in Figure 10-17, justified text has the advantage of creating the same margins on the left and right. It appears well-structured and visually stable, unlike the other alignments.

Text can be aligned in four ways: left-aligned, right-aligned, centered, and justified. The most common type is left-alignment, which is also the default alignment in Internet browsers. The main disadvantage of using left-aligned text is that the rows differ in length, which may make it difficult to locate the next line and increases eye strain.

Justified text has the advantage of creating the same margins on the left and right.

As an example, compare the left-aligned paragraphs against the justified ones in Figure 10-17. However, this disadvantage is less serious than the drawbacks of the other alignment options.

right-aligned text

Text can be aligned in four ways: left-aligned, right-aligned, centered, and justified. The most common type is left-alignment, which is also the default alignment in Internet browsers. The main disadvantage of using left-aligned text is that the rows differ in length, which may make it difficult to locate the next line and increases eye strain. As an example, compare the leftt-aligned paragraphs against the justified ones in Figure 10-17. However, this disadvantage is less serious than the drawbacks of the other alignment options.

As shown in the right-hand image in Figure 10-17, justified text has the advantage of creating the same margins on the left and right. It appears well-structured and visually stable, unlike the other alignments.

Text can be aligned in four ways: left-aligned, right-aligned, centered, and justified. The most common type is left-alignment, which is also the default alignment in Internet browsers. The main disadvantage of using left-aligned text is that the rows differ in length, which may make it difficult to locate the next line and increases eye strain.

Justified text has the advantage of creating the same margins on the left and right.

As an example, compare the left-aligned paragraphs against the justified ones in Figure 10-17. However, this disadvantage is less serious than the drawbacks of the other alignment options.

centered-aligned text

## Anti-Aliased

—

When fonts or graphics are displayed at different resolutions, distortion called “aliasing” can occur. Anti-aliasing is the process of inserting pixels of intermediate colors along boundary edges to minimize the distortion and smooth the images or type. It is useful for large display type but is not suitable for small type sizes, especially type that is 10 points or smaller. As shown in Figure 10-20, aliased small font sizes are easier to read than anti-aliased text.

Conversely, Figure 10-21 shows how anti-aliasing large text improves the text quality.

Anti-aliasing is the process of inserting pixels of intermediate colors along boundary edges to minimize the distortion and smooth the images or type. It is useful for large display type but is not suitable for small type sizes, especially type that is 10 points or smaller.

Antialiasing: Verdana Regular 10pt

Anti-aliasing is the process of inserting pixels of intermediate colors along boundary edges to minimize the distortion and smooth the images or type. It is useful for large display type but is not suitable for small type sizes, especially type that is 10 points or smaller.

Non-Antialiasing: Verdana Regular 10pt

Anti-aliasing is the process of inserting pixels of intermediate colors along boundary edges to minimize the distortion and smooth the images or type. It is useful for large display type but is not suitable for small type sizes,

Antialiasing: Verdana Regular 20pt

Anti-aliasing is the process of inserting pixels of intermediate colors along boundary edges to minimize the distortion and smooth the images or type. It is useful for large display type but is not suitable for small type sizes,

Non-Antialiasing: Verdana Regular 20pt

1
2

1 Figure 10-20. Anti-aliasing causes blur in small text

2 Figure 10-21. Anti-aliasing large text has a smoothing affect

# Design Studio: Visual Text Design

This activity involves the manipulation of letters to create a visual text design.

The guidelines for this activity follow:

- Manipulate the letters of the word so that they visually represent the word's meaning and the average person's common understanding of it.
- Use only Verdana (Windows) or Helvetica (Macintosh).
- Use only black and white.
- Do not add any graphics or images.
- The finished work must be readable.

**Choose one of the diseases or symptoms listed below:**

- Obesity
- Asthma
- Toothache
- Insomnia
- Pneumonia
- Anorexia
- Dementia
- Headache
- Somnambulism
- Schizoid

If someone is obese, they are extremely overweight. Figure 10-22 is an example of a visual text design for the word "obesity." The visual weight of the typeface is heavy and rounded to represent the condition.

Figure 10-23 is another example of a visual text design, this time using the word "anorexia." Anorexia is an illness in which a person has an overwhelming fear of becoming obese, and thus does not eat properly and becomes increasingly thin and malnourished. Figure 10-23 illustrates this disease with a typeface that is very thin and curved and seems too weak to stand upright.

1 2

1 Figure 10-22. The word "obesity" in a representative large, heavy font

2 Figure 10-23. The word "anorexia" using a thin, weak typeface

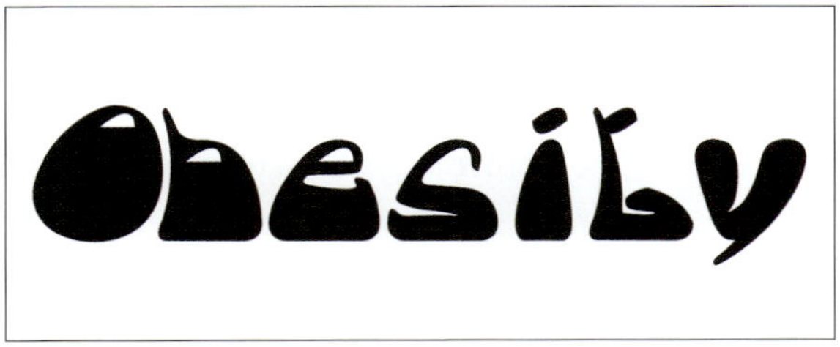


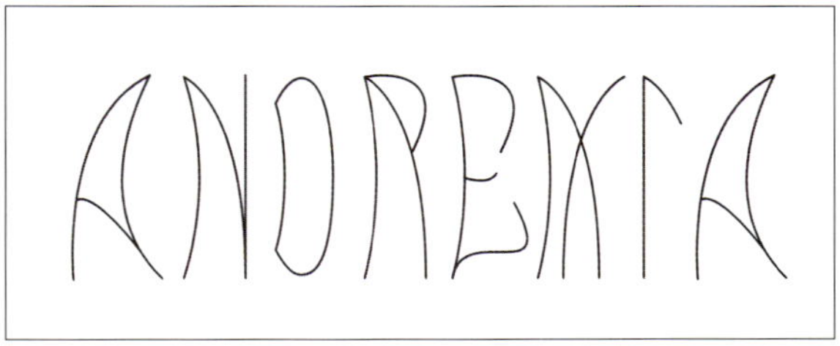


## Mock Testing

This exercise introduces a way of assessing a design in the real world. Create the front cover for a fictitious magazine. Decide on a name for the periodical and create a logo for it. Follow the layout format of other magazines by including the name, logo, graphics, and an issue number.

1 Figure 10-24. A cover design for double eyes magazine

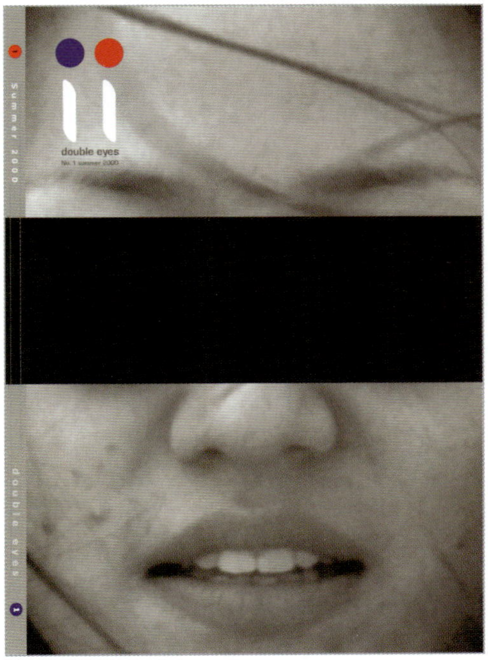


Figure 10-24 is a mock cover design for a fictitious magazine called "double eyes." The layout looks stable and balanced, and the background image presents a strong impression that attracts the viewer's attention.

In Figures 10-25, 10-26, and 10-27, to truly test the effectiveness of its composition, the magazine design has been placed among issues of real magazines as they are displayed on actual magazine stands.

This allows a new perspective to better judge the cover design in terms of the viewer's visual experience.

It is important to determine whether a design will work in a real environment. The viewer's perspective is the primary concern in commercial design. Those designing for web display should also test the design using the most common browser types, screen resolutions, and Internet bandwidth speeds of the site's target demographic.

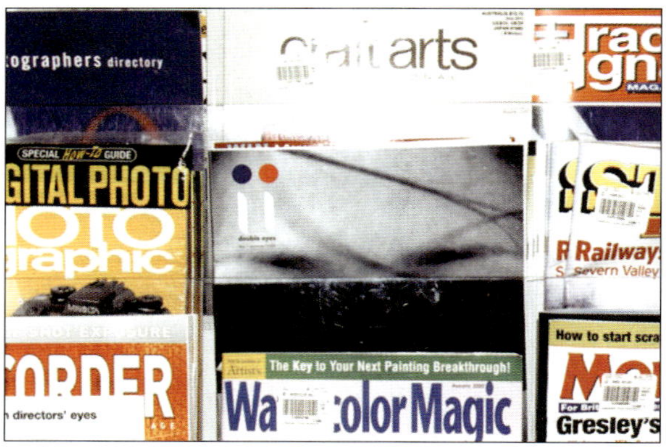


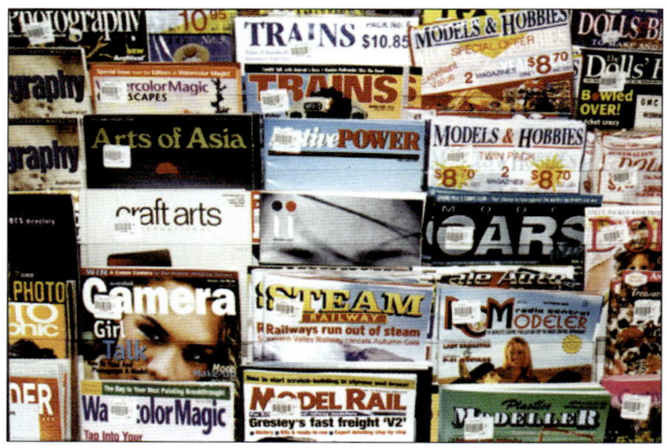


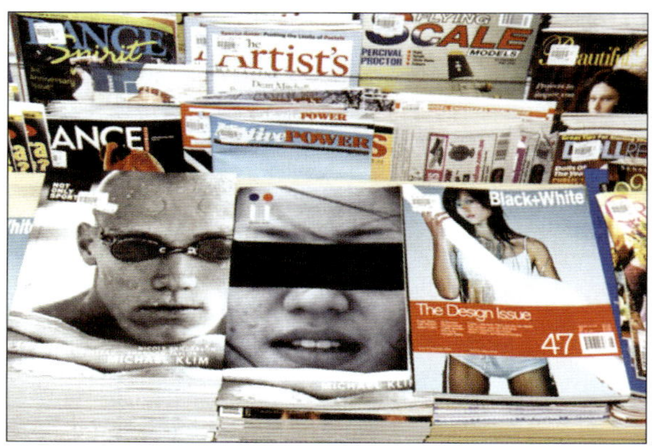


1 2
3

1 Figure 10-25. Double eyes squeezed in beside other periodicals on the stand

2 Figure 10-26. Double eyes magazine vies for attention among competitors

3 Figure 10-27. Double eyes more prominently displayed, laying flat and fully exposed

# Student Gallery
## Visual Text Design

You need to choose one of the words provided and manipulate the word to create a typographical design.

- Use that word only and do not add any other graphics or images.
- Use only Verdana (Windows) or Helvetica (Macintosh).
- Black and white version only
- The finished work must be readable

- Software: Adobe Illustrator CS2 and Photoshop CS2
- Dimension: Within 500 x 500 pixels
- Format: publish a gif format. Choose one of the following words;

| | | | |
|---|---|---|---|
| Happy | Love | Hate | Sad |
| Death | Life | Family | Friends |

### Marking Criteria (possible marks: 10)

Student will receive one of the marks in the following:

- 9 – 10: Successful design with creative solutions and professional finish
- 7 – 8: Successful design, but insufficient creativity and finish
- 5 – 6: Adequate, but lack of experiment or creativity
- 3 – 4: Inadequate, partly misunderstanding
- 2 – 0: Wrong theme or no submission

### Student Works - Dynamic Layout

- Karina Maree Voss 2007

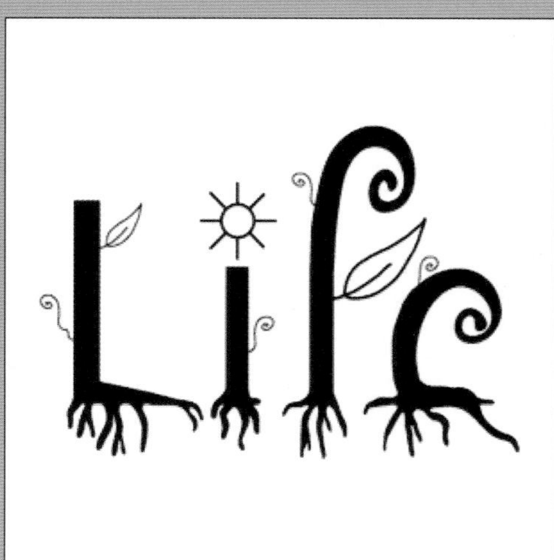


It is not easy to create a good visual balance between letters in typography because each letter has its own visual weight and size. The activity required visualizing the characters of the chosen word according to its word meaning. The work to the left done by Karina Voss completely expresses the meaning of 'life' by adopting the metaphor of plants.

Kaylene Court 2006

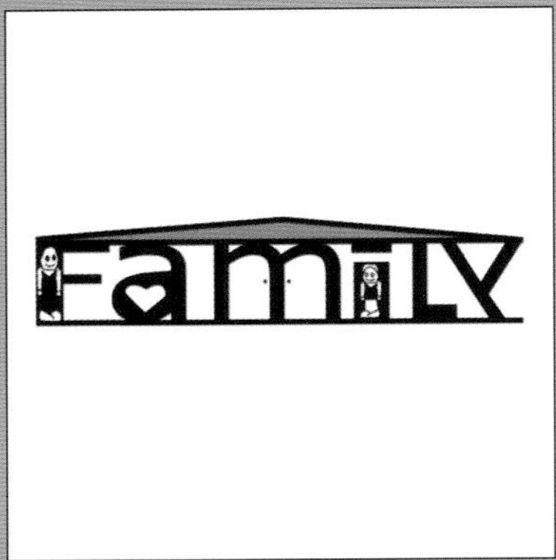


Michael Ignatius Horoba 2006

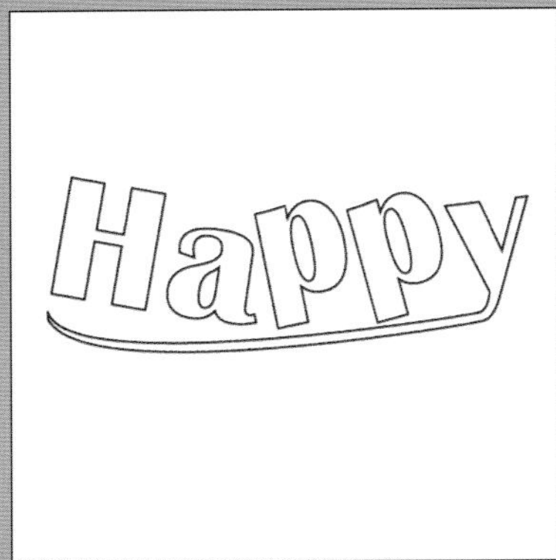


Joy Reynolds 2006

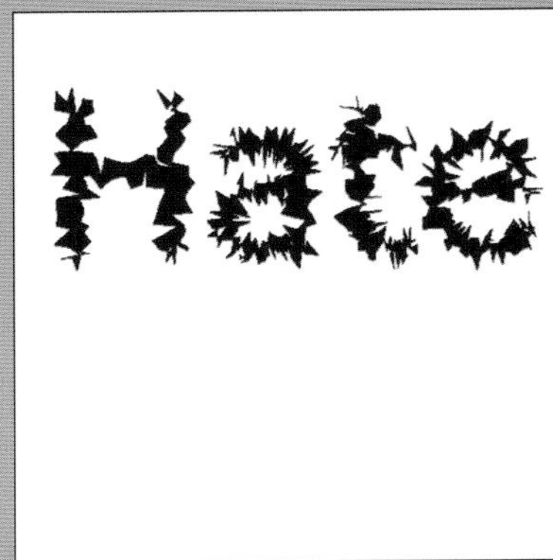


Douglas (Chak Cheung) Tsang 2006

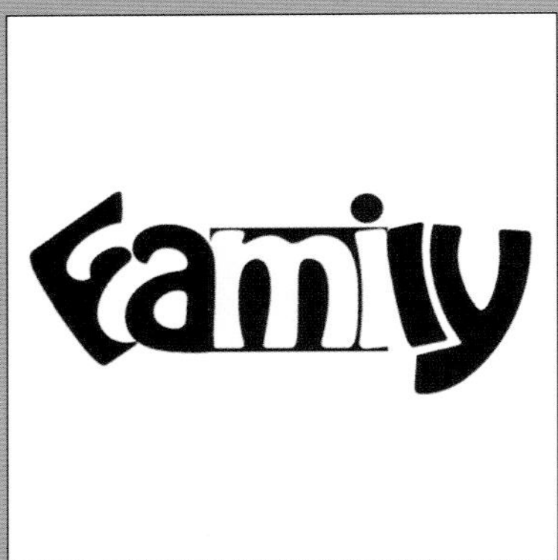


Krista Avila 2007

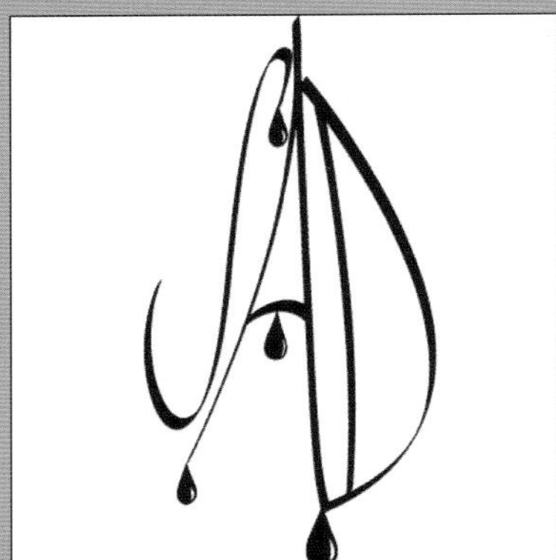

Natalie Gaye Clarke 2007

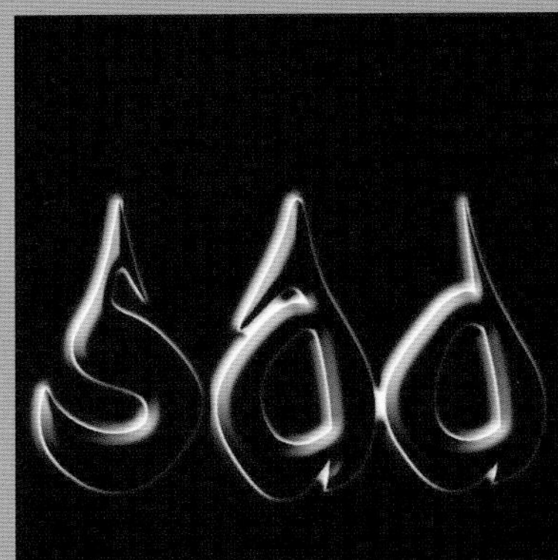


Justin Andrew Hawley 2007

Elise Sondergeld 2007

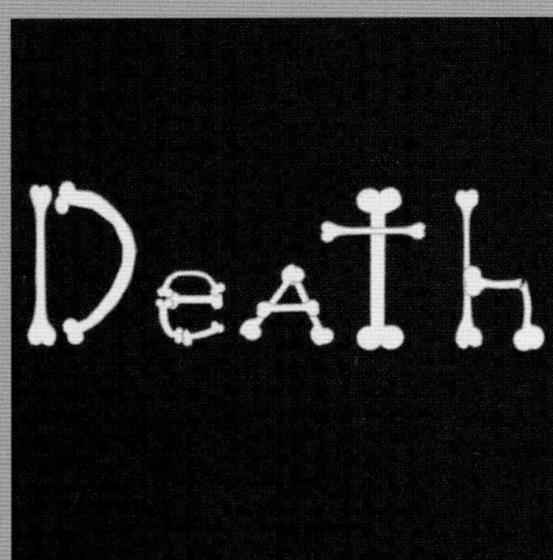

Chapter

# [ 11 ]

# Web Versus Print

The key difference between the print and web mediums is that the print design is based on paper and the web is a place where people actively exchange information. Visual communication in web design supports creating an interactive user experience in relation to the user engagement and communication.

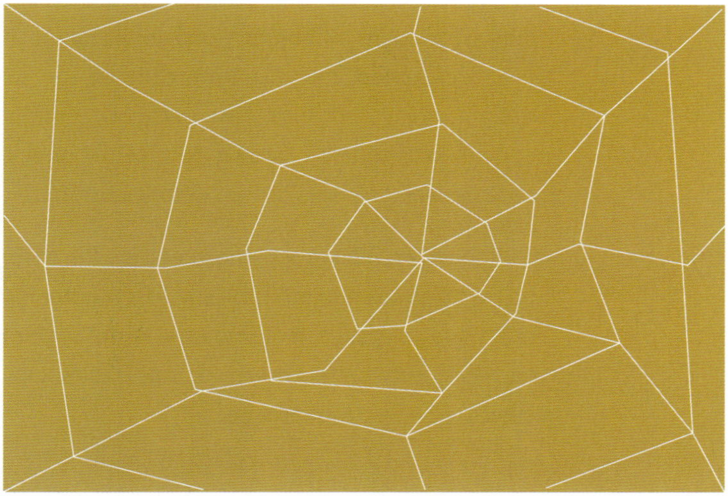

# Differences between Web and Print

Seeing is believing. What you see on paper is what it is. However in digital media, what you see on the computer screen may not be an accurate reflection of the original design.

There are important differences between print and web design that can affect the success of visual communication. Some principles of print media design cannot be successfully applied to digital media. The following tables illustrate some of the differences.

When a color appears in printed form, it can be viewed the same by everyone. However, not everyone sees the same color on the web due to variations in monitors, image resolution, and graphics cards. By the same token, not everyone can see the same fonts on a web design unless they have that particular typeface installed in their computer. In addition, people may see the same font in different sizes because web browsers allows users to customize the font size.

As shown in Table 11-1, the message (or theme) of an artwork is delivered to the audience through visual communication. On the web, the visual message is combined with functional communication because users often control or manipulate the design elements to meet their own requirements.

**Table 11-1.** Communication methods compared

| Print | Web |
|---|---|
| Visual communication in a predetermined layout | Visual and functional communication; design elements can be navigated by the user |

As explained in Table 11-1, resolution of images is different in both media. Print media requires much higher resolution than the web. However, both print and the web call for the best quality image. Web design is impacted by the image size (file storage) as well. For example, an image at 72 ppi (pixels per inch) should be appropriate for the screen view. More than 72 ppi does not improve the resolution, but it does increase the file size. However, an image suitable for the web usually does not have sufficient resolution for printing. This requires at least 150 ppi, and 300 ppi is common.

Table 11-2. Image quality compared

| Print | Web |
|---|---|
| 1200dpi * | 85 dpi: all web graphics should be no bigger than 72 ppi |

- Dpi is a measurement of printer resolution that measures in dots per inch, whereas ppi is a measurement of image resolution measured in pixels per inch. These are often used interchangeably, but there are important differences. Ppi can fluctuate, in that an image could be set to 72 ppi, 150 ppi, or 300 ppi, whereas dpi is the resolution of the printer, which is not flexible.

File formats of both media have to be chosen according to the purpose and the quality of the image (see Table 11-3). For example, only a GIF format supports a frame-by-frame animation.

Table 11-3. File format compared

| Print | Web |
|---|---|
| **TIFF**: Tagged-Image File Format<br>• Used for bitmaps only<br>• Stores the attributes of image data through tags | **GIF**: Graphics Interchange Format<br>• Limited to only 256 colors<br>• Supports transparent backgrounds<br>• Short time to release compression<br>• Creates animation<br>• Compression rate is 2:1<br>• Uses transparent color<br>• Creates Interlace image |
| **EPS**: Encapsulated PostScript<br>• Used for both vector graphics and bitmaps<br>• Embeds additional important data about a PostScript image or document | **JPGE**: Joint Photographic Experts Group<br>• Used for photographic (continuous tone) images<br>• High compression rate (variable compression rates)<br>• Creates Interlace image<br>• Loses quality when editing and saving<br>• Supports 24bit (16,000,000 colors) |

According to Table 11-4, there in no limitation in choosing typefaces in the print media, but the web has many limitations for not only choosing typefaces but also manipulating them. In most cases, however, the most important issues are the readability and legibility of text.

Table 11-4. Typeface compared

| Print | Web |
|---|---|
| Any typeface | Users must have the same typeface installed on their computers or the browser will substitute with the default typeface. For this reason, typeface selections are limited. Designers may convert an unusual typeface to an image, but this may cause technical and aesthetic complications. |

The color modes vary widely between these media. For web-based design, color modes can be converted at any time, but the variations in the color ranges may produce different results (see Table 11-5).

Table 11-5. Color mode compared

| Print | Web |
|---|---|
| **CMYK**: Cyan, Magenta, Yellow, and Black for full-color printing | **RGB**: Red, Green, and Blue for the digital screen. Technically, this mode can produce millions of colors, but web browsers may not be able to support those colors. But there are 216 colors that are known as web-safe colors. |

The final stage of graphic design is publication of the media on paper or electronic platforms. As shown in Table 11-6, print media considerations include paper thickness and texture, while web media is concerned with screen size and color quality.

Table 11-6. Paper versus screen

| Print | Web |
|---|---|
| • Paper thickness<br>• Texture<br>• Color<br>• Absorbency<br>• Inks | • Screen resolution (pixels): 800×600, 1024×768, 1280×1024<br>• Screen size (inches): 15, 17, 19, 21<br>• Color quality (bit): 8, 16, 32<br>• Monitor brand: Macintosh is brighter than Windows (high gamma display) |

# Considerations

For building a successful web design, the designer needs to concern the following issues: visuality, loading time, screen size, typography, browserability, image format, navigation, and visible area.

A print design is completed when it is published, but a web site requires maintenance and updates. The web site design is never complete, as it publishes constantly. The web is a much more interactive experience than print media. The user controls and manipulates the design elements and sequence of web pages. Print media focuses on communicating information to the audience while web design considers the user's spatiotemporal experience. The following items are some considerations that may affect a web design.

- **Visuality**: Not everyone will view the web site under the same environment. They may see different colors, typefaces, graphics, and images than the designer originally intended. These are determined by the monitor, the browser, and resolution. Designers often preview their design in a variety of browsers and with different monitor resolutions to ensure that the design works in different environments.
- **Loading Time**: File size and the user's Internet bandwidth determine the speed at which web pages load. Smaller is faster, but smaller is not always better. You may need to create a loading function for a page or a design object to optimize the user's environment and experience.
- **Screen Sizes**: Monitor sizes (15, 17, 19, 21 inches) and resolutions (800×600, 1024×768, 1280×1024 pixels) determine the visible

area available for web design.

- **Typography**: In general, readability on a computer screen is less than in print. Direct factors of readability are typeface, font size, and font color; indirect factors include monitor size, screen resolution, browser (including scrolling function), and platform. (See Chapter 10 for a detailed discussion of typography.)
- **Compatibility & Plug-ins (browsers)**: A plug-in is an application that provides added capabilities to the Internet browser. There are a number of plug-ins, such as Adobe's PDF reader, JavaScript, CSS, Flash player, Shockwave, QuickTime Player, Real Audio & Video, etc. A plug-in may not be installed on the user's computer (by choice or inexperience, or the computer's limited capacity).
- **Vector vs. Bitmap (Raster)**: Bitmap images (or raster images) are made up of different colored pixels in a grid. A pixel is a little tiny square dot that is the smallest unit in a digital image. It is difficult to resample (increase or decrease the size of) the bitmap image without losing image quality because the pixel is a fixed and solid data. For instance, increasing the size of a bitmap image means that new pixels will be created, which in most cases, makes the image appear jagged. Vector images are based on mathematical equations which makes them scalable and renderable at the highest quality. Vector images are editable so that changing the attributes will not reduce their quality. The primary disadvantage is that vector images are not suitable for realistic imagery such as photographs.
- **Navigation**: A book has a typical sequential pathway known to the reader. The reader knows how to open and close it, and can tell how big it is. The reader can calculate how many pages there are to read. The form and the structure are lucid and its navigation is linear. A web site seems to be placed in a rectangular shape (browser), but it is amorphous (formless) so that the user has to navigate from page to page to understand the whole structure. Therefore, web designers should organize and manage given content and the design elements with the user's navigational needs in mind.

- **Visible area**: A browser window (or Internet browser) consists of tool bars, status bar, and frame (borders). To design a web page that fits into the real size of a desing area, you need to confirm the working area in the window rather than simply designing in an area of the same size as the screen resolution. Table 11-7 lists common screen resolutions. (The resolutions can vary in LCD monitors).

If you design a web page by trying to match the resolution to the screen size, the result may differ from what you expect. The actual area of your design will be smaller than the resolution of the browser window. There are no standard equations for the working area, but the following table (Table 11-8) will is a useful guideline.

Table 11-8 shows the actual working area for web design in Explorer and Netscape browsers on Windows and Macintosh. The results are measured in the maximized browser mode and do not include the scroll bars on the right side of the browser. If necessary, deduct 16 pixels of the scrollbar width from the browser width. However, the visible areas vary in LCD monitors and laptops. In addition, many Mac users have a tendency to not use the browser in maximized mode. Table 11-9 presents the best average size for design in the browser.

| Screen (Inch) | Resolution (pixels) |
|---|---|
| 14 | 640×480 |
| 15 | 800×600 |
| 16 | 1024×768 |
| 17 | 1152×864 |
| 18 | 1280×1024 |

| Resolution | Explorer 6 | | Netscape 7/8 | |
|---|---|---|---|---|
| (pixels) | Windows (pixels) | Mac (pixels) | Windows (pixels) | Mac (pixels) |
| 640×480 | 640×304 | 628×304 | 628×283 | 628×326 |
| 800×600 | 788×425 | 788×423 | 788×403 | 788×445 |
| 1024×768 | 1012×592 | 1012×592 | 1012×571 | 1012×614 |
| 1152×864 | 1140×710 | 1140×710 | 1140×710 | 1140×710 |
| 1280×1024 | 1268×860 | 1268×860 | 1268×860 | 1268×860 |

1 Table 11-7. Screen and resolution
2 Table 11-8. Working area in browsers

Approximately 40 to 70 pixels are deducted from the width and 170 to 180 pixels are deducted from the height of the original resolution to fit the visible area within the browser. These are general estimations, not absolute guidelines. In addition there are margins within the browser that vary by brand. Table 11-10 lists the margins of common browsers.

If designing a CD-Rom or for Web TV, the visible area may be considered differently. In the case of a CD-Rom design, you can follow the resolution of the screen so long as you design within the full screen mode. For Web TV design, follow the standard size, 544–378 pixels.

| Resolution (pixels) | Design area (pixels) |
|---|---|
| 640×480 | 600×300 |
| 800×600 | 760×420 |
| 1024×768 | 955×600 |
| 1152×864 | 1082×695 |
| 1280×1024 | 1210×855 |

| Margin Property | Explorer 6 (pixels) | Netscape 7/8 (pixels) | Firefox 1.5 (pixels) |
|---|---|---|---|
| margin-bottom | 4 | 4 | 1 |
| margin-left | 3 | 4 | 1 |
| margin-right | 3 | 4 | 1 |
| margin-top | 3 | 4 | 1 |

1 Table 11-9. Best size for design in the broswer
2 Table 11-10. Margin values in the browsers

# Design Studio: Web Page Analysis

Your visual assessments should not remain in instant feedback or emotional responses. Different analytic approaches and critical assessments of visual works will improve your visual communication and enable you to be more creative.

Choose one genre of web sites, such as news, game servers, banks, or commercial sites, and select four large or well-known web sites in that category.

- Analyze the homepages and one sub page with your visual assessment of the layout design. Examine carefully all visible design elements such as logo, login, and columns.
- Reproduce the layouts with grayscale value and add your measurement results (see the following images).
- Make a comparison chart to reflect the data as shown in Table 11-11.

This example uses news web sites to demonstrate the activity. The objective of news web sites is to present a large amount of information within a limited area. They show how to use space effectively and aesthetically.

The four news web sites selected include the Washington Post, USA Today, the Telegraph, and The New York Times. The homepages and sample article pages were examined for layout design.

- Washington Post (www.washingtonpost.com) (viewed May 2006)
- USA Today (www.usatoday.com) (viewed May 2006)
- The Telegraph (www.telegraph.co.uk) (viewed May 2006)
- The New York Times (www.nytimes.com) (viewed May 2006)

As Table 11-11 shows, three columns are standard for reading a large amount of text information. Although The New York Times divides its homepage into five columns, text appears in only two and the other columns are advertisements. Similarly, four newspaper web sites use only two columns for news in the homepage and the rest of the space is reserved for advertisements. Comparing the width of the columns of their article pages, maximum width is 474 pixels in the Washington Post and minimum is 344 pixels in the Telegraph. All four sites use only one column for the article page, which assists readability. As a result, they all use 30–40% of the available page space for advertisements, which is proportionally less than the text information, but it may still visually overwhelm the whole page. Ideally, the space allotted for advertisements would be no more than 20% of a page to preserve the visual aesthetic.

**Table 11-11.** Layout analysis

| Features | Washington Post | | USA Today | | Telegraph | | The New York Times | |
|---|---|---|---|---|---|---|---|---|
| | Home Page | Article Page | Home Page | Article Page | Home Page | Article Page | Home Page | Article Page |
| Columns | 3 | 3 | 3 | 3 | 3 | 4 | 5 | 3 |
| Page width/ text+ads (pixels) | 977 (641+336) | 977 (474+320) | 770 (470+300) | 700 (420+350) | 740 (614+126) | 740 (476+264) | 959 (578+381) | 985 (625+360) |
| Headline/Article width (pixels) | 2 columns (317+280) | 1 columns (474) | 2 columns (221+405) | 1 columns (350) | 2 columns (289+195) | 1 columns (344) | 2 columns (279+201) | 1 columns (431) |
| Others elements | logo, login, banner ads, navigation bar, search, date/time, weather, main photo | | logo, banner ads, navigation bar, search, main photo | | logo, banner ads, navigation bar, search, main photo | | logo, login, banner ads, navigation bar, search, date/time, weather, main photo | |

In layout design for information-driven web sites such as news sites, the dominant design principles should be stability and proportion. Effective delivery of textual information to users requires a very stable structure, providing visual comfort. It also requires careful arrangement of the design elements of text, images, and advertisements to produce a balanced proportion.

1 2
3 4

1 Figure 11-1. Washington Post homepage analysis
2 Figure 11-2. Washington Post article page analysis
3 Figure 11-3. USA Today homepage analysis
4 Figure 11-4. USA Today article page analysis

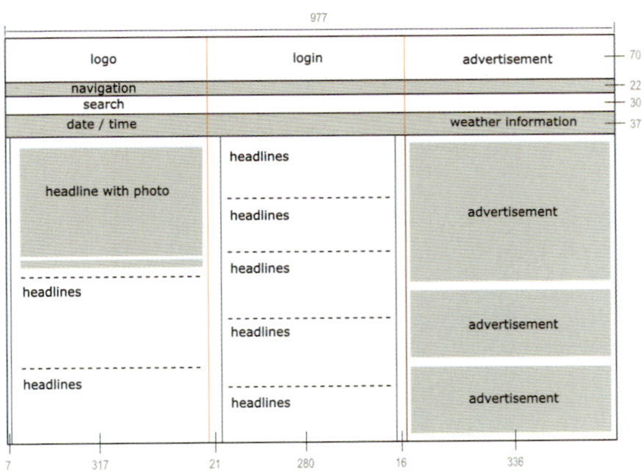


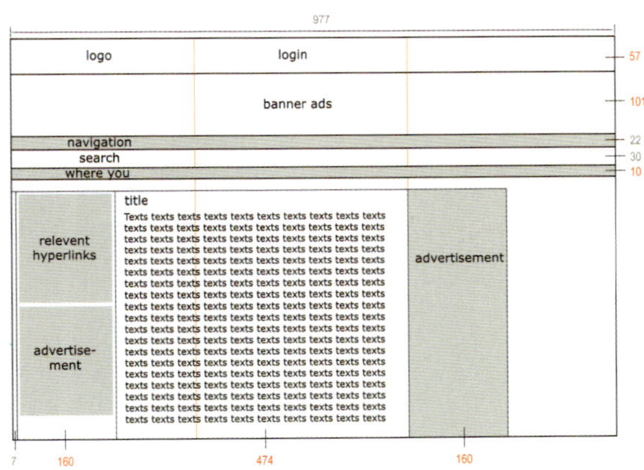


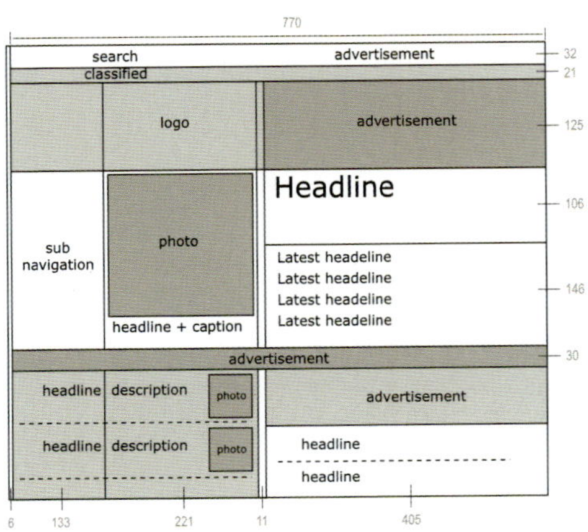


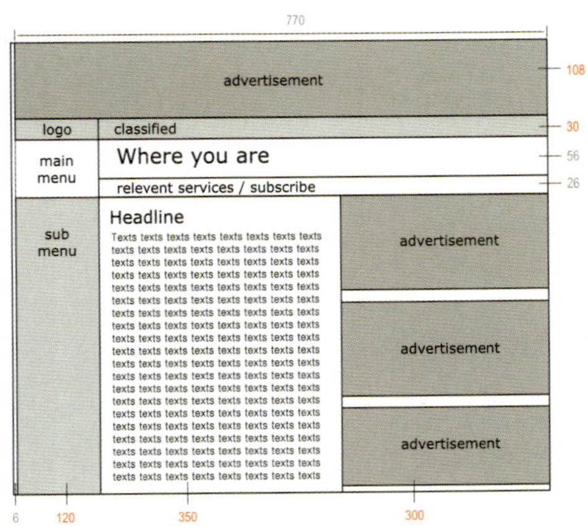

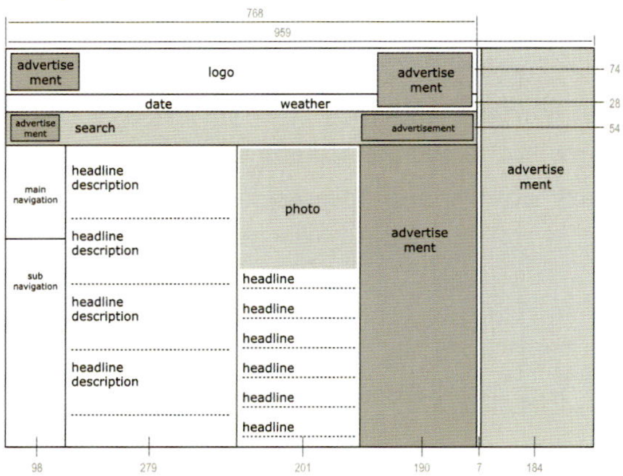


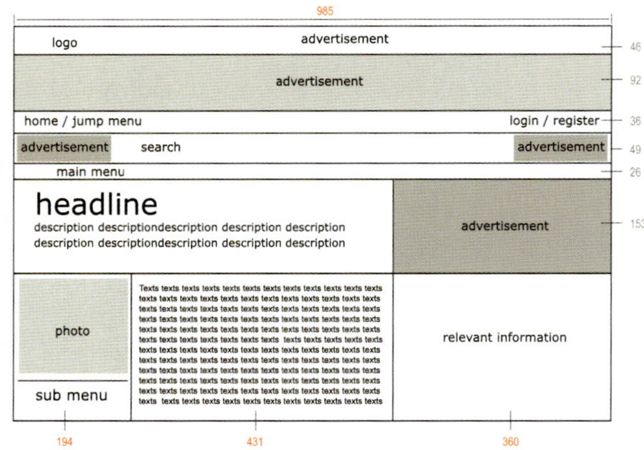


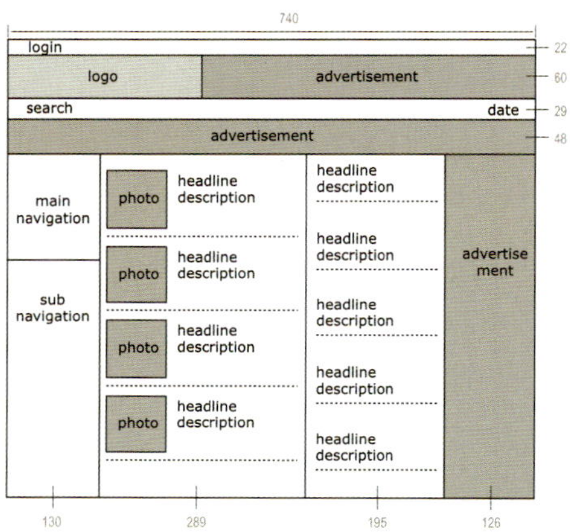


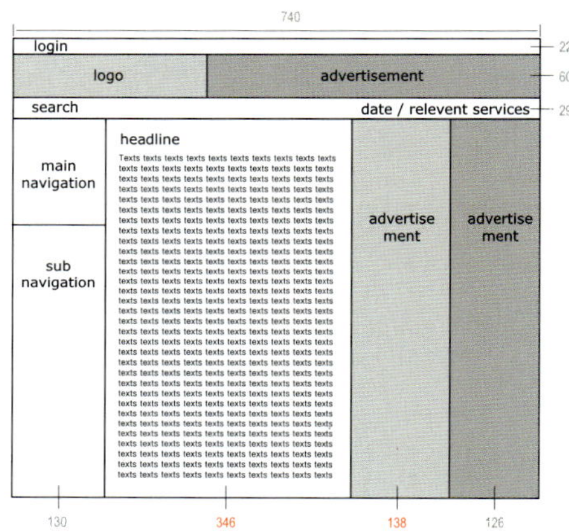


**1** Figure 11-5. Telegraph homepage analysis
**2** Figure 11-6. Telegraph article page analysis
**3** Figure 11-7. The New York Times homepage analysis
**4** Figure 11-8. The New York Times article page analysis

# Student Gallery
## e-Card Design

The activity is to create an e-card for the font page of your portfolio that arranges, and presents, the previous 10 works. The e-card is similar to an invitation card that represents yourself or style of your design. It can be an icon, an image, a symbol, or a caricature of your face.

- Logo, symbol, or image (which represents yourself or theme of the portfolio)
- Your name
- E-mail address
- Copyright (to insert copyright symbol © in Photoshop and Illustrator, hold down Alt and press 0169)

- Software: Adobe Illustrator CS2 and Photoshop CS2
- Dimension: 400 x 250 pixels
- Format: publish a gif or a jpg format (depending on the image quality and file size) from your work and insert it into the marking sheet provided.

### Marking Criteria (possible marks: 10)

Student will receive one of the marks in the following:

- 9 – 10: Successful design with creative solutions and professional finish
- 7 – 8: Successful design, but insufficient creativity and finish
- 5 – 6: Adequate, but lack of experiment or creativity
- 3 – 4: Inadequate, partly misunderstanding
- 2 – 0: Wrong theme or no submission

## Student Works

- Krista Avila 2007

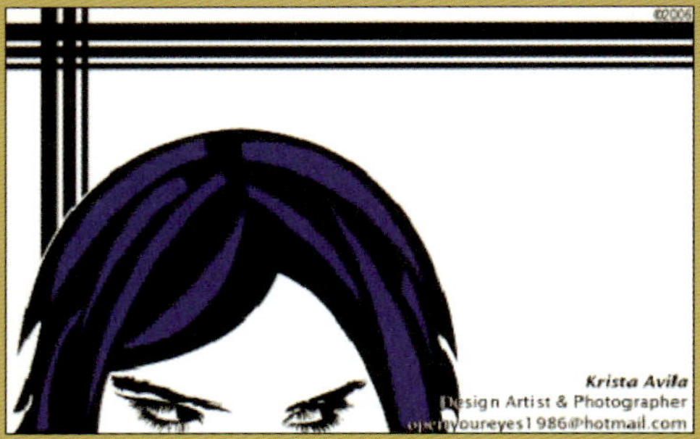


The work to the left creates a strong visual interest by using a visual line via the lady's gaze. Furthermore, the elements are arranged well with a gird system and the blue hair keeps the balance of the layout by holding the visual weight in the middle vertically.

- Kaylene Court 2006

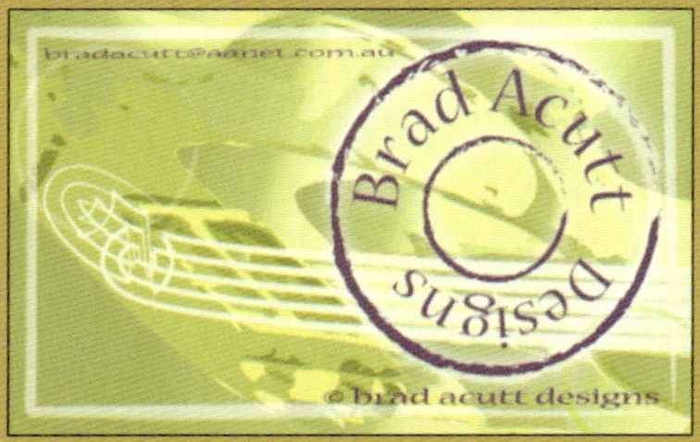


- Kaylene Court 2006

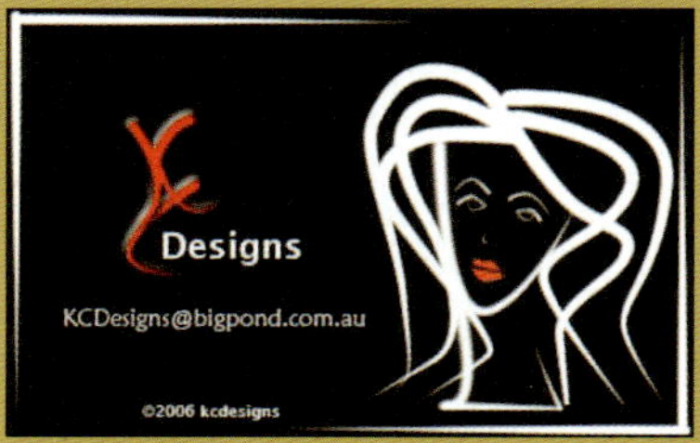


- Joy Reynolds 2006

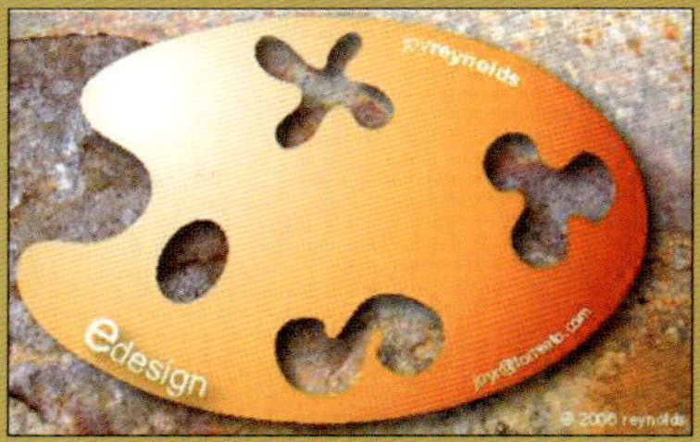


- Douglas (Chak Cheung) Tsang 2006

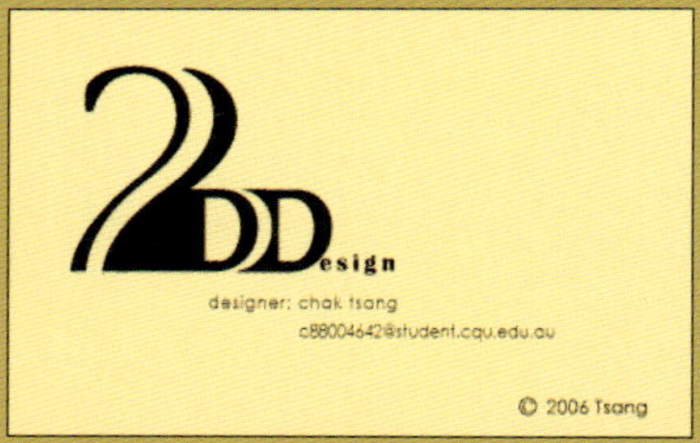


- Natalie Gaye Clarke 2007

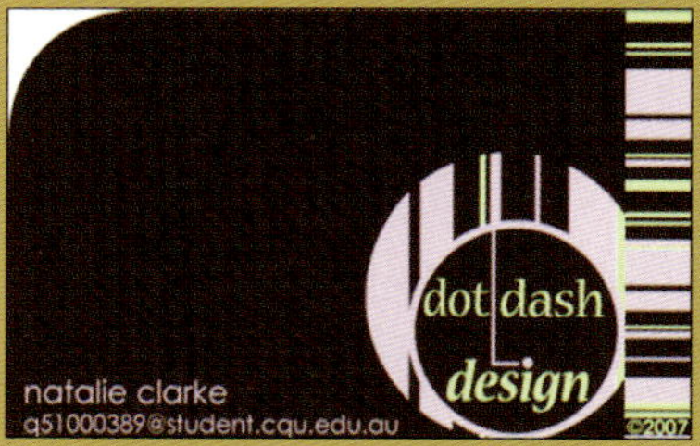


- Justin Andrew Hawley 2007

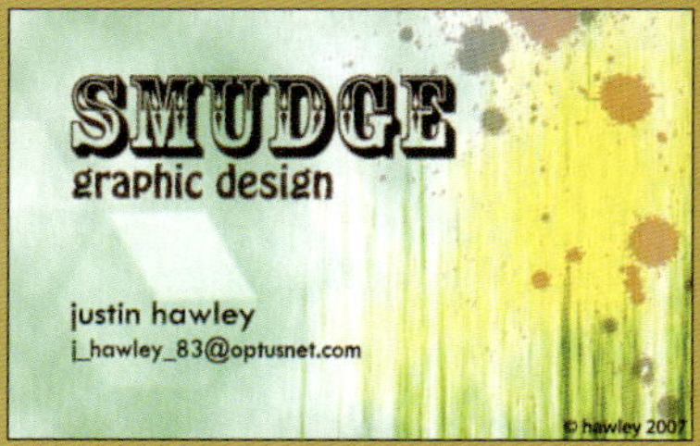


- Elise Sondergeld 2007

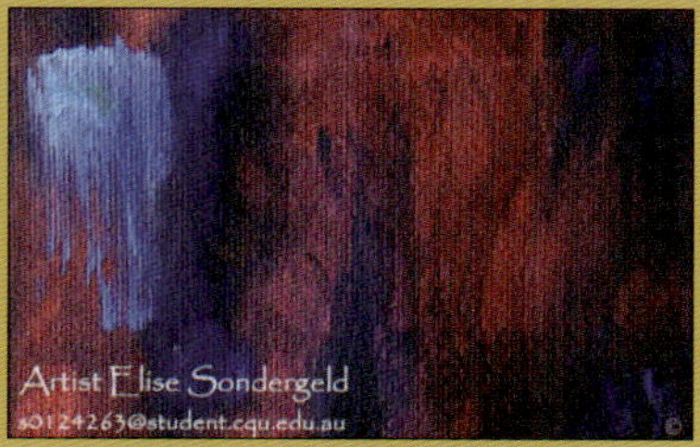


- Chelsea Sutherland 2007

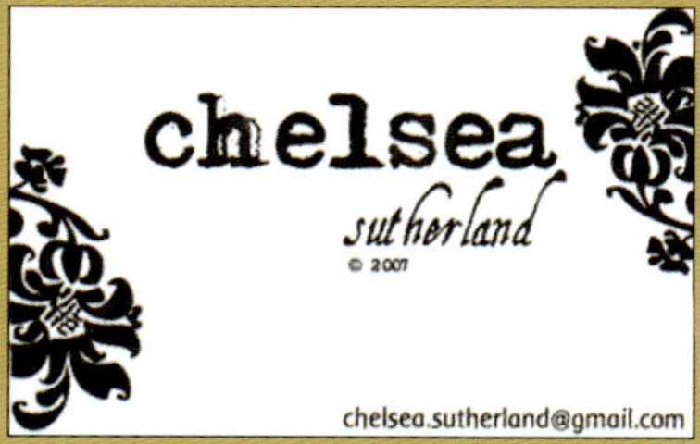


- Karina Maree Voss 2007

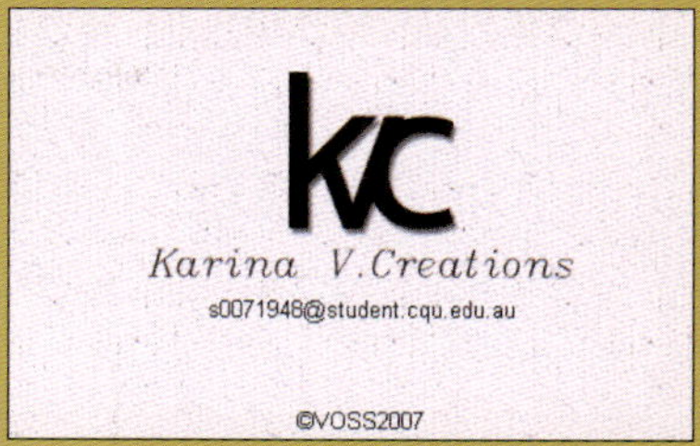

Chapter

# [ 12 ]

# Visual Communication

Visual communication refers to the communication of ideas or thoughts by using visual elements. It basically requires knowing features of various visual elements and it is ultimately to understand the target users, to arrange the design elements in order to create a particular use experience.

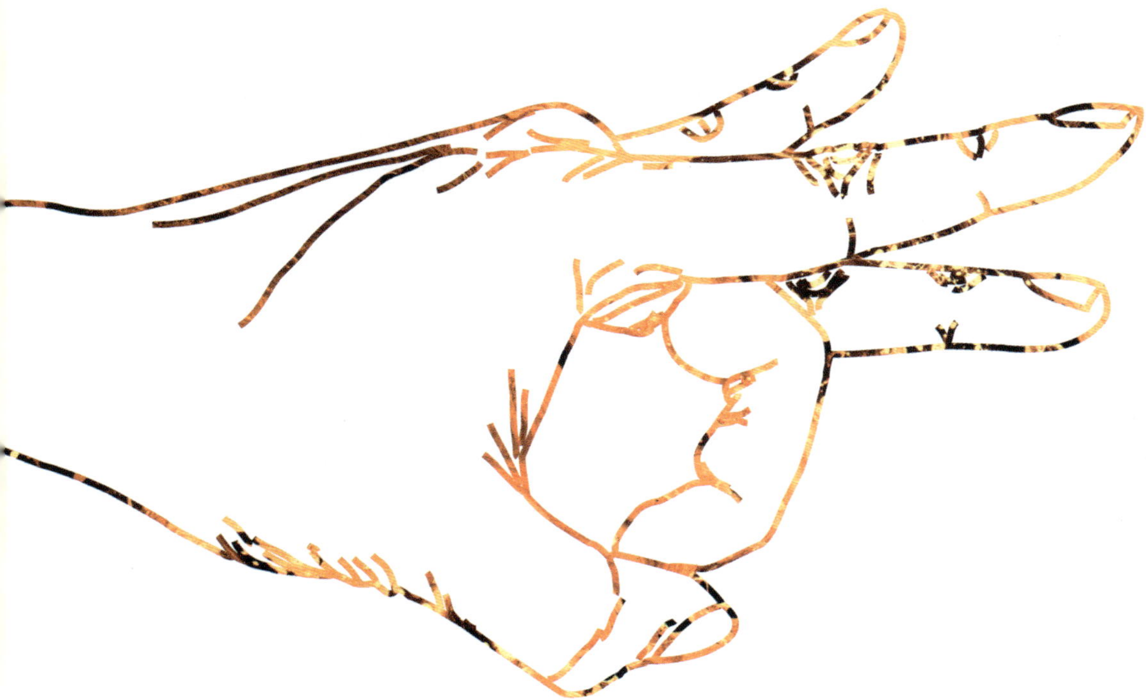

# Defining Visual Communication

Graphic design is a process of combining various design elements to visually convey a message. Superficially, graphic design creates a certain "look."

Graphic design is a process of combining various design elements to visually convey a message. Superficially, graphic design creates a certain "look." Fundamentally, it is a process of visualizing given data. The core objective is to develop a visual structure that communicates the designer's objective, and then to dress it up with design elements.

The designer's job is to systematically interpret the user's association with the information to be conveyed and then translate those associations into visual design using design principles and tools. In web design, this is particularly complex due to the interactive nature of the online environment. Visualization implies these three important processes:

- Observing the user experience
- Organizing the user experience
- Visualizing the user experience

## 1 | Observing the User Experience

The user always exists prior to visual design. Observing the target user assists the designer in ascertaining what the user expects and how viewers perceive particular design elements such as color and font. This observation process is akin to researching the user's preferences, which prevents the designer from narrowly confining the user to the designer's own aesthetic perspective.

Aesthetic also precedes visualization. Aesthetic is a more comprehensive and primitive concept than visualization. Observing the target user's visual experience suggests an aesthetic framework that helps the designer to tailor the design elements.

This observation step identifies the target user's visual experience in relation to the designer's intended theme and elements. This helps the designer to integrate the user experience and the design objective, and to determine an appropriate strategy for manipulating the design elements. Good commercial layout design develops from the target user's needs rather than designer's imagination.

### 2 | Organizing the User Experience

The wide range of user experiences and available design elements can produce a tangled thread. The observations of the user experience must be well managed in order to effectively connect the design elements. That is to say, components of the user experience will be rearranged or manipulated within the visual structure (layout design) to support the designer's intended communication. However, this does not mean that the user is a passive factor. Rather, the user must be capable of perceiving the visual language to be able to receive the communicated information. Interpreting and organizing the user experience links the viewer and the design objective to create the most effective visual design.

### 3 | Visualizing the user experience

The final step is for the designer to actively visualize the user experience. After identifying and organizing the user's experience of the design elements, the designer strives to engage the user in the design.

At this stage, the design elements have to be transformed to fit the aesthetic and functional needs of the user. An emotional motif, extracted from the user preference, is often adopted as a visual trigger that leads viewers to a particular message.

In addition, visualizing implies that the design should be tested by a group of the target users. The designer's imagination and creation may be too overwhelming or too remote from the user's visual experience.

These three steps of visualization enable the designer to create a rich and interactive user experience.

# Design Tiers

The 10 principles of design—stability, balance, dynamics, variety, emphasis, scale, proportion, harmony, rhythm, and movement—were introduced in Chapters 2 and 3. These principles are the key concepts for layout design. Three principles in particular—stability, dynamics, and scale—are the most comprehensive and inclusive concepts. They constitute the primary tier in design principles (see Figure 12-1).

These three principles coexist in good layout design with balanced importance. For example, a stable layout can contain a dynamic feature used for a visual accent, and a scale layout might include a stable feature in terms of visual balance.

The remaining seven principles are secondary. The secondary tier can be independent in a layout design, but its main purpose is to supplement the primary principles.

The tertiary tier is formed by combining primary and secondary tier principles, usually in a ratio of one primary and two secondary principles. For example, a layout may look stable with strong variety and rhythm.

Designers often become absorbed in their work and forget to emphasize the theme. The 10 principles will help the designer to determine the type of layout design desired. The key to continued progress and successful layout design is to strike a balance between a layout's thematic objective and the creative, experimental methods that fulfill the design's objective.

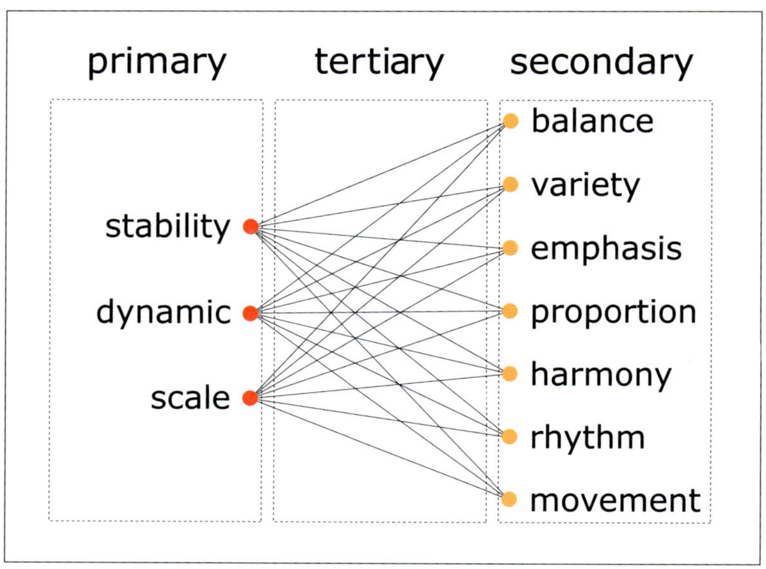


**1** **Figure 12-1.** Tiers of design principles